IVAN MARKS
THE PEOPLE'S CHAMPION

His greatest ever stories

I have often said that if you want to be a successful angler - pleasure man or matchman - you must think like a fish.
Ivan Marks, August 1976

First published in October 2011

© Text - Bauer Media

© Pictures - Bauer Media

© Design - David Clow

ISBN NUMBER 978-0-9567015-9-6

Unit Four, Ashton Gate, Harold Hill, Romford, RM3 8UF

CONTENTS

CHAPTER ONE MATCH FISHING

CHAPTER TWO FISHING FOR ENGLAND

CHAPTER THREE TACKLE

CHAPTER FOUR TACTICS

CHAPTER FIVE BAIT

CHAPTER SIX IRELAND

CHAPTER SEVEN EVERYTHING ELSE

INTRODUCTION

Ivan Alec Marks was born in Leicester on April 13th, 1936. The angling bug bit early in his life and by the age of 12 he was taking part in local club matches, but soon found himself facing a ban - not because of any wrong-doing but because he was just too good. The seniors simply couldn't face taking a bashing from a schoolboy.

In 1954 he joined the area's foremost match team of the time – the Black Horse Pub Angling Club – where its captain, Eddie Allen, recognised the burgeoning talent and taught Ivan the intricacies of bream fishing. It was to shape his life.

Having completed National Service, Ivan joined the open match circuit and soon established himself as one of the most potent names on the scene. Leicester became a hotbed for angling talent and Ivan, along with Roy Marlow - who Ivan was to run a tackle shop with for many years - Dave Rossi, Brian Envis, Dave Downes and Howard Humphrey, Leicester AS became known as the 'Likely Lads', a nickname that was to follow the team throughout the 1970s.

Big honours – both at team and individual level – soon followed. Individually, he won the Nene Championships in 1967, also taking claiming top spot in the Great Ouse Championships in 1970, 1972 and 1973. He also grabbed first place in the Welland Champs, both in 1970 and 1972. These, remember, were huge contests, some upwards of 1,300 pegs, and his consistency was unprecedented.

Ever the team man, he was the cornerstone of winning Likely Lad sides in the 1971 and 1974 National Championships. His growing profile in a booming sport made him angling's first real superstar. He wrote his first column for Angling Times in 1972 and for the next eight years he was a regular in a newspaper selling 170,000 copies a week. Voted 'Angler of the Year' three times in succession, he became the most famous fisherman in the country and regularly drew crowds in excess of 200 wherever he fished. England, inevitably, beckoned. Ivan's first cap came in 1972 when, under the leadership of Stan Smith, he fished for his country in Czechoslovakia. Eleven caps followed, but despite individual silver in 1976 and six team medals, he never got his hands on one coloured gold. It was to be his greatest regret in fishing.

By the early 1980s, the Likely Lads had disbanded and Ivan had joined the Barnsley Blacks, a team that was to dominate the scene in much the same way Leicester had done in the previous decade. His international career though came to a close, the appointment of Dick Clegg and a new era spelling the end for Ivan.

Despite continuing to fish to a high level, ill-health was to beset much of his later life. He only started smoking at the age of 35, but became addicted, often smoking upwards of 40 during a five-hour contest. At 51 he suffered a heart-attack before, in 1993, undergoing a heart transplant.

Despite slipping somewhat from public eye, his popularity remained undimmed and, in 2005, he was voted third in an Angling Times poll to find the UK's greatest ever anglers.

Ivan still fished every week up until his death, helping out with Leicester Sensas, and his enthusiasm was as keen as ever. He died, after a short illness, on December 5th, 2004, leaving a wife, Linda, and son, Chris. He was 68.

Tributes were plentiful. The great and good of his own - and the current - era of match fishing were in attendance to say their goodbyes and even today a memorial match in his name takes place every year. A monument on the banks of the River Welland was also erected, inscribed with the one quote that symbolises the great Ivan Marks.

It reads: "At the end of the day, I was just an ordinary bloke who could fish a bit."

Brilliant, innovative, likeable and, above all, humble, he wasn't just a great angler, he was a great character, too.

THE MAN,
THE ANGLER,
THE LEGEND...

DAVID HALL
Chairman, David Hall Publishing

"When I first launched Coarse Fisherman magazine in the winter of 1975, a fellow journalist asked what my motivation had been. I replied, 'to meet Ivan Marks.' It wasn't strictly true, but it was pretty close.

I loved his column in the Angling Times and his weekly banter with Dick Walker. Ivan would write about catching bream on the River Welland, fishing with a 1lb breaking strain hooklength and a size 20 hook. The next week Dick would reply saying that Ivan was crackers and that you should fish with at least a 4lb line and a hook no smaller than a size 14. It was great fun and while the reader could be forgiven for thinking they were the worst of enemies, they were in fact the best of friends.

I first met him only a few weeks after I had launched Coarse Fisherman. Talk about a baptism of fire! I drew between him and Roy Marlow in a 500-peg Dave Downes open on the River Welland. As luck would have it we'd drawn in a poor area and none of us caught, so I hadn't disgraced myself. With an hour of the match remaining I got up from my peg and walked down and introduced myself. Little did I know that this was going to be the beginning of a wonderful friendship.

Ivan was one of the kindest men you could ever wish to meet. He had tremendous generosity of spirit and made friends wherever he went. Largely because of his tremendous winning record and his column in Angling Times, he would gather a crowd behind him wherever he fished, and he loved a crowd. He was also a great showman - time and time again I saw him light a cigarette while playing a bream or a chub and all the time he would be turning round and talking to the enthralled crowd.

The 70s were Ivan's time, but then so were the 80s and 90s. The Leicester Likely Lads, as they were known, were winning all before them under Ivan's stewardship. They won the last 'weight' National, or the All England Championship as it was known then, on the River Severn in 1971. It was fished by 116 teams and a total of 1,392 anglers. That truly was the golden age of match fishing and Ivan was at the very forefront.

He even had his own barmy army. Every weekend Ivan, Roy Marlow, Tom Bedder, Stan Piecha, Stu Killen, Graham Barry, Joe Roberts and any one of a dozen anglers would rendezvous at some motorway café or Little Chef on their way to the Trent, the Welland, the Severn or some Fenland drain, to fish an open. Ivan would happily share any information he might have gleaned during the week from one of the local cracks, which was his way.

I look forward to the publication of this book and to re-reading all those wonderful articles again. Ivan Marks, my hero and my friend."

PETER DRENNAN
Founder of Drennan International

"Charm is an enviable characteristic and Ivan Marks had it in abundance.

When it's combined with true angling genius, you really do have something very special and absolutely unique!

Ivan had everything: massive in-depth expertise, intuition – the proverbial sixth sense, and the physical abilities to go with it. I could never beat him at anything, from table-tennis to throwing groundbait; he was always faster, sharper – that little bit more accurate.

Of course, he looked like a scruffy individual and seemed to be as careless about his tackle as his appearance. In later years, he even took an inverted pride in pulling a tangle of reels and catapults out of the bottom of a dirty tackle box in front of a bankside gallery. But that was all part of the show, part of the appearance. In practice Ivan's attention to detail, where it mattered, was acute.

I have been fortunate enough to have kept company with great anglers and charming, charismatic, angling celebrities, but never with anyone in whom this was all combined to such effect: that's why we all loved him!"

TOMMY PICKERING
Former World Champion

"The biggest compliment I can pay Ivan Marks was that he was the true 'People's Champion'.

I recall the huge crowd at his funeral and to a man they all had their own personal story to tell - the moment Ivan had dedicated his time to help and listen.

Ivan Marks was a great angler, who did great things, but it was his generosity that took him to the next level. He taught me a lot about this sport, but above all he gave me a lesson in how to treat fellow fishermen."

KEITH ARTHUR
Journalist, radio presenter and star of Tight Lines

"On a 'rest day' during a match in Ireland our hosts took the group of us to Killykeen on Lough Oughter to fish for bream. Ivan opened his wicker basket on the bank and removed a bait box. Among the jumble of contents was a sheep's heart full of maggots - gozzers as they were known. They had travelled on the plane, in the hold luckily.

We realised that he also had another 'trick up his pocket' (an Ivanism) when we found a pillowcase full of pinkies hidden in the telephone seat in the hotel lobby. Talk about 'Be Prepared'; he must have been the ultimate Boy Scout."

TIM KNIGHT
Editor, Angler's Mail

"Ivan Marks was a god when I grew up in the 1970s and 80s. Like most fishing-mad kids of the day, I was inspired by his tactical advice. As I mixed with veteran London matchmen, one of the very few outsiders they spoke in awe of was Ivan. To them too, he was a genius.

They say never meet your heroes but in Ivan's case I was glad I did – he was so warm and helpful, with a cheeky glint in his eye. A true angling legend."

RICHARD LEE
Editor-in-chief, Angling Times

"Ivan might have won more big matches than anyone else alive but statistics aren't the only measure of his popularity. What set him apart was something else altogether.

This was a man who had the ability to touch people in a way no-one has done before or since. Ivan's greatest attribute, and the reason he was so universally loved, was his everyman approachability."

Chapter One

Ivan Marks on...

MATCH FISHING

> Now, I've got a reputation for a
> 'golden arm' when it comes to picking
> a good swim. For however talented
> the angler, his knowledge is useless if
> he draws a duff 'un....

THE GREAT PEG DEBATE

[April 6th, 1972]

I AM giving away no free pints of casters for guessing the name of my favourite stretch of water. It's that wonderful Nene below smokey old Peterborough.

Where else could you find a possible 280 winning match pegs out of a total of 400? It's the fairest match water in the country, and the Leicester lads just can't fish it enough.

In their wisdom, the Nene and Welland River Authority have spaced permanent concrete pegs roughly 18 yards apart. These stretch along the river's North Bank from Fitzwilliam Bridge down to the Dog-in-a-Doublet sluice...several 'golden' miles of fabulous fishing.

Now I read that more than 40 miles of Norfolk's Broadland rivers are also to be permanently pegged. That's just great. It will ease the burden on clubs organising matches and stop anglers wandering the banks searching for their swims.

The North Bank, lower Welland and Great Ouse Relief Channel are all waters where there are permanent pegs. And the sooner all River Authorities fall in line with this trend, the better it will be for anglers.

The Likely Lads gave the Witham the cold shoulder last season. The pegging there is so close at times you can hear the next man breathing. If the river is running and you fancy trying for roach, you can't do a lot with ten yards.

We suggested to the various Witham match organisers that we were prepared to pay more entry money if fewer pegs were put in the bank. But they weren't interested. They can get a sell-out every time. So until the anglers are allowed more space on the Witham we'll be staying away.

Unfortunately, the situation is rapidly getting as bad on the Trent. Take Winthorpe as an example. Here there are 100 permanent pegs, a good distance apart. But when a big match is on - such as the Holme Marsh open - the organisers put out an additional 200 pegs.

If you draw one of the permanent pegs you are in with a chance. But if you are crammed in the other stretch forget it. An additional two yards on your swim is extremely valuable on the fast-flowing Trent.

Fishing will always improve with better pegging. None of us is an angel. We will always try to draw away the next man's fish. And if two swims are too close together, this will kill it for both anglers – especially if they are good.

If you are fortunate to have a vacant peg below, then you can afford to smile. But how many times does this happen?

In time I hope that all match waters will be permanently pegged, and the spacing apart of swims will not depend on the suspect strides of a local bailiff.

On rivers such as the Witham where the water level is some distance from the top of the bank, you can lose or gain vital yards depending on how you are drawn. If pegged on the outside of a bend, then competitors will find they have more water to fish when they get their baskets down in the mud.

The converse is true if you draw on the inside of a bend. Make a little sketch and you should quickly see what I mean.

Another big match which is not permanently pegged is the Middle Level drain near King's Lynn. Often you are left struggling to fish from a hole in a rush bed! One man gets 18 yards another only 10. It makes a mockery of the match. Yet they are always sell-outs.

Complaining to a steward won't do any good. All you can do is fish and make the best of it. This is where the luck of the draw plays such an important part in deciding the outcome of a big match. A percentage of the crack anglers will always draw the best pegs. Permanent pegging makes match fishing fairer for all concerned.

One river which doesn't need permanent pegs is the Severn. There, every angler gets at least 25 yards of river to fish. The trees make sure of that. And the results confirm it as one of the most consistent rivers in the country.

If a big match is arranged on the river, the organisers never struggle to push in extra pegs.

I've certainly no grumbles about the Nene. The Leicester anglers can sit next to each other on the North Bank and still catch fish. But I believe that in fairness to everyone those 40 pegs on the South Bank above Fitzwilliam Bridge should not be included in open matches. Always protected from the prevailing wind, those swims are the best on the river. Fish are there in quantity, yet no one seems to know why.

Roy Marlow won the Nene Championship there and Robin Grouse the Henson Memorial Cup. I've only drawn it once, but I was eight pegs away from the fish. I picked Roy's peg number for him and he won with 24lb. That's match fishing!

The mighty Welland has 800 permanent pegs, and they act as useful markers for keeping tabs on those elusive bream shoals. Let me explain. After the Welland Championship in July I carefully note the peg numbers that provide the winning weights. A week later are the CIU Championships, which Roy won last year with 32lb. By working out the peg distances between the winning areas we can see how far downstream the bream shoals have moved in a week.

The fish tend to follow a pattern as they swim from their upstream spawning grounds to the feeding areas in the coloured water of the lower Welland. Their rate of movement allows us to predict what areas the shoals should have reached in future matches. This would be extremely difficult to work out if permanent pegs weren't spaced out along the bank. They are also a boon to pleasure anglers who can 'sit on' the fish during the week if they fish those match winning areas.

Between pegs 192 and 210 has been a consistent winning area over the seasons, and I am happy to go for bream if I draw between 300 and 320. There are always bream between 530 and 660 too.

The Relief Channel is a fickle water at the best of times. But a ring to bailiff Cliff Cawkwell will tell us the producing pegs. You've probably seen those cards that are left on each bridge at the end of a club match. They tell the bailiff the numbers of the winning pegs.

The only time I don't complain about close pegging is when the lads go down the 'Smoke'. The matches there are rovers and you can end up sharing a swim with three other anglers! But I don't take them seriously, although the money is just as good. The lads treat those matches as a laugh.

You can get away with cramped swims on the London lakes by oucasting and outfeeding the opposition. What we lose on a peg we gain on distance. That's how I won the South Ockendon and Marcos Lakes last season.

In the Marcos match I 'filled in' the swim with groundbait, had a 30-minute kip in my tent and then slaughtered the bream. Simple when you know how.

Of course you can come unstuck if you draw next to one of your mates. Roy Marlow and Howard Humphrey sat next to each other in the HAS match. Their tactics were ruining it for them both. So Howard sportingly agreed to pack up and let Roy have the fish. That's how strong the team feeling is among the Likely Lads. Roy finished a creditable third.

Bad pegging can ruin many a day out. Last season the Likely Lads fished the team match on the Dorset Stour at Throop. We took two teams down, and our B team drew number one. Those four found their swims but the A side that drew end peg 53 spent most of the match looking for theirs. Roy Marlow finished fishing next to Johnny Essex; Dave Rossi fished his swim for two hours and was then moved to a non-existent peg. And I was stuck on the end of a section. As 25 per cent of the pegs were only a foot deep anyway, we will be leaving that match alone in the future.

If I do get a bad peg, I don't run complaining to the steward. I just have a laugh and a joke with the next man. That's what fishing is all about!

WINNING THE GREAT OUSE CHAMPIONSHIPS

[July 6th, 1972]

EVERYTHING went wrong for me the Saturday before the match! By the time I got to bed in the early hours of Sunday morning I was shattered. I wanted to sleep for a week. But sharp at 5.30 that morning the alarm jarred my jangled nerves into consciousness. I woke from a nightmare that my tackle shop was being consumed by an army of pinkies and remembered it was the day of the Great Ouse Championship.

Luckily I had prepared the bait the night before. So, being careful not to wake the wife, I tiptoed downstairs to pack my basket. Roy Marlow was soon hammering on the front door loud enough to wake the dead. And we were away, bound for Norfolk. Five of the Likely Lads travelled down in one car while the tackle went in a van. There's nothing worse than travelling long distances with a swingtip poking in your ear.

By the time we arrived at the draw, I was beginning to feel a bit more enthusiastic. Conditions looked good for bream... but would I get a good peg? Now, I've got a reputation for a "golden arm" when it comes to picking a good swim. For however talented the angler, his knowledge is useless if he draw a duff 'un.

I put my hand in the box, and fished out the envelope. I was still joking with the lads when I opened it and read Section Two, Peg One. I knew that this was a good fish holding area just below Denver Sluice, and I hoped that I would be fishing open water with no angler pegged opposite.

Phil Coles was drawn in the same section and as we walked together along the Channel's East bank we came across two anglers legering for eels. One of them told us he had caught a bream on a lobworm. So that was some encouragement.

My peg was in the rushes with an empty swim on my right, but I wasn't so happy to see I was sharing the Channel with another Leicester angler pegged opposite. On top of that cheeky Phil Cole pinched a bag of my groundbait before the start leaving me with only a stone.

I tackled up with the new swingtip rod developed by my old mate Roy and fixed a three-eighths of an ounce Arlesey bomb paternoster style six feet from the hook. Reel line was 3lb and the hooklength 1.7lb. Now I knew that Relief Channel bream were big, strong fish but I decided to kick off with a size 20 hook - a decision I was not to regret.

I had not brought much bait with me by bream-fishing standards. Just some gozzers for the hook, a pint of casters, a gallon of squatts and the groundbait. Before the whistle, the steward came down for a chat. He said he was fishing the Second Division National on the Welland and asked if he could watch. Then he told me this section had produced the winner for the last two Championships. I was beginning to get interested...

The whistle blew and I let the angler opposite make his play. He threw his groundbait my side of the middle and to my right. So I cast out only a third of the way across to my left. In went four balls of groundbait and I sat back on my basket to see if a bream would pick up the two white gozzers.

In that first hour I had one eye on my swingtip and the other on the anglers opposite. I saw them catch their first bream and waited hopefully. I was just beginning to think I should have stayed in bed when out of the corner of my eye I noticed a bream roll 30 yards above me. Nothing to lose, so in went another ball. Still no bites so I tried another three balls.

Then the swingtip flicked and shot up. A line bite. But the bream had moved in! A second line bite followed and I hovered over the rod butt. Third time lucky and I felt a good bream kick deep down against the hook. My first fish, and it was a good one. At least 3lb 8oz.

The next quarter of an hour kept me busy as I put six fish in the keeppnet. The contest was starting to warm up and big match fever started to grip. Perhaps I had a chance after all?

I pushed my umbrella into the water to shield the swingtip from the downstream wind, and waited for action. Three more bream came before the second hour was up and I was thinking of a place – if they would keep feeding. The next 20 minutes passed slowly. No fish. Thoughts raced through my mind. Should I put on a bigger hook and fish bread? But as if in answer, the bream returned and out came another four. They were strong, fighting fish but I was reluctant to change that 20 hook. I was catching well but each time the hook was just in the mouth. I had to use the disgorger only twice.

The bream were obviously moody and wrong goundbaiting could frighten the shoal. For me this was obviously the make or break time of the match. If I put in too much, the shoal could take fright and swim off to another angler's peg. But if I didn't feed, I could still lose them.

I had to take a chance while they were still on the feed so I put four balls on top of their heads. As I feared, the bites stopped. Had I killed the swim? But then one or two line bites told me the shoal were still there, disturbed but reluctant to leave the feeding area.

After a blank 15 minute spell, I started to catch again. Phew! I was never so relieved to see a swingtip move. From then on it was plain sailing as the bream came steadily. Every so often I would toss a couple of balls at them which they now seemed to accept.

As the match progressed I got keener and keener. I seemed to sense that I could possibly win if I kept them coming. When the bomb was out there I had to make double sure I was going to catch. I couldn't afford to miss a fish just by striking too soon. When Norfolk bream take, they really pull the swingtip out straight. So I contained my excitement by folding my arms and sitting back with a cigarette.

My best fish must have been pushing 5lb, and that's some fish to hold on a 20 hook. It's difficult for me to judge how fast I got the bream out. But I felt that I beat them reasonably quickly. Once hooked, I could keep a bream coming until it was under the rod tip where it fought hard. But I lost only three fish and they came off after only two of three turns of the reel handle.

Anyone watching me might have thought my casting wasn't accurate. But I was deliberately putting my bomb beyond or short of my groundbait. The fish were never settled in one spot, but preferred to move around the baited area. Sometimes I also twitched the bait along the bottom to give it another lie and pick up a fickle fish.

In the final hour the tension built up. I even fished with my hand on the rod butt – and that's unusual for me when legering.

I took five bream in the last 20 minutes of the match, and this is when I believe I added those two vital ounces to beat my old friend Geoff Bibby. It was just a matter of one cast. But I never guessed at the time that I had caught more than 60lb. I thought the net held more like 40lb. I had used only two pints of my squats and less than 10lb of groundbait. I suppose I had between 25 and 30 bream for my 62lb 10oz, the smallest about 1lb 8oz. Then I heard there had been another 62lb weight. I couldn't believe it. But I remember thinking I was the right side of eight ounces.

When I was walking back to the headquarters I saw Geoff driving along in his car. I asked him what he had got and he said 62lb 8oz. I told him my weight and we both laughed. Neither knew whether the other was kidding! Geoff joked that he would throw me in if I had pipped him. I'm glad he didn't!

ONE BREAM COST ME THE WELLAND TITLE

[July 20th, 1972]

ONE bream cost me the Welland Championship and a chance of winning the Grand Slam – the Ouse, Welland and Nene major river opens.

But I've no grumbles. The best man won on the day. And

21

that's what fishing is all about. The Likely Lads won the team event and proved we are just as dangerous as ever.

Last week I said legering was the best method to tackle big bream in matches. Perhaps I should have qualified that to say the 'bomb' has an advantage over the float when the wind is against you. But the float is certainly better than the 'bomb' when your swim is choked with weed. On the Welland I had the worst of both worlds - a swimful of weed and a strong downstream wind!

Just before Roy Marlow and I left Leicester, a lorry delivered a big parcel at our tackle shop. I had to open it there and then. Inside was a consignment of our new float rods. I picked one up, hoping to try it in the Championship. I couldn't forget my success in the Ouse match two weeks before when I christened our new swingtip rod with the winning catch.

I could have kissed my casters with delight when I saw the peg I had drawn - number 746. I thought it was opposite the willows. But I wasn't so happy when I arrived and saw I was nearer Crowland Bridge.

I reckoned I was at least 15 pegs short of where I needed to be. Dave Rossi drove past and saw me sitting long-faced on my basket.

"You're on," he whispered. Dave had drawn this area so many times in Welland matches that he spoke from experience. This cheered me up a little.

I took my time at the start and let everyone around me play their hand with groundbait. I picked up the float rod to plumb the depth. I knew before I started that a large weed bed covered the river bed on the far side. Anglers were legering right on top of that weed, so their maggots were just wriggling in. With float tackle I could keep the bait out of the weed.

Upstream of me was a young lad, and downstream an angler legering. I cast across the river but couldn't see the float. The black background obscured the tip, so I reeled in and increased my depth. A small shot was pinched near the hook. Now the float would stand well out of the water.

I tossed a couple of small balls as near as I could to the far bank. Two white gozzers went on a size 18 hook and I was fishing.

The antenna zoomer had hardly settled when it rose out of the water. Cursing the bleak, I struck casually and was amazed to find I had hooked a good bream. But no sooner had I got it out of the water than the angler next door hammered in some hefty groundbait to draw my fish.

This had the opposite effect. The bream disappeared to a swim two pegs away. The angler there caught one and in went some more groundbait. So back came the bream into my swim! And this time they stayed put.

I took seven bream for about 18lb in the first hour and a quarter. By fishing my float top and bottom I was able to lift the line from the water and control the bait correctly. And remember that I was casting only a rod length away from the opposite bank.

I shot into such a quick lead that I ran out of wind! Or perhaps I should say the wind ran into me! It blew up from nowhere, coming downstream and across. A big bow in the line kept pulling the float under. So I had to resort to the 'bomb'.

Line bites on a swingtip told me my swim was still full of bream, but weed repeatedly fouled the bait. Eventually I hit a fish only to have the hook pull out at the last moment. The maggot had doubled over and obscured the hook. What a day for that to happen.

I made no mistake with the next fish. As weed was still a problem I switched to bread and landed another, but I felt I still needed at least another three fish to be sure of winning.

As the wind and rain dampened my hopes, the weed became more of a menace. I tried the most unlikely baits to keep the hook clean, but I knew I was struggling. The only bait usable was bread.

I took one more bream, plus an eel, in the last three hours. Before the end I 'filled-in' the swim just for something to do. People kept coming up to me and saying that a Sheffield angler upstream was catching fish. They said he had about 12 fish. I thought I had around nine. We were both one fish out.

Then, when I heard he had weighed 28lb 6oz 8drm, I knew I was beaten. But only when they weighed my catch in at 26lb 4oz did I realise how close I had run Johnny Talbot.

Before the Championship, the Leicester anglers thought the winner would come from a peg above Crowland Bridge in the region of 770 to 780. But I would have needed smelling salts to revive me if I had drawn peg 851, which turned out to be the winner.

We usually regard this area as 'no-man's land', but this season the late spawning has obviously kept the bream up-river. When this area performs it cannot be beaten. The bream will gradually move back downstream when rain splits the shoals.

THE FIRST DIVISION NATIONAL WILL BE FARCE!
[August 31st, 1972]

I MAKE that prediction because of the state of the Bristol Avon. The river doesn't call for a First Division National. It may have done four years ago when the roach were present in force. But the lower reaches are certainly fishing badly now. I predict that between 300 and 400 anglers will catch under a pound of fish. And most of these will be in sections A to F.

Seven of us from Leicester went down to practise last week and fished a match in E and F sections. Now, we are as good as most anglers in the country, and usually reckon to catch a few fish, even on a strange water. But five of us caught under a pound each of tiny bleak, dace and bream in a six-hour competition. That's how bad it was.

It's going to be very hard for a team to catch right the way through the match stretch. Under the points system, any team which weigh in a pound a man from the bad sections should finish incredibly well...two pounds a man and they will paralyse the match.

The poor sections will decide who is the winning team. Yet they could also provide the individual winner! Odd shoals of big bream live at certain pegs, and the right man in the right swim could finish the day with 40 or 50lb. Yet these bream holes do not stretch for several swims. One peg away will be out of sight!

Bream are in every section, but they rarely show in matches. And there seems no set pattern as to how they feed. They could be on the bottom; they could be on the top.

You can be fishing away for roach, chub or dace and go clump into a bream. Then it's up to the angler to change tactics. Fish for them from the start and if they don't feed, you will blank out.

The locals say the Arlesey bomb doesn't work with the Avon bream. But Leicester anglers have caught odd ones on the bomb in practice. Just because we don't fish the river a lot - it's more than 100 miles away - doesn't mean Leicester can be discounted.

We've plenty of friends down there who are helping us with information, and next time we are practising on the better sections. We've heard of 20 to 30lb pleasure catches.

I will have no team instructions for Leicester. Each man will fish his peg for what he thinks it's worth. It will be up to him to decide his approach.

We go for an individual win first, then for a team. How can you tell a man to go bleaking for the first hour and perhaps throw away the chance of £1,500? I'd be kicked all over the car park if a Leicester angler lost the individual title through following my team instructions. Anyway, which is the bigger honour? As a team we like to collect the top prize, but only by fishing it our way.

I've noticed that the Bristol anglers seem very confident. I've no doubt they are extremely good anglers, but you don't get the big names fishing the Avon matches.

When Cofton Hackett used to fish the Avon team championships, they won the title so many times they stopped entering the match. And even in the competition we fished in practice, only one Bristol angler appeared in the top six. The rest were five outsiders - two Londoners, two from Leicester and one Witham angler.

The National might open the Bristol lads' eyes to the fact that 'foreign' methods could be better than their own. Surface fishing is no challenge.

But there is one great advantage which the local anglers have over all the cracks, and that is a sound knowledge of the water. As soon as they draw, they will know the swims they are fishing. And for that reason, I pick Bristol to finish in the first four.

Along with them should be Birmingham, CALPAC, Bradford or Leicester. One of these five teams must be the winner. Both Bradford and CALPAC can catch a lot of small fish - which it pays to do under the points system.

Ray Mumford has been fishing extremely well this season, and he will push and push his team to back him up. The London anglers have been winning a lot of competitions on the Avon in recent months. And I know Ray is hungry for a team win.

I rate Birmingham as the country's best all-round side, while Leicester are as good as the river will let them be. The side has performed on every river in the country, so I don't see why the Avon should be any exception.

There is, however, one more cloud on the horizon. In places, the Avon looks no wider than a brook and the fish definitely won't stand spectators. The top teams will take a slaughtering from the crowds, so don't think I'm being mean when I say I hope it pours with rain on Saturday week.

NATIONAL STRANGLED BY POINTS SYSTEM
[September 21st, 1972]

THE points system has killed the National. This isn't sour grapes because Leicester didn't win - despite catching the top weight. It's just stating the case for the smaller associations who I believe will never again climb the rostrum to collect the team trophy.

The NFA has turned the National into a super league. Big name sides like Birmingham and Leicester will always be in the top ten places. But under the points system, the unknowns are doomed to fail.

Leighton Buzzard shot to fame in 1968 when young David Groom won the Broads National with 37lb 6oz 4drm. His exploits helped his team to victory, but under the new system Leighton would probably have finished well down the list.

The only alternative is for teams to import big names into their sides. And I can foresee a lot of anglers in the future switching from team to team.

My prediction that the river would fish badly was certainly borne out by results. Nearly 500 anglers caught less than a pound - more than half the total field! Even in the top sections there were plenty of dry nets, although some excellent weights were recorded.

The Avon holds 'slotmachine' bream. They are so tight in certain pegs that catching them is like feeding two bobs into a fag machine. The next man could be struggling to catch but the more he tries to get the bream away from his neighbour, the more he ruins his own swim.

I drew in B section where I knew that I hadn't a chance of winning the match. But under the points system it was vital that I should catch anything that swam. I was netting roach of 1oz 8drm to make sure that they didn't escape - something I never normally do.

My first cast went straight into a tree, but as soon as I got rid of the initial nerves it was down to business. There were a lot of spectators behind me, but I wasn't bothered. These people had travelled fair distances to watch me, and I hope they enjoyed themselves. They were a good-natured crowd and we had a laugh and a joke together. I had to ask some little girls to move, but only because they were in danger of being hooked.

My 4lb made me second in my section, but although the Leicester team had another two seconds, plus a win, we still totalled a horrible 333 points. We held our own right through the bad sections but blanked-out in those where we expected to do well.

We were winning the National until you come to these last two sections. A look at last week's results table will show you what I mean.

Birmingham had collected 245 points, but were penalised with only three points from L and M. Leicester had only 215 points but were flattened with a massive 118 points from the last two.

Now make no mistake, we were there to win the team prize as well as the individual. But we were a little unlucky and the points system beat us.

The team plan was to struggle to catch anything in the lower sections and go for a win if it looked possible in the better sections. We all had wasp grub but virtually nobody caught on it.

If we had drawn next to Birmingham we would have matched them bait for bait. And we even had a secret bait which we knew Birmingham hadn't got. But Birmingham won on the day, although we were 14lb clear on weight.

Young Phil won the National with 33lb 8oz but a mere 15lb would have ensured he still collected only one point from his section.

As the NFA are obviously sold on this points system, why don't they go the whole hog and adopt all the Continental rules? For example they could ban legering in the National. This would certainly make things a lot easier for all the top teams, which they seem intent on doing!

Then there's the system where they decide individual

placings on section results. This happened to Percy Anderson in the French Championships. He caught the second highest weight and finished 6th!

This method is just as farcical as the points system. It's not as if the rest of the country's matches are fished to points. The sooner the small clubs realise the dangers of the new system and vote it out at the next Conference, the better for matchfishing.

But I shall always remember this National as the day Phil Coles grew up. When I got off the bus and they first told me that Phil had caught 33 lb8oz, I was so stunned that at first I thought they were joking. But really I just wasn't surprised. Phil is a natural at fishing like other young men are born footballers, cricketers or golfers. If I could find another dozen like Phil I'd pack up work and become their manager.

Provided he looks after himself and meets a nice girl who understands fishing, Phil's got a great future. Angling is an up-and-coming sport and if professionalism is ever introduced, Phil is just the right age to make it a career. He's only 18 but we've fed so much water knowledge into him that when it comes to angling he's got a head on his shoulders like a 40-year-old. Phil's father, a greyhound trainer, used to take me fishing when I was a lad so I knew young Phil from an early age, and used to watch him play football.

Two years ago Phil lost his father and since then he has virtually lived in my shadow. I would take Phil along to open matches, pay his pools and give him just one bait. He couldn't actually win the match, but he would find out what I wanted to know about the water.

Older anglers took no notice of a young boy fishing, and I could trust him to discover how the fish reacted to certain baits. I used Phil as a guinea pig for 18 months, until I knew that he was ready to tackle the big matches.

He still needs a little bit of confidence pushing into him, but his record this year shows that he is growing in stature match by match.

He finished 10th with 29lb on the Huntspill a few weeks

ago, besides winning the close-season open at Marco Lakes. He still asks me what to do before a match, and I hold nothing back. This likeable lad could grow into the greatest angler of all time.

SPONSORS AND BOOKIES MAY GET US ON TV
[October 26th, 1972]

MORE people go fishing on a Sunday than cram into the terraces at Anfield, Highbury and the rest of the country's Football League grounds on Saturday afternoons. Yet try telling that to a TV producer or a sports editor. They'd laugh!

Angling is Britain's Cinderella sport, and it is still waiting for a Prince Charming. But I believe that we could witness a revolution in the next few years that might put match-fishing on a par with golf.

Walk into any bookmakers and you will see odds quoted for all the big stars competing in major tournaments. Any member of the public can have a flutter on Lee Trevino or Tony Jacklin. So why shouldn't a similar scheme work for anglers fishing any of the river championships or big opens?

Rotherham bookmaker Jim Wooding ran successful books on this year's Gladding Championship and Woodbine Final - the only two sponsored matches. And I can foresee this growing, especially when more tackle firms step in to sponsor other big-money competitions.

Giving the angling public a chance to bet on the cracks would be the best way to drum up interest in a big contest. It would increase the number of spectators and win the maximum amount of publicity for the sponsoring firm.

Who knows, in time we might even see matches televised on World of Sport. But in the meantime anglers have to be grateful for any publicity they get, however small.

When Phil Coles won £2,000 in the National Championship you needed a magnifying glass to find a mention in our local paper. Yet if an 18-year-old golfer or show jumper had won the biggest tournament in England the news would have been splashed right across the sports pages.

Look at the publicity given to soccer star Trevor Francis, hailed as Birmingham's boy wonder. Yet Phil's achievements are ignored by the popular press.

When Leicester won the National Championship on the Severn last year, we had to apply for a reception with the Lord Mayor. But if Leicester City had won the FA Cup the team would automatically have been given a civic reception. The Mayor gets a ticket for the Cup Final, but he's very welcome to come and watch Leicester fish the National.

It was the same when I was picked to fish for England. There was very little coverage in the local press. Yet it's headlines if a Leicester soccer star is selected by Sir Alf.

Leicester anglers certainly made an impact in last week's Nene Championships - we had the top three anglers plus the first three teams. How did we do it? Well, take it from me there's no 'magic' involved . . . just good fishing and careful homework.

Both teams of likely Lads knew where they wanted to draw to stand a chance. We had practised on the North Bank during the week and found the river moody. But the area between permanent pegs 270 and 320 produced some good bream for Roy Marlow. Now if you cared to look back over match results for the North Bank for several previous years you would find these pegs consistently producing the winning weights at this time of year.

For some reason the big bream - which have been absent in Nene matches so far this year - move into this feeding area. Luckily Roy drew peg 292 in the actual match and walked it. Before the start I thought that 16lb would clinch the championship, and so it proved with Roy taking 19lb 13oz. He knew the fish were in front of him and mid-week practice had given him the confidence to catch them.

Brian Dexter drew just three pegs away and finished second while Phil Coles at 316 was third. Phil got his fish later in the match and I thought that he might beat Roy.

I drew a peg in the 60s where I thought that I would either catch a lot of fish or none at all. Two RAF chaps rang me before the match and asked if they could watch me fish. But when I saw where I had drawn I told them to go and watch Roy. It was a good job they did as I weighed in only 2lb 2oz.

It's a great shame that we aren't able to fish more matches on the North Bank as we regard this water as a second home. We understand its fish and its moods.

But to anyone who regularly matchfishes this water without much success, I would say make a note of the winning peg numbers of the matches you either fish or see reported in the Times. Then over the months you may notice a pattern of fish movement or catches. This way you will be able to make full use of a good peg if you draw one, rather than grope blindly for that first couple of hours.

SECRETS THAT WON THE GREAT OUSE MATCH
[July 5th, 1973]

GROUNDBAITING is just common sense, but dozens of anglers still persist in attacking shoals of bream with balls of bait like concrete. In last week's Great Ouse Championship, I saw anglers making three or four balls before the whistle. The bread was baking hard in the sun and no doubt had a similar effect to house bricks when thrown at the fish.

I noticed an angler opposite who had four of these rock-hard balls in the air at the same time. Fortunately I wasn't next to him! I took 20lb of dry with me, and got through 10lb. That might not seem much, but it was enough to keep the fish feeding on the day.

Some anglers just throw in everything they've got, catch-one fish, and then sit and wait for five hours. This is good for the tackle dealers who sell the groundbait, but no goodfor fishing.

If the man who took the most stuff with him won the match, then I'd start loading my car at six in the morning. In the summer, the rivers are stale and gentle cloud groundbait is all you want. The heavy stuff should be used only when the river is "batting" along in times of flood.

Some anglers seem to be suffering under the delusion that the man who throws in the most groundbait is going to win. Well, I wish it were that simple. Just how many fish do these anglers want to catch? Judging by the amount of groundbait they use, you'd think they were after two hundredweight. All I want to do is catch enough fish to win. It's still the same money whether you win by 10oz or 10lb.

I thought the record would go on the Channel last Sunday week, but I guessed a catch of 40lb would put me in the first four. And, as it proved I was well on target. After I had drawn my peg, people told me that I was in a good section, but in the wrong area. And when I saw my peg, I had the feeling that I wasn't going to catch. There wasn't a sign of a fish moving in the Channel below Stow. So it looked as though I was going to struggle badly.

The whistle went and I put in five balls of cloud bait laced with squatts. Out went my bomb taking two gozzers on a size 20 hook on a six-foot tail to the middle. I put my swingtip rod in the rest and waited. Other anglers round me continued the cannonade, and as if in protest, the bream started to show five pegs away by rolling and splashing on the surface. The fish were obviously unsettled and started coming my way up the Channel.

Would they settle in front of me? The answer came soon enough, when my swingtip shot up. I struck, but with the maggots untouched I presumed it was a line bite. I had four line bites on my next cast which I left alone, putting in the odd ball now and again.

Slowly the bream started to settle, and I started to catch odd fish - nothing fast but they kept feeding. A gallery slowly grew behind me and it was the spectators' presence which kept down my weight. My tip was going up and down like a yo-yo with line bites. And I knew the crowd behind were expecting me to strike.

If I had waited for proper bites every time before striking, my style would have looked ridiculously crude. A fish taking the bait would pull the tip out straight, and keep it there, whereas a false bite from a fish swimming into the line made the tip drop back quickly after straightening.

Under these conditions, with bream moving about in the swim, I like to sit with my arms folded. This stops me striking and dragging the bomb back through the shoal, hitting the fish and scaring them.

But the crowd was expecting me to strike when the tip lifted as many as three times. So every so often I would have a go, even though I suspected they were only line bites. As a bonus I foul-hooked a couple of bream. Normally I wouldn't have had so many strikes, and I could have caught a lot more fish.

I didn't expect to win when they weighed my catch at 53lb 3oz because a huge weight is always a possibility on the Channel. The angler on one side had an eel, and the chap on the other had about 10lb.

This angler - I don't know his name - is my lucky mascot. Last year, when I won the Championship, he was drawn next but one to me!

THE FRENCH ARE SMALL FISH MASTERS
[September 19th, 1973]

FRANCE have the best international match team in the world- but if those crafty continentals had entered a team of 12 to fish the Witham National they would have stood no chance of winning! They would have finished in the top six but the style at which they're masters would have defeated them. When it comes to matchfishing our methods and those of the top continental teams, France and Belgium, are literally poles apart! And any group of anglers who manage to perfect our methods of legering and long range float fishing, as well as the European tactics of pole fishing, would clean up week after week on the match circuit in England.

If a French team had fished the Witham they would have stuck to the methods at which they're best. In the low weight sections and those where fish were hard to come by, they would have picked up a lot of section points by catching small fish. But they would have failed on the sections which produced the big bream weights - they just don't have the necessary experience of bream fishing.

A lot of nonsense has been trotted out in the past about the way the French are just 'tiddler snatchers' fishing with tiny hooks that have to be whipped under a microscope.

To understand their tactics you have to understand their match rules. In a French open, section performance is vitally important - just like the new National points system. They will split a 400 peg match into say four sections and the top four individuals in the match will be the four section winners in descending order according to weight, and not the four individuals with the four heaviest weights.

The fifth, sixth, seventh and eighth individual placings are then taken by the men who finish second in each section, with the fifth place being taken by the section runner-up with the heaviest weight.

This is the key to French consistency - they go flat out for a section placing. But at the same time it means they can't afford to gamble on 'blowing out' on big fish - and that's why their tactics are geared to speed fishing for small fish.

Their tactics are gradually changing and in a few years' time they'll be fishing like English anglers. They've realised they can learn a lot from our methods - and make no mistake when they switch to rod and reel they'll be a force to be reckoned with. We might even let French manager Robert Tesse join the Likely Lads!

There are two essentials for success in match fishing today - line control and feeding. If you have mastered one, but not the other, you'll have a limited amount of success. If you've mastered either you'll be lucky to win anything. You can have the best kit, the best bait and the best groundbait in the world - but if you can't control your line you might just as well fish in the field behind you.

The French have mastered these two essentials - and geared themselves to catching what we would call 'small' fish. Their poles give them better line control than even the best English angler can ever attain with a rod and reel. The best pole angler in England just couldn't live with the French or Belgians - it would be like matching my 13-month-old son against Benny Ashurst or Billy Lane. It's their method, and they've had years to perfect it.

Their feeding is brilliant too - but I don't think it would make much impact on our open match circuit. They mix concrete hard balls of groundbait studded with bloodworm and jokers. It works well - but only because French conditions are different to those on our rivers. There's no such thing as a hook-shy French fish. Nearly every fish caught there is taken home for the pot.

On the Welland or Witham you're after fish which may have been caught as many as four or five times before - and they don't take kindly to having balls of concrete lumped on top of their dorsal fins.

Many French rivers take in open sewers - and these are a natural source of bloodworm. Fortunately, our major rivers don't have open sewers running into them - and consequently our fish aren't quite as willing to get preoccupied with bloodworm.

French matches are shorter than ours, and the French feeding pattern is geared to producing a golden half hour when they produce a fish a cast. They don't keep fish feeding as long as English anglers. The fish go off after that half hour spell because they've gorged themselves on bloodworm.

Contrary to popular opinion, the French don't fish all that light. They fish a lot heavier than our own bloodworm experts and their usual hook sizes are 16, 17 and 18. Their preoccupation with section performances means they won't hesitate to scale down to a 22 or 24 for tiny fish if the going is really hard – but they prefer to catch larger fish if possible.

They don't bother about catching fish on the drop - their aim is to get the bait to the bottom as quickly as possible and they bunch their shot accordingly. The Leicester Lads are always looking to take fish on the drop - and-that French tactic intrigues me.

Anglers only get to the top in the match world if they're looking for new ideas all the time. You can't say that fishing on the drop is a better method than getting the bait down quickly or vice versa. On their day, both methods are match winners. And the angler who can perfect both methods, and know just when to use them, is going to be a consistent match winner too.

A large amount of French match tactics have little relevance to the English open circuit. But the anglers who master the French styles which could be adapted for our rivers will be smiling all the way to the bank. The first man to master English and Continental tactics will be a real world beater!

ROBERT TESSE – WHAT A GREAT ANGLER
[October 31st, 1973]

GETTING Robert Tesse to reveal his secrets is one of the best things Angling Times has ever done. This Frenchman is among the greatest anglers in the world and we must listen to what he says. His groundbaiting methods are fantastic and there's no doubt that they are deadly on his own waters. But I have my doubts about whether they would work to the same extent here.

The stuff they make their groundbait from is ridiculous - ground nuts, ground hemp, ground everything. But I am convinced that their real secret is in the little red jokers. Their whole philosophy is different. They feed their fish where we do our best not to. We just tickle their fancies, so to speak.

I've watched these Frenchmen, and they can get those little fish out a treat using their special groundbait. This is why I think it works. The French pack millions of tiny jokers into their exotic groundbait, carefully blended from ingredients chosen to allow the jokers to burst from the little groundbait balls at exactly the right depth. Depending on what fish are sought, release of the jokers at varying depths can be controlled.

Another thing, they are dead keen on getting the right colour, whereas our groundbait is nearly always bread based and simply brown or white.

Although I agree with Tesse about colour, we must remember that in France fish don't get a chance to learn. The French kill everything they catch. Our fish have been caught dozens of times before, so we've got to kid 'em along every time. Their killing fish does mean that everything they catch is in perfect nick, while many of ours suffer from rough handling. But I just can't bring myself to kill a fish. They are precious things.

Anyway, you can judge for yourselves how good the French really are when they come to fish the Nene's North Bank next year. Their techniques will be good, very, very good. It will take us all our time to beat them. I really rate them, and they've beaten us twice already, don't forget.

If we fish to our rules we can go right out and beat them on the float or leger. If the bleak don't show, it will give another chance. It's nice to know that Tesse himself is dead interested in our methods and rates us higher than ever before. So we can't be bad!

But if Guy Herbert, the Tesses and Henri Guiheneuf bring their poles to the Nene, be prepared for some fantastic angling. We don't want to see them with rods and reels. That way we'll learn nothing.

The Nene will suit them down to the ground. Nothing will stop them whipping out double figures of roach, bream or bleak. But we will see if their long poles will scare the fish off. I have a feeling the shadow might frighten our fish, which have good reason to be shy of anglers. We're back to their killing fish again.

It will amaze you to watch them really splash their tackle down on the water when they are after bleak and small fish on the top. They're not being crude, just clever.

Think about it. Their joker-packed groundbait goes in in little hard splashes. My theory is that the fish quickly associate these little splashes with easy food. So when their tackle lands the same way, bingo, the same reaction.

How many of our bleak anglers who lay their tiny float and shots carefully across the water have thought of that? I've seen Guiheneuf whip out between three and four hundred bleak an hour fishing like that, so how can they be wrong? This is the sort of thing we have got to pick up if we are to beat them at their own game.

This tactic should work well on the North Bank with small roach. I've tried it on a larger scale in Ireland where I pack my feed into concrete-hard, Jaffa-sized balls. Within three or four minutes the fish are right on top of it, queuing up for the stuff in the groundbait.

There is also the advantage of only having to feed every 20 minutes or so. But again that's in Ireland where the fish are only rarely caught.

I would like to see the French beat us on the Bank. Then we could admit that it was their superior groundbaiting which did the damage. Our methods don't call for bloodworm. You couldn't buy a pint of casters in France for £2. But this money would get you a similar amount of jokers.

Bloodworm has been tried successfully on the North Bank when Graham Joynt and Roy Meredith of 'The Firm' sat between Roy Marlow and myself and gave us a bit of a hammering. Then we changed to the right style and turned the tables. But we learned something from them. If they had beaten us all the way, we would have learned even more!

SPECTATORS CUT MY MATCH WINNINGS BY £1,500

[January 9th, 1974]

I HATE to say it, but spectators who crowd around me in big matches are costing me very dearly. I am convinced that spectators have cut my winnings by as much as £1,500, as well as a golden chance of qualifying for the Woodbine event this year.

But the spectator problem is one I, and other names who attract the crowds, have got to learn to live with. It's a real dilemma, and one which must be solved. But how this can be done escapes me.

Angling badly needs those spectators who are prepared to turn out in all weathers to watch their heroes, and I would never back any move to ban them. It would be like having a Cup Final at Wembley without crowds.

It would help a great deal if spectators in the National and championship matches kept away for the first half hour or so to give anglers time to settle down on these big occasions when nerves are pretty raw. Spectators gain very little from these early minutes anyway.

I am always prepared to show them how I fished, how I fed and things like that...after the match. It will be worse than ever for this year's Welland National, especially for myself and the Leicester Lads. We have all done well on the Welland, and crowds are sure to gather around us to see if we can win.

The majority of Welland pegs are backed by a very high bank, making crowds stand out like skyscrapers. The National could well be a roach dominated match. Big crowds will kill off the chances of anyone lucky enough to draw a good bream peg.

To be honest, I would much rather have 500 people behind me and none behind the other lads, simply because I think I can take spectators better than they can.

If the match was judged on weight, it would not be so bad, as I would be prepared to catch less just to give them a spectator-free pitch. But we must all get the best from each peg on the points system and no team can afford to carry anybody.

The National and the chance of winning the Ouse Championship for four years running, are titles I badly want to achieve this summer. But I am really afraid that attention from spectators could well prevent me from winning either.

To be honest I enjoy having spectators around me, being a bit of a showman. If they didn't gather behind my peg, I would be really upset. They are all out for me to win.

Unfortunately they don't help me a bit. I love it when they clap and even tell me when to strike. Then matches often turn into a bit of an exhibition. Because they enjoy watching the big names so much, how can you tell people to keep away or moan afterwards that they've cost you the match.

Angling is not like any other sport in this respect. In football the crowds can shout and call you all the names under the sun without having any effect on your game. You've got the ball, and it's all up to you.

I am sure in time there will be big events like the Woodbine or Gladding featuring all the top men in say a three series competition. This would really pull in the crowds and I can't understand why it hasn't been done already. Then we will all have to learn how to live with the crowds, and why not?

They come to watch you catching big fish or lots of small ones at a fantastic rate. But the sheer fact that they are crowding behind stops you doing either. This is the real problem.

Would golf addicts be prepared to watch Tony Jacklin playing golf without a ball, or watch Barbra Streisand on television with the sound switched off? I doubt it.

I would hate to see spectators roped off. This would only have the even worse effect of creating crowds not only behind the star, but also around the poor anglers at adjoining pegs, who perhaps can't cope with spectators chatting and stamping about.

Another match I badly wanted to win but was prevented

from doing so by spectators was the Middle Level National. I had taken several 20lb-plus nets in practice from the same peg I drew. In the match itself, I caught only 4lb from the close in swim. I suppose it's the penalty the big names must be prepared to pay.

Going back to this year's Welland National, I could suggest that the NFA make only four access points on the lower river for spectators. This would thin the crowds out along the bank and give every competitor a chance to get going.

Many people don't realise that the Coronation Channel chub could easily win this National. But again, chub, which are probably the shyest fish swimming, will quickly head for home if even six spectators stand behind the angler lucky enough to draw the chub peg.

I can only ask any spectators who do want to watch either me or other anglers, to sit down and not to move about on the skyline then all of us will get the best out of these big attractions.

CONFIDENCE IS OUR EXTRA MAN
[October 2nd, 1974]

WHY are Leicester anglers so consistent? Why are we the most feared team in Britain? I'll tell you why. In every team contest we fish we have an extra man in our side.

In teams of four there are five of us. In Nationals we have 13 instead of 12…and break no rules by having this additional assistance. Let me introduce you to the man whose name has never appeared in Angling Times – although he's won more matches than anyone else in Britain. It's impossible to calculate how much cash he wins in the course of the average season.

His name is Mr Confidence. He's good…and he knows it. That's the main reason for his success. And it rubs off on the other members of the team. Leicester would rather drop

Ivan Marks than drop him.

In fact, as you know, I had to fish for England last weekend instead of in the National, but Mr Confidence stayed with Leicester.

Stan Smith wants him badly for the England side. He hasn't fished for England yet – which is one of the reasons why the team hasn't done as well as we would like against the Europeans...but the day isn't far off now.

How does this fellow exercise his influence? I'll tell you. He makes us fish from first to last, from the opening to the dying seconds. He never knows when he's beaten - and that's the lesson he has driven home to all the Leicester anglers.

One man can win or lose a National for his team in a matter of seconds. Mr Confidence knows that and although he sometimes finds it difficult to be at every Leicester peg all the time, his influence works wonders.

How did Mr Confidence prepare Leicester AS for last weekend's Division One National? He impressed on us all that we were the form team. He reminded us that only two of our anglers have yet to top 20lb in big Welland open matches. Some have done it many times.

How many other teams can say that? And the two who haven't yet quite topped 20lb – Pete Jayes and Trevor Tomlin – my stand-in, have both finished high in Welland match placings. So we were well prepared on that leg.

Of course it wasn't easy to get Mr Confidence to nominate for Leicester in the first place. Here's what we did which finally won him over.

Imagine you are a Leicester National man. You've been picked to fish, so clearly you've got the makings of a good matchman. You're at a team meeting - one of six we have every summer to discuss National tactics. Dave Rossi is in the chair. Dave and I are rated the most experienced in the squad so we control the discussions and push them the way we think they should go. It's all very friendly but there's a bite to it. Out of the blue Dave will announce a peg number, one in the National match length. Every man present is given a sheet of paper and is instructed to write down exactly how he would fish that swim, the bait he would use, his feeding rate, why he would go for one species instead of another and many other assorted details.

The writing done, Dave collects the sheets and then calls up one of the team to talk about what he has written down. He has to explain exactly what he would do when fishing that peg. And whatever he says must relate to what he has already written down.

That way we can burrow deep into a man's personal knowledge of a water - or we can assess whether or not he is conning us. It brings out his secrets and, just as important, his flaws. That way we destroy the doubts any man might have about his own knowledge and the team gets the complete picture from every man in it. That's Mr Confidence at work.

But it's a waste of time indulging in these capers weeks before any big match - whether it's a river championship, a big open or a National. The planning starts 18 months in advance of the fishing date. The team must realise its deficiencies long before the date looms large so that there's ample time to take advantage of the realisation that there are gaps in our knowledge.

Other, perhaps more defensive, reasons play a part in this early assessment and practice. We don't want our serious rivals to spy on us days before a big match, do we? We could so easily give the game away.

Our tactics in the end are our own. We want to keep them exclusive if we can for if every team starts a contest with as much knowledge as we have ourselves then they will beat us...if they get a much better draw than we do.

We pride ourselves on being the most professional outfit in match fishing today. We are determined to win everything that's worth winning...and if we don't quite succeed we get closer to a maximum return than anyone else.

We were favourites in the National just ended. We shall be favourites again next year on the Nene. And if people rated us this year because of our record on the Welland they must be equally confident of us on the Nene.

If anything, our record on the Nene is better than on the Welland. I've lost count of the wins we've had there in recent years. There are that many, and against the best of the opposition too.

So Mr Confidence is in the team for next year. We haven't got to renew his contract. He's there already.

HOW I'LL KNOW WHEN TO QUIT
[October 16th, 1974]

OUR Leicester AS and Great Wigston teams to fish this year's Trent Division of the Angling Times League are going to look mighty strange. Roy Marlow, Dave Downes and Dave Rossi won't be in either of them. No, they haven't been dropped. They've dropped out. To their way of thinking, the cash prizes in the Division are not really worth fishing for.

This is no mutiny. It's a simple application of our logic that poor fishing needs big cash prizes to compensate. When the fishing is liable to be less enjoyable, money talks and we all tolerate the poor fishing for the 'brass'.

I don't expect anyone except match anglers to see the point. And clearly some of those won't either for, after all, the Leicester proposal for amended pools for the Trent Division didn't find favour with most of the other affiliated outfits.

We believed that by changing the pools set-up, the top individual prize for the winner could be stepped up from £80 to £150. And that would have been worth fishing for.

We wanted the abolition of the puny team pool. This called for a 50p stake from every man involved with it, but gave the winning team an average of only £3 a head. As a betting proposition it just isn't on as far as some of our lads are concerned.

Our suggestion was for a £3 pools total which would have

included the match peg fee, but the majority wanted to stay at £2.50 and to continue this daft team pool. If anglers want to bet, why stop them? There's nothing compulsory about optional pools. Anglers who don't want them, or who prefer a limited wager, are free to make their own choice.

Let's have bigger individual pools. I think Dave Downes has been on the right lines with the open matches he has run. Dave has paid out 30 per cent to the individual winner, 25 per cent to the second man, 20 per cent to the third, 15 per cent to the fourth and 10 per cent for fifth. That's it.

I'm looking beyond the Trent Division to the Trent National in two years time. So Leicester and Great Wigston will be making some enforced changes. Leicester must make some changes for the Trent National. We already know that - even if we fish an unchanged side on the Nene next year. This will be a perfect opportunity to blood some of our youngsters in readiness for the National.

We must not make the same mistake as that famous Coventry team of the middle 1960s. Those men all grew old together. The same team fished year after year with little or no change. The time came when changes had to be made - and there was no one to step into the older men's shoes. That won't happen at Leicester.

This is all about team building. Don Revie can't teach Leicester anything about that. We won't be caught like Sir Alf with no replacements and a series of failures as the result. It's no good building one team and expecting that to stand for all time. I am now regarded as the senior professional at Leicester, I have no plans to retire, but I shall know when to step down. That, I trust, won't be for a long time.

There are plenty of years left in Ivan Marks. There's only one thing that can finish me and that's deteriorating eyesight. Once your eyes lose their sharpness it really is time to quit the big-time open match scene.

Good youngsters can't be blooded soon enough. Just look at the Leicester AS record. Phil Coles won the National for us when he was just 17. Trevor Tomlin, who fished for us on the Welland this year, was just 19. We set out to breed the winning instinct into the youngsters. Stuart Killen is an unknown now - although, of course, he was a member of our Junior National-winning side. Give him a couple of years and he could be ready for the Trent National.

When age kicks me out, it will be Roy Marlow or one of the other younger anglers who takes over as senior professional. And when Roy's day is done, then Stuart or another of the present crop of youngsters will take over. And so it must go on. Just so long as Leicester maintain this attitude, we shall be up with the top flight. We shall be in front for as long as it takes other teams to realise that our policy is the only one which can keep the team winning.

When he's 50, Stuart will have bred this will to win into other youngsters. Leicester will continue to be hard to beat. We can't win them all - but we shall get closer than most. So, as Roy Marlow, Dave Rossi and Dave Downes step out of our winter league teams, the door opens for others.

What will they be doing this winter? Remember what I told you last week...unobtrusive practice! That's how the big wins are made and wherever the National goes, we shall be ready for it.

THE GREATEST MATCHMEN OF OUR TIME
[April 23rd, 1975]

WHO were the great matchmen of the last era? I have no doubts at all about the four men I rate the best we have known - both for their contributions to angling by way of tackle and techniques, as well as their superb match records.

My quartet has to be Benny Ashurst, Billy Lane, Sammy Buxton and Fred Foster. They were the giants when I was a young lad first taking an interest in match fishing. All took a lot of prize money out of match fishing. They also put a lot into it that others have benefited from.

I wouldn't like to have to place those four in any order of merit. But with Fred Foster's death so recently, I must tell you a story about Freddy. It's my tribute to a man I shall always regard as the King of the Witham. And I speak for everyone I know in Leicester when I say that.

Dave Downes was desperately keen to learn more about swingtipping the Witham. That he did learn was apparent in the last Witham National which Dave lost by a gnat's whisker with over 40lb of fish in his net.

We have always believed that a shortcut is to sit behind one of the acknowledged stars of any river. So Freddie was the man to watch for the Witham.

Dave hurt his arm and couldn't fish one weekend – at least that's how I remember it. His arm bandaged and wearing his best hang-dog look, Dave asked Fred if he could follow the maestro to his peg and sit down and watch.

"You can come and sit behind me any time you like, son", said Freddie. He then explained what he hoped to do.

"I won't catch bream until 12 o'clock. The water will start to pull after and that's when the bream will come", he said.

He wasn't quite fishless when 12 o'clock arrived but immediately after he began to catch the occasional bream, finishing fourth out of more than 300 with 12lb-plus.

Maybe Dave would spot the bites Freddie saw now but at the time, with limited experience he missed most of them. Dave came back to us after and admitted he was puzzled. How had Freddie seen his bites? We talked it over. Freddie was probably watching his line, not his swingtip, for indications of a bite. We dismissed every other possibility.

For me Fred Foster had to be the King of the Witham. I can't see anyone else in the future giving the sustained performance that Fred put in. Jim Wooding reckoned Freddie's open match wins at 80. I don't pretend to know Freddie's exact record but he had that uncanny knack of winning at unrated pegs.

A stretch in the match length would have fished badly for weeks but more often than not when Freddie was drawn there that stretch showed a sudden improvement.

Freddie was never in a hurry. He did things methodically, not quickly, and as a result he kept his mistakes to the minimum. I believe his clangers could be numbered on the fingers of one hand during the six-year period when he seemed to be winning almost at will.

Remember the year Coleshill won the Division Two National on the Welland? They were drawn next to Barnsley - and Freddie was in the Barnsley side. He drew D Section, next to Norman Haynes. The bream didn't show anywhere in the area. Norman didn't get a bream, Neither did dozens of others. But Freddie got one. With that sort of ability it was obvious that when Freddie had a good draw, everyone else was fishing for second place. Worms, maggots, bread; Freddie was master of them all.

It isn't widely known that Freddie was the master of the float in his younger days, but he realised long before most that a float couldn't compete with the bomb for big weights on the Witham. The finesse he had acquired for floatfishing made him equally fussy when he switched to legering.

Freddie Foster's record, perhaps more than anyone else's, should help convince those people who down-grade legering as an inferior aspect of match angling, requiring little or no skill, that this is far from the case.

WHY THE SEVERN IS AT THE TOP OF MY LIST
[April 7th, 1976]

I AM frequently asked to name my favourite river. The answer is simply that I haven't got one but my results over the past season suggest I should prefer the Severn.

My own table of merit for the primary rivers used in the open match circuit, based on my results for the 1975-76 season, is this:

1 - Severn. 2 - Warwickshire Avon. 3 - Welland. 4 - Trent. 5 - Witham. 6 - Great Ouse. 7 - Nene.

Why do I put the Severn at the top of my list? Simple, I fished it eight times last season and weighed in 6lb, 9lb, 15lb (twice), 17lb, 19lb and 20lb. The only blemish was one waterlicking. That lot gave me a match average of 13lb. I won a bit of money on the river but, just as important, I caught fish even when I couldn't make the frame.

My weights from the Warwickshire Avon were spotty, just like the pegs I drew. Of six match pegs, three brought blanks but the others gave me 10lb, 17lb and 21lb - an 8lb average over the six matches.

In 14 visits to Brummieland I recorded eight double-figure weights. And every 10lb-plus catch won money.

My conclusion has to be that the West Midlands fished far better than Eastern England throughout the season. Why? Because the West Midlands had flowing rivers at times when the east had no flow at all.

Both the Severn and Avon are natural rivers. Man hasn't messed them about too much and they have what I call the grand slam to fish for: roach, dace, chub, bream and barbel. They've got everything.

Dave Downes, my Leicester AS colleague, fished the Severn just three times for a 38lb total so Dave's average is about the same as mine. If this year's form starts to repeat itself next time then I shall see more and more of the Severn and much less of Eastern England.

I put the Nene right down at the bottom of the league. In four matches on it my weights were 6lb, 2lb, 10lb and 2lb - an average of 5lb. That doesn't sound too bad but considering that my track record on the river over the years is about the best I have, I rate it a very poor return.

In fact I reached the stage where I cheerfully opted for a day on the Loughborough Soar rather than fish the Henson Memorial match on the Nene. I weighed 7lb for 6th place on the Soar, so it's a fair bet I did the right thing.

The Nene has gone back terribly. There's got to be something wrong with it but no one is talking. The reduced flow hasn't helped. Neither has the fact that many of the bankside trees have been felled, but the decline must be for deeper reasons than those.

In ten visits to the Welland my match weights were 6lb, 9lb, 9lb, 15lb, 8lb, 3lb, 3lb, 4lb, 7lb and 11lb. That's a total of 75lb for a 7lb-plus average.

I would have done better on the Welland had I been drawn in better sections. I've no complaints about the number of section wins achieved. It's just that they were the wrong ones! I was never in with any real chance of a bream weight on the Welland the whole season…but the law of averages says that things could be better for me there next season.

Results were not, of course, helped by the fact that the river backed up far more often than it ran. Like the Nene it needs flow if it is to produce fish.

I won money nine times out of ten on the Welland - but with the weights consistently much lower than those I managed on the Severn for a lower success ratio.

Visits to the Witham were curtailed to three last season. The Witham is going through a bad patch in which close pegging has played a big part and it isn't now as popular as it used to be. My weights there were 7lb, 6lb and… 6oz. And that 6oz weight won me a section!

I put the Great Ouse low in the placings because again, here is a river man has messed about far too much. The flow is erratic. Sluices now control the flow to the extent that there's still water for hours. Then, suddenly, and out of the blue, the river is allowed to run like stink for an hour or more - or less. If the flow was allowed to be continuous through each 24 hours at whatever pace the backwater imposed we should be very much better off. The fish would be and so would we.

Goodness only knows why we should have to suffer such stupid control of the flow rate. It seems obvious that no one who knew anything about fishing was involved with the decision-making. Or that anyone involved with fishing cares!

So, the Severn is top of my league for 75 - 76. In all I fished 29 major contests, winning cash 19 times for a total of

£1,400. Considering I didn't win any major prizes I can't really complain...but I hope to do better next time.

THE WINNERS IN THE MONEY LEAGUE
[April 14th, 1976]

THE money league recently published in Angling Times revealed once again that it is the consistent anglers, the mature men over 30 years of age who stay the pace year after year.

Over the 1975-76 season Ken Giles is the most notable example. He topped the league with £3500 in match winnings. But take away his mammoth £2,500 payday in the Woodbine Challenge and he still gets into the listings.

If you've made a habit of studying the placings year after year there are some recurring factors that are well worth remembering for anyone hell bent on getting himself a nitch in next year's table.

Two of these stick out a mile. The first is that the regular winners come from areas where fish are plentiful. They fish rivers where there is a better chance of making something of a swim; where ability counts. And the other prime point is that they get there via floatfishing. There are bomb anglers in the top placings every year but it is most noticeable that few if any bombmen figure two years on the trot.

To some extent at least this has to confirm there's more skill in floatfishing than in legering...how else can the top float men consistently do so well yet the bombers dip out? To be brutally honest about it, many of the top-flight leger men have made their reputations via the hat. They've drawn well and picked up big money.

The float angler has to fight hard all the time. He's not handed so many winning pegs but sheer craft gets him through often in the face of intense competition from other cracks.

Mind you, there's always an exception...and that's Fred

Bailey. I thought there would never be another Fred Foster but there is...Fred Bailey. At one time Fred was christened 'Fred the Bread' since bread was the key to much of his early success. But the Kidderminster crack has all the craft that's needed these days. When he sits right he can't be beaten. His leger tactics will beat the float men every time...when he has drawn well.

It isn't widely known that in his younger days Fred was a fantastic float angler but he is 57 now. He recognised some time back that if he wanted to stay a winner he would have to change his style. Reduced eyesight beats the best in time. So Fred made the switch and everyone now knows how successful that has been for him.

Fred is the only man who has ever given me a rollicking on the river bank for making a tactical mistake. It happened late last season when I was making up my mind how to fish a Severn match. Everyone else said that the feeder would win. All the renowned float men were dogmatic that this was one occasion when swimfeeder tactics would triumph. Everyone except Fred Bailey.

Fred made the point that I had been enjoying a good run with the float and said he thought I was daft to change... but change I did. I used the feeder and finished second in a match I would have won if I hadn't switched styles.

That wasn't my only error last season. I made one in the Lawden Masters that I'm sure pleased Jim Wooding. I had a big bet that day. The odds were 12-1 and I don't expect to get that price again in a field of only 30 anglers. So I plopped £100 on a straight win...and lost the match by ounces.

Had I won I would have pocketed £2,400 - £1,200 from Jim and £1,200 from the prize money. Instead I picked up £400 for second, paid Jim £100 and finished with £300. Not a bad day's work, but £2,100 less than it might have been.

What I haven't told anyone before is that I laid my rod down for three minutes during the match to talk to people on the far bank. Expensive, that. Shows how important concentration is, doesn't it.

The bloke who owned the garden and bank on the opposite side of the river had stuck up a notice - "25p TO WATCH IVAN MARKS FISH". That notice was in fact taken down before the match started but to some extent the damage had been done.

I'm not bleating about it. I should have won I think. But that, after all, is match fishing. At least the Brummies now acknowledge that I shall always be a threat to them on their own river. That in itself is no mean accolade to win.

We are still a long, long way from the days when match anglers win as much in a season as the top golf pros. Each year more and more men top the £1,000 mark in match winnings but it will be some years before anyone grosses £5,000 in a season. To do it next year someone would need to win at least two out of the Woodbine, the National, the Tetley Gala and the Lawden Masters – and put up a good supporting sequence everywhere else. I can't see that happening.

Three years ago only six men topped £1,000 in a season. Last time 18 did it. Next year the total could rise to anything between 20 and 25.

The Gladding Masters is, of course, one big booster contest. The prize pick-up amounts to £500 for the winner but with Jim Wooding in attendance it is possible to take home £1,500.

At the end of the season though, when all the reckoning up has been done (by those who take the trouble), everyone has to face the fact that there are no wealthy match anglers. In most cases, the cost more than consumes the winnings. Only the fun and memories remain for long.

TAX THREAT NONSENSE

[June 29th, 1977]

IT SEEMS that at long last all this chat about the huge amounts of money won by match anglers has percolated back to the taxman. Not, I think, that anyone has anything to worry about. If anything, we may be better rather than worse off as the result of it.

It is though first of all important to get two things into perspective - the cost and the winnings - and to establish the relationship between the two. For there's no taxman in this country who can consider one without the other.

I haven't done my sums seriously, mainly because I don't think it will be necessary, but I reckon it costs me £650 a year for match fishing. Could be a bit more. There's no way I can ever hope to win big match paydays without spending that money. We have to fish a lot of matches to be sure of ever getting a few pegs that provide the chance of winning. So the taxman really must allow us expenses to set against winnings.

My first question to the taxman has got to be this: if you want to take your share of my winnings when I win, do I get a tax rebate when I fail? In other words if I win less than it has cost me to fish a full (tax) season, I am as much entitled to a rebate as Inland Revenue is entitled to a cut out of my takings in a good year. That's fair, isn't it?

I reckon that my matches average out at a cost of £8 to £10 a time. Nationals obviously cost a great deal more than that. Then there's the cost of practice sessions. Can a tax officer legitimately separate the cost of practice (practice to win) from the cost of actually fishing In the match? Of course he can't.

In essence one does it in order to have a chance of the other. So we must be entitled to show match fishing practice as a perfectly legitimate expense.

Clearly there is no way that the Inland Revenue can attempt to tax winnings from a bookmaker: from Jim

Wooding and Ladbrokes. There is already a betting tax in existence that gets the taxman his whack from that source and it would clearly be most immoral to crop the same source twice.

If they tax us then expect the winning punters at Newmarket to have to pay up too. And that won't go through without a massive fight!

I really think the taxman may have been inadvertently conned into believing that the money involved is in fact much bigger than it is. Look at the big money league Angling Times publishes every year and you see the results for yourself. On average no more than 20 men win £1,000 or more in the course of a season. Although figures have never been put together for people winning lesser aggregate totals I believe there could be as many as 100 anglers who 'win' £650 a year. In my view everyone who wins less than £650 could not be eligible for any sort of tax.

Let's be generous and assume that everyone who topped £1,000 won £1,500. That gives a grand total of £15,000. And the 100 anglers who topped £650 but didn't make £1,000. They could have won a total of £80,000...making a grand total of £95,000. But we must deduct £650 expenses for each man: total £18,000. Which leaves Inland Revenue with a potentially taxable £17,000.

Assume they took half; leaving £8,500. They've got to have staff, premises and all the expense factors for interviewing and checking and it is absolutely clear that it just isn't on. Even more so when every failed matchman - everyone winning less than £650 that is - can claim a rebate.

There's no way that the Inland Revenue can simplify the business by just taxing people who win, say, National Championships and the Embassy Knockout. Mind you, it might not be such a bad thing for us if they taxed all matchmen. I've got ten rods I use for matches. At present day prices those cost an average of £30 apiece. That's £300. I've six reels at some £20 a time: £120. And a basket full of quite expensive miscellaneous gear. There must be another

£100-worth there. So my tackle costs £500. And of course, you'll agree, there's not much point in going fishing without tackle…so assumedly the Inland Revenue must give me an allowance on the cost of my tackle every year if they expect me to earn them some money!

So, there's no need to worry about it lads. There'll be no tax on match winnings. It would be nonsense in every respect…although, come to think of it, there's an awful lot of nonsense about these days.

Picture the scene at, say, next year's National. A taxman is on the bank measuring your maggots for quantity to set against your income tax returns. There's another testing monofil to see just how long it lasts. It really is too ridiculous to contemplate. It just isn't on.

VERDICT ON THE 1977 OUSE CHAMPIONSHIP
[July 6th, 1977]

MY COMMENTS on the Great Ouse Championship in which I inquired about the £1.50 cost of a ticket to fish didn't go down at all well with at least some of the organisers of this annual event. In fact one of them gave me a bit of stick on match day.

I don't really think he got very far for he tried it in public - and it was clear that if the issue had been decided by vote that what I said was a popular reflection of public opinion.

I still say £1.50 is too much for a match ticket…and there must have been some belated rethink by the Great Ouse Consultative officials for the prize money paid out of the entry fee was doubled.

The Daily Mirror has detailed the miscellaneous expenses that eat so heavily into the cash available in this contest. Let me say here and now that I have no objection, none whatsoever, to GOFCA, the local angling consultative organisation, getting a £250 backhander. It's an angling organisation from which, assumedly, anglers benefit. So it's 'fair dos' anglers should have to help defray the cost.

No one though can be quite so happy about the £400 paid to 29 stewards...why that's £13 a man in round figures! Not a bad day's pay, is it? I would have thought there are easier ways of getting the work done at lower cost: all sorts of ways. Try some of these for size GOFCA, you may find them worth considering:

Let's begin by recognising there's nothing so special about running a river championship. It's just another match. It can be run efficiently without so many paid helpers on the day.

Scheme One: Limit the paid men to one per set of scale and recruit unpaid assistance from the competitors. They can draw a steward's card...as happens in most other open matches. And, without attempting to suggest I am being tightfisted, realistically, £10 a day is good pay for a steward in a river championship.

So, say, one set of scales to 40 pegs. Six hundred pegs need 15 sets of scales. Fifteen scalesmen at £10 a time and the expenditure is £150, cash saving: £250.

Scheme Two: No paid scalesmen at all. The match stewards are all competitors...three every forty pegs. Every competitor enters on the clear understanding that he is obliged to assist the weigh-in and stewarding on the bank as required. To compensate, there could be a special contest run for the stewards. Several ways of doing that: Three prizes either for the stewards who weigh-in the individual champion or a contest within a contest especially for those stewards. No charge on entry but three prizes (say £20, £15 and £10) for the best match weights made by stewards.

Certainly there are numbers of ways of rewarding otherwise-unpaid workers which would save most of, if not all, the £400 that went to the match stewards this year.

Clearly the match officials have got to do something. The match entry has fallen disastrously in recent years. At some 580 it was marginally better than I expected but a long way short of the days when close to 1,500 fished. I can't think of another river championship which has suffered such a drastic loss of public appeal.

To be scrupulously fair, it must be said that the Relief Channel itself is not now so popular as it used to be...for a number of reasons. Firstly it costs too much to fish it and anglers are stopping away in protest.

It is no secret that match bookings on the Channel have slumped to a fraction of what they were a few years back and the abortive bid to flog half the fishing didn't help. There was never any chance that any organisation would be interested in renting one bank from the Anglian Water Authority. But that wad of uncertainty helped shatter the Channel's popularity with the result that it is now little better than a pink elephant.

The Channel is now stuffed out with little skimmers. The water will continue to contain a massive stock of bream and its future as a potentially-great coarse fishery is assured. We must though continue to wonder if that potential will ever be exploited.

It is, of course, right to say that at least on paper its catch rate has been in decline in recent years. But those people who say that this last championship was the worst on record should make a detailed comparison with last year.

Last year 20lb won it but 8lb took third place. This time 13lb was the top weight but 8lb made only 10th place...so this year's was a marginal improvement. It would, I believe, be wrong to read any stock deficiency into the recent low championship results. True, there hasn't been so much sign of running bream in recent years. The remarkable incidence of line bites once so very frequent is not now so common, but there remains an exceptional head of big bream. I'm sure of that.

It certainly didn't help this time that the flow was constantly changing direction. I reckon it changed five times in the contest. Small wonder then that bites are scarce when the flow direction changes five times in five hours. Can't something be done to control factors like this on big match days? You'd think so!

Strictly, the water needs to be examined in detailed form to establish its potential. Small things have been done already. There's a couple of good car parks now that we didn't have years ago. But a similar park is badly needed at Downham Market to get cars off the main road. Anglian Water Authority should recognise that the 67p day ticket and massive season ticket cost hasn't worked. In fact, even in their terms, it must have been counter-productive; less income despite the high charges.

If form is any guide though the day ticket is more likely to rise to £1 than drop to 50p. Fishing is getting too expensive.

I can't sign off this week without some reference to the massacre Leicester AS suffered on the Nene at Barnwell Lock from Kettering. Why did it happen? No excuses, but we went in green. We took it too easily and didn't do enough homework. Kettering, on the other hand, worked at it in the days before the contest. Full marks to them.

Winning can never be taken for granted. It's about motivation...and no one has to be inspired to fish their socks off when they're drawn against recognised top-notchers. On the other hand the attitude that 'these are easy' can prove costly, as many of the big clubs in the Football Association, never mind the East Anglian Cup, have discovered to their cost.

So we have paid the penalty, and it hurts, but I reckon there were a few grinning at NFA headquarters last week. Can't blame 'em for that. After all this is exactly what the East Anglian Cup is all about.

YES WE ARE A CRAFTY BUNCH... BUT IN THE NICEST POSSIBLE WAY
[July 13th, 1977]

I CAN never quite understand why some match anglers should from time to time have a verbal bash at other match anglers. The game we are all involved in isn't so large, so popular and so widely-supported that people like

Ray Mumford can hope to gain anything either for themselves or for competition fishing.

It is so very easy to create the wrong impression. People will assume we can never agree about anything and that there is no natural link between all match anglers. Just a few weeks back Ray was knocking some sections of match anglers, notably those from the Midlands. There is really nothing to gain from doing this. As I read it, his main push was against the Brummies. Certainly he was setting out to draw a line between north and south when there's really nothing to gain.

So the Midlanders are 'crafty, clannish and bait mad', he suggests. No doubt everyone will happily plead guilty to point one since craft is vital. You can't hope to do much without being a craftsman.

Clannish? Yes, why not. Realistically I suppose we are clannish. That's really the reason why our teams have such a good long running record, why we are almost always difficult to beat. I take my hat off to the Brummies. They've got a lot of spirit and as much ability as it takes. They're not mealy-mouthed either. If you are good enough to win on their patch they give you full marks for it.

Of course we're out to beat each other, that's what it's all about, but I've never found them short on sportsmanship. And they give you their respect too, once you've earned it!

I wonder who Ray meant when he talked about the people who could only fish the Warwickshire Avon in such disparaging terms. In my book the regular winners at Evesham and elsewhere on the Avon include Max Winters, Ken Giles, Clive Smith, Barrie Brookes, Lloyd Davies and Ken Smith. Can anyone really suggest that these people are one-river men only, that they can't win anywhere else? That's the biggest heap of nonsense I've read in years.

If the Brummies can't fish other people's waters it is certainly difficult to explain how they've come to win the last two National Championships. And If they win again this year (and only a fool would say they can't do it) then they will have set up the first example of three-on-the-trot the National has ever known.

I can summon up a smile at the comment that Midlanders' tackle preparations take second place to the work they do on their bait. Matches aren't won by the newest, shiniest floats, the flashiest rods, the newest anything. The best of tackle is usually positively drab in appearance. That's my excuse - and I'm sticking to it.

Why are the most successful teams resident north, usually a long way north of the Thames? There are many reasons for that. I'm not knocking the south. They've never really had big-time match fishing on their actual patch and they've really got to travel to meet the tip top opposition...yes, even to the Warwickshire Avon.

Some of the south's individuals are better than they've ever been...and the numbers will increase. There will be more very good men down south. Why, you've only got to look at their team in this year's Super League. It's a better team than last year, I think.

Southern match anglers of outstanding ability are not splintered; splintered was the word used. They are thinly spread through a very big area...but the numbers are increasing all the time. And it will continue to grow.

The new-look NFA has perhaps helped and the return of the London AA to the National Federation is another plus factor.

It certainly isn't helpful to attempt to drive wedges between one section of match anglers and any other. We're all in the same game.

Why do the Brummies fish their local rivers a lot? That's a question they can answer better than I, but I do know the choice is theirs. Their match weights are good. They catch fish. Why should they be criticised for fishing the best waters instead of the second-rate ones? The Severn is the best river in the country. That's a fact. Match weights confirm that year after year with unfailing regularity. Can you blame them for fishing their own river...when it is the best in the country? The Severn and the Warwicks Avon are both well stocked with quality fish and there is, after all, something to be said for catching fish that have the size, the strength and the environment which helps them to fight back.

The really top-rate anglers all respect each other. They know the relative strengths and weaknesses of the best of the opposition just as well as they know their own limitations.

Take Kevin Ashurst. He's my big brother. We've never had a serious cross word between us in 20 years. Kev will give me a friendly rollicking if he thinks I've fished badly and I may do the same to him. But it's all fun. It's all about match fishing. It happens on the bank, in the cafe afterwards. It isn't newspaper talk. There's nothing to put into print. It's just that we have a harmony of interest. We're pals in competition.

Good anglers should always talk to people who ask questions. They should help other people. No one has ever heard me say to them "Why don't you clear off!" Sometimes people can be a nuisance, but there are two ways to react. I find it's much better to point out that if they want to watch me fishing they're better off sitting down rather than standing in full view, or walking about.

After all they want to see me catch fish. If they sit down I've got a chance. But I never tell them to buzz off! I actually enjoy helping people. And I like talking to them. I'm sure that my feelings are echoed by most of if not all the better known anglers.

Years ago the top names were Benny Ashurst, Sammy Buxton, Fred Foster and Billy Lane. That, at least is my top four from yesterday. They would all talk about their fishing... if you approached them properly. They all helped me and I'm sure they would have helped anyone else who wanted information and advice.

And so it is today. The anglers are the same. Only the names are different. I am really chuffed to see Phil Coles showing up so well this year. I expected it. And said so... and he's now again justifying all the confidence I ever had in him. I've helped make a great match angler in Phil...and other well-known men have done the same with other people. Does that make us clannish and crafty in any derogatory sense? I doubt it.

90LB-PLUS – WHAT A RIVER THE SEVERN IS!
[August 10th, 1977]

'VE SUNG the praises of the Severn enough recently so perhaps the river concluded it owed me a good day! Whatever the reason, I drew a good peg in the Kidderminster Open. What else can I say...I got 90lb 7oz from it....to finish second!

I've got a lucky hand so far as the Severn is concerned. I fancied the early 80s in this 100-peg match on the Winterdine length at Bewdley and that's what I drew, peg 80.

What's a good peg in the middle Severn worth these days? Fifty pounds? Sixty, even eighty, perhaps, and there are some of the local experts who are quite capable, I believe, of knocking .out an all-time match weight record, beating Ian Heaps' 166lb in Ireland earlier this year.

It's a question of the right man in the right peg on the right day. That permutation could be four years in coming - or it could happen next weekend. Hauling out these enormous match weights isn't quite the crude fishing that so many people imagine. There's a need to match the tackle to the occasion, of course, but it has still to be sensibly handled if the fish are to keep coming without too many dropping off on the way.

I don't think I fished particularly well to bag 90lb. If I fished the same match over again (how many times do we all say that?) I could get into three figures with some comfort but I don't know just how much better it could be. That's impossible to predict.

I do know though that the next time I fish this middle Severn I shall do so with three rods all set up. All of them with the 'big feeder' on, but each with a varied length of tail for the hooklength. I wanted rods with tails of 16inches, 2ft and 3ft but I had only the rod with the 16 inch tail. The great snag was that the barbel would keep having a go at the feeder itself.

The swim was only 3ft deep and if I had been able to fish a slower 'drop' I would have sharpened up the scoring rate. Not, of course, that it was slow as things were but it could have been better.

I had used the biggest swimfeeder I'd got. It had its holes opened up to allow the contents to evacuate at speed and I reckon it was absolutely empty within 20 seconds of every cast. It had to be because I used up between 13 and 16 pints of maggots in that match. I can't give an accurate amount simply because I filled the feeder so hastily that I must have 'lost' three pints during the day as they spilled out.

That 90lb 7oz was between 55 and 60 fish. I didn't keep an accurate account simply because there were so many fish. I reckon that 40lb was chub, 50lb barbel. The biggest chub weighed around 3lb 8oz to 3lb 12oz, the best barbel 2lb 4oz. The smallest fish of each species weighed 1lb but there were more small chub than small barbel. The catch included just two other fish: an 8oz roach and a 4oz dace.

How did I tackle up? This will make you blink. No, I didn't use a size 20. I settled for a 14 and fished that one eyed hook for the whole match, the first cast apart. On that first cast I hooked a biggish fish and the hook simply halved. Bad temper, no doubt.

Line breaking strain? Yes, again things were rather different. I settled on 6lb line...all the way through to the hook. When in Rome...

Tell you something else, I didn't use a landing net all the match. There's really no problem playing out fish on that sort of tackle and then grabbing them one-handed at the back of the head. Tom Bedder reckons that a 3lb 12oz chub is just about as wide a fish as can be lifted out that way!

If this is the week for surprises, I had better tell you about my hookbait. It was either a single or two maggots on that size 14. No need for three, four or five maggots, that was unnecessary - and took too long. When I tried caster, as seemed to help the scoring rate from time to time, I fished a single caster or a caster and a maggot on that same size 14 hook.

The trouble was that after a while the fish slowed down on maggot. A switch to caster brought them back again and when that too inevitably slowed then a change back to straight maggot brought more fish.

I had to try the float at one time in the match. I wouldn't be Ivan Marks if I didn't. I tried after about an hour but couldn't raise a fish although I trotted over the feeder-fed patch which was located just beyond the middle of the river.

Was it though just coincidence that after the break from swim-feeding I got the biggest chub next fish after the switch back to legering? I don't think so.

While the action was fast and furious the relatively small fish took over the swim. When the action slowed the bigger fish got a look in. On average I suppose the fish I got weighed in at 1lb 8oz apiece.

The continued use of the swimfeeder in the middle and lower Severn has produced some strange behaviour by the fish in the river. I am convinced the chub and barbel have become so accustomed to virtually feeding out of swimfeeders that they actually home in to the sound, sight and vibration of the swimfeeder hitting the surface after casting.

In some casts while running up that 90lb weight I had takes within 15 seconds of the feeder hitting the surface. It can't be contrived much faster than that - although I've got to concede there are better men at this than me. I'm not, mind you, saying they would remain so far out front as they are at the moment if I fished their river more regularly.

I have, of course, made an early move to the Severn this year simply because the eastern rivers are fishing so badly. Would you believe, you eastern area anglers, that some Severn match anglers won't fish the chub and barbel sections unless they think they can catch 35lb or more at a sitting. They rate anything less than that a waste of bait. Thousands of East of England match anglers haven't caught 35lb of fish all season! Which when considered in relation to what's happening on the Severn leaves only one conclusion to be drawn...and you know what that is.

My longest wait for a bite came when I stopped to light a cigarette. There have been days when I could smoke a packet on the Welland and still not get a bite!

I travelled to Bewdley in a party of six anglers. Here's what happened to us. Me, 90lb, Dave Downes 38lb, Mick Field 37lb, Leo Sayer 25lb. Tom Bedder reckoned his swim was only worth 20lb so he packed up to watch me fishing and Graham Barry didn't rate his worth any more than 20lb either. He didn't even fish. Graham went off to another match and finished third, admittedly with only 18lb but in that one the ceiling weights were never likely to rival these Kidderminster weights.

There are people around who will tell you it's 'only' the middle of the Severn that's fishing this well. Well I can only say there's one helluva length of middle to the Severn...from Shrewsbury all the way down to Holtfleet in my book. There may be a few bad areas in the lower length but collectively it's so far ahead of the rest of the rivers there's really no comparison. And it's likely to last, I would guess.

The barbel are keen. They are hooked quite regularly. Two of mine had hooks stuck in them and it's anyone's guess how many had been in a keepnet before.

BRINGING HOME THE DANISH BACON
[October 19th, 1977]

I T STILL hasn't sunk in properly. I know it's true, of course, that I've just won £3,000, more money in one fishing match than anyone has ever done before but it really hasn't registered.

People tell me I fished well. There were plenty of spectators at the Embassy Challenge final in Denmark and a lot of them were full of praise. I wonder if I deserved it. Anyone can look good when he's catching fish. It's more difficult to gain any sort of credit rating when the fish aren't feeding and you are trying your heart out. It is easier to fish a winning peg than a bad one. You think something ought to happen and it does. It's the bad pegs that upset your logic.

Yes, I'm having a good year. My cash winnings for the season currently stand at £6,700 - that's over two thousand more than anyone has ever won in a season before. Ken Giles is the only other angler to have topped £4,000 in a season. If the breaks continue to come, if I get the chance to win again, I can easily top £7,000, maybe even £8,000.

It's daft really, but I never really fancied that peg on the Guden. Everyone who claims to know the river has always said you want reeds over on the far bank. All I'd got was somebody's garden and a new concrete quay. That quay was brand new. The concrete was white. It couldn't have been there more than three or four weeks. I thought that under the water it must have been the kiss of death.

The Guden was about the width of the River Thurne at Martham Ferry - but it was running just as hard as the Bure at Acle Bridge. Not a pretty sight.

We don't get much opportunity to fish rivers running at that speed - when they're only 2.5ft deep and stocked with bream but that slack patch of water near the concrete made my day.

The real task was bringing the bream across the fast water. Foul-hooked fish were impossible. I fouled five and lost the lot. I couldn't get their heads down. The current took charge. I played the fish I landed out of the slack by the far side and then eased them through the fast water. Most came across eight yards downstream, the current acting almost as a pendulum and swinging them over for me. Good job they weren't big fish. The best weighed about 3lb 4oz.

I had time to feel sorry for the chap pegged downstream of me. The crowds that came to watch me put him off. He would probably have fished a good match if he could have fished in solitude. It just wasn't his day.

I made a very slow start to my 110lb. I had four small roach in the first ten minutes and although I had one bream in 40 minutes it wasn't until I got the second bream on the hour that I put myself in with any chance of a decent weight. After that, I changed from float to quivertip and it began to happen for me.

Mind you, I wouldn't have won if I hadn't kept switching the hookbait. That really does help keep up the hooking rate. I would get three or four bream quickly on a single worm, then it slowed. A switch either to two worms or three maggots then bucked things up again. Oddly though, the change would first bring two or three roach up to 8oz before the bream renewed their interest. Then two, three, four or five more on successive casts and it was time to switch again.

At the end I put my weight at between 60 and 70lb, I really hadn't a clue because, most unusual for me, I lost count. When the bloke upstream weighed in 65lb I realised I must have more...and when I tried to lift the net I knew there was 100lb inside. Once I'd weighed in that 110lb I thought I must have won - although you can't take the Guden for granted. But there has never been two three figure bags in one knockout final on the river, so I felt quite hopeful.

The river fished very well under the circumstances but I'm surprised that more of the anglers didn't use the leger rather than stick to the float.

This is my first-ever 100lb plus match weight. It couldn't have come at a better time from the cash point of view but there are contests I'd rather win. Individual fishing is sudden death stuff but I really prefer team fishing. My great ambition is to be part of an England team win in the World Championship.

Lots of people will wonder why I had the 'stupidity' to back myself £100 to win at 20 to 1! That was a big bet. I'll tell you why I did it. This was my first final for four years. It may be another four before I even qualify again and ten more before I have any chance of winning. The odds were fair but they weren't by any means exceptional. Imagine a horse race with 80 runners...the favourite would have to start at 20 to 1. I'm surprised that more competitors didn't see it my way. Some of the 50 to 1 people could have picked up £5,000 if they had won.

There are one or two people who would have preferred me to lose it but it struck me just how many friends I've got. That's really wonderful. Barrie Brookes was on the phone, Clive Smith sent me a telegram. Lots of others gave me their good wishes personally or phoned in to the shop.

SET YOURSELF A MATCH TARGET!
[October 26th, 1977]

SEEING that full page of match results in Angling Times every week has made me stop and think of the time I used to operate at small club level. Most of the men who now work the big open match circuit began their fishing at club level for this is the first proving ground for up and coming anglers.

These matches cater on average for 30 anglers a time. They are the traditional bus-load and most of the big towns have a dozen or more such clubs fishing every weekend.

This sort of fishing is usually very amicable. There is less of the out-and-out will to win on show. Many of the anglers want to get to the top but so many haven't really absorbed the basic lesson - which is a great pity. They could do so very much better with very little extra effort.

How does a club angler, operating in, say, 30-a-contest events set out his stall if he wants to win regularly? Well, I've just done some homework on his account and the results are fascinating.

I always thought that if a club angler gave himself a 5lb match target each week and set out to make that weight he would win very many more than he would lose. So I checked the theory out against a full page of Angling Times club results.

In one week there were 193 match results listed on that special page. Now an angler who had weighed in exactly 5lb in every match would have won 141 of them and been beaten in 52. And, here's perhaps the really significant bit, his 5lb would have given him second place in 36 of those 52 matches he wouldn't have won.

So, on one week's showing, exactly 5lb is worth first or second in 176 out of 193 matches. Only 17 failures...and although I didn't check it out any further, some of those 17 would have been thirds. Now this information is most revealing. After all, admit it, you'll happily settle for 141 wins and 36 seconds in 193 contests. In fact you'd be rated the best matchmen who ever walked if you could achieve that sort of performance!

Obviously it is much harder to get 5lb in some matches than in others; canals, for instance are difficult, but equally, other waters are much easier - the Severn for example.

So perhaps the 5lb target is one that every club angler who wants to win should set himself. Whereas the big open match circuit angler requires anything from 10lb to as much as 60lb and more for a win, the club angler can set a more modest target...and therefore has a much better chance of achieving it.

With the need to go for really massive weights eliminated, the club angler has no need to adopt the muck or nettles attitude so necessary in the big time on say the Welland, Severn or Relief Channel. Which equally means that he doesn't wreck his swim going for broke. He can afford to feed more gently, take his time and pursue the various opportunities each swim offers.

After all, club contests, like the bigger events, usually run for five hours. Some, in fact, last even longer, but taking five hours as the average, that simply means you need only 1lb of fish every hour - to win 141 matches out 193!

Now a pound an hour isn't always easy...but it is by no

means as difficult as 5lb an hour! And if this small club contest fishing is further examined I'm prepared to wager that most of the fish are caught in the first hour. That always used to be the case in my time...so I doubt if it has changed.

After the first hour there are usually only two or three anglers still catching fish with any consistency - and they usually take the top places. So the first tactical point to take into account is the importance of not busting the swim and of carrying on catching fish through the full duration of the event.

Recognising that fact makes other points become equally obvious. There's a clear need to equip yourself with groundbait and feed to last a full five hours, of course, but both the cereal and the maggots or whatever you use needs to be of the right type and quantity to help ensure that the fish do continue to feed right through.

Other things also become clear. Since the target is a mere 5lb there's no need to risk everything on a swingtip approach to a bream water. If statistics were available to prove the point I'm sure we would see that floatfishing is usually the better way of ensuring you reach a low target weight.

Maybe the leger is the better bet if you're after 25lb from a bream water or from the middle Severn but that's not the problem. I am guessing, of course, but I'm prepared to say that of those 141 winning weights of 5lb, no fewer then 130 could have been made on the float rather than on the bomb.

There's no way of telling the real proportion but we are concerned only for the best overall or tactical approach to winning small matches.

TOP OF THE MONEY LEAGUE
[April 5th, 1978]

D IDN'T I do well - to coin a phrase! The name Ivan Marks sitting on top of the big league of money winners for last season probably gave me more satisfaction than anyone else. It certainly gave me more money!

In truth - and this seems absurd - I had greater difficulty winning the last £10 to push the total to around £7,000 than I had in winning some of the bigger sums that helped boost the total.

I've a feeling that this is one record I shall own for a few years at least. It will be a long while before anyone can better £7,000 in a single season. Must happen eventually, of course, inflation will see to that, but if anyone imagines he's going to take that record off me next year he ought to realise it amounts to winning the Gladding Masters, the Embassy Challenge, the Tetley Gala AND a National Championship all in a single season.

By my reckoning the accumulated value of those four paydays would be seven and a quarter grand...just enough! And I here and now offer to carry anyone who does that around on my shoulders for half-an-hour in tribute. He will have earned it!

The guts of my winnings came, of course, from the Embassy Challenge. The existing prize money, £3,000 for the winner, was augmented by a further £2,000 I picked up as the result of a £100 bet with Ladbrokes at odds of 20-1. People thought I was mad to stake £100 on a contest in which I already stood to pick up three grand for a win. A lot of anglers won't see that my way, but it was a chance too good to miss.

Okay, I could have been drawn right out of it with no chance and my money would have been right down the chute but that's the luck of the game. In truth I've had a number of quite poor seasons - at least in relation to standards I set earlier - and I thought it was only a question of time before fate gave me a better deal.

It must, though, be clearly understood that a comparison of the amount of money won in no way relates one angler to another. It doesn't figure that because I have just won more money than anyone has ever done in a single season before that mine was an outstanding year. It could have been much better.

And, had today's prize money been available at yesterday's matches I have little doubt who would show at the top of the table. It would have to have been the late Freddie Foster. There were seasons when Freddie won so many big East of England Opens that he seemed to attract winning pegs wherever he went. And it wasn't until the closing years of his life that he ever said much in print about his fishing.

Freddie's ability has been handed on to Stuart and Russell. Both get a regular high billing in the money table. Russell finished about fourth last time with some £2,500.

Money seems to be getting tighter and open match entries showed a marked reduction last year. Money was just one of the reasons. Another was the poor quality of the fishing that was generally available. On average most open entries dropped by getting on for a third last year and if the drop continues next time then it is clearly going to be that much harder to win big amounts.

We haven't heard so much recently about the mammoth amount of profit match anglers make on their season's activity! The accusation - somehow it is made into an accusation - that there are lots of professional anglers around has lost credence. No one believes that any more - simply because no-one makes a living at it.

Okay, my £7,000 from last season would have given me a living for a year but I can't bank on the same return next year. So what happens then...

Clive Robinson, winner of the Division Three National, grossed £3,100 last year, which put him into second place in the table. He had a good year but even Clive - at number two, remember - could hardly expect to live on his earnings.

Match fishing expenses get stiffer by the year. Petrol, pools and bait are the most expensive items, with tackle still trailing. People don't realise that today's tackle is still quite cheap in relation to prices charged as long as 20 years ago. Many fixed-spool reels, lines and even rods show nothing like the percentage of price increases seen with, say, petrol and food over the same period of time.

Even so, match fishing in a fully committed fashion costs a lot of money - if you are prepared to fish whenever possible. In total the cost of a full year's activity can't be a long way short of £2,000. Which, in effect, means you have to win a National Championship just to break even.

I HAVE 100 YEARS OF MATCH FISHING EXPERIENCE
[July 11th, 1979]

I DON'T ever sit down and work out just how much my match fishing costs me. It was therefore something of a surprise when I did try to estimate the cost when asked to do so. I discover that I must fish not less than 100 matches every year - an average of at least three a week. I can't think many people fish as many, most would average rather less than two each week, I think.

The cost of these contests - and they are a varied collection, including evening events, full day contests, river championships, even close season contests in Ireland – is incalculable. I estimate though that my total pools bill for the year can't be much less than £400. If that is a frightening amount it is no worse than the average smoker's bill...and I know which I would give up first if the pressure was on me!

If I had a bad run that lasted longer than my cash resources I would give up smoking before I packed in match pools. And I advise others to do the same. Non-smokers? What should they give up? I can't answer that!

We all get bad sequences when nothing goes right. You get them, I get them. We have to accept them as a fact of match fishing life. And, just as inevitably, there are good spells when things go well. I remember one year going all through the summer with next to nowt (less than £100) to show for the matches I'd fished... and I then won a river championship and another very big event on successive contests.

I am sure that the present season won't cost me anything

of my own money since I'm £1,300 into pocket thanks to the Embassy and Irish contests. So, in round figures, my season's fishing is already paid for.

The money isn't that important, though. I must stress that. It's the competition that turns me on. I need that with my fishing, otherwise, I suspect, I might become lazy and not make the full effort. I enjoy winning - in the right company. I enjoy being watched. I wouldn't talk to the crowds quite so readily were it otherwise. If people say I'm no good, that they can whack me, I will happily have a go at them.

I suppose my real ambition is two-fold - to be a member of a World Championship winning England team and to be the individual winner...in that order.

The youngsters, those breaking through and heading for the top, are the ones who keep me geared to top level performances. I've always got to try to keep them back. Encourage them, yes, but beat them, too. Billy Lane always used to say (before he was 50) that top flight match angling ended at 50. He could be right, but I hope not...I'm 43!

As I've said before, eyesight is the crucial factor. If your eyes remain good then there's no problem. Your reactions are guided by your eyes' ability to see so they remain as fast as is necessary.

I do believe, though, that experience must make up for at least diminishing eyesight. There's obviously a point where performance does fall off, but I reckon I'm 100 years old in match angling experience.

I have accumulated the best knowledge of Billy Lane, Benny Ashurst, Eddie Alien, Sammy Buxton, Freddy Foster and Fred 'the bread' Bailey. That is a lot of knowledge.

Billy Lane used to say: "When you can't see the little sod he's dangerous because he's catching fish. When he's not catching he's sitting beside you picking your brains!"

I suppose I was a bit brazen by normal standards. I was never afraid to ask. And if people didn't always give me a completely straight answer I had enough up top to be able to sort the fact from the semi-fiction.

That's how today's youngsters ought to be. I don't mind being asked by anyone...and the answer is always straight. Lots of people will see me this season. If they've got any questions all they've got to do is ask them.

Youngsters are the least ready yet, perhaps, the most deserving. Almost invariably the smallest lad is bullied into putting the first question. Then, when the ice has been broken, they all realise how easy it is. Not, of course, that learning ever stops. I can't answer all the questions 100 per cent accurately. I can only tell you what I know. I drop clangers, too.

Which is why I'm by no means unhappy to repeat that, in match angling terms, I'm a hundred years old. You can be, too, if you acquire and store all the knowledge that's available.

[Chapter Two]

Ivan Marks on...
FISHING FOR ENGLAND

*This summer I shall be fulfilling
my greatest angling ambition when I
go to my swim on the river
Berounka in Czechoslovakia...I
certainly shan't be taking time off
for a stroll round in this match.
They will have to blow me up before
I take my eyes off the float.*

MY FIRST ENGLAND CAP
[May 4th, 1972]

THIS summer I shall be fulfilling my greatest angling ambition when I go to my swim on the river Berounka in Czechoslovakia.

Ever since Billy Lane became World Champion in 1963 on the Moselle in Luxembourg, I have wanted to fish for England. Now at last the opportunity has been given to me.

I certainly shan't be taking time off for a stroll round in this match. They will have to blow me up before I take my eyes off the float.

People have asked me if I am excited at the thought of crossing the Iron Curtain. I'm there to fish, not sightsee. There will be time after the match for celebration, if we do well.

Everything's got to go right on the day. We'll be fishing as one man and if our style is wrong we could finish last!

But I regard that as extremely unlikely, especially as we will be practising on the river four days before the match. Each team member will fish his own way and try to come up with the method that will give us the best chance of winning.

Kevin, perhaps will try a stick float, I'll try a peacock (waggler). After a couple of hours we'll see who is catching the fish. Once we've hit the method on the head the team will stick to it. All of us will carry enough floats to cover any situation.

Last year the England team ran into bait difficulties. Each Italian threw in more bait than our whole team could scrape up. This year, I hope, it will be different. Team manager Stan Smith will take enough bait with him for practice. When we find out in the first two days what bait is catching fish, Stan will telephone home and arrange for a further supply of fresh bait to be brought over, for the match.

Even if we find the best bait is bloodworm I'm confident each team member will have sufficient for the match. I don't think we'll be bothering with sweetcorn this year.

The England team wants to see sizeable fish of 4oz and above. The Continentals are very fast with small fish and we would be unlikely to match their speed.

But by using poles they will have to net fish that we would swing in on our tackle. This will slow them up and give us the speed advantage.

Our team will be taking poles as well and will try them in practice. If we found they gave us the best chance of winning then we would use them.

I'm a great believer in practising on a water as near to the match as possible. To win a match you've got to hit on the right method pretty quickly. Conditions can often change overnight, but knowledge gained in practice is never wasted.

This year we have the best team that England has ever sent to the World Championships. But there is one factor that might upset the applecart....the limited-line restriction.

All of the team have got a big cast, but they will have to make do with just 51 feet of line. This is from the reel to the hook, so if you were fishing the North Bank you would reach just over halfway.

This means that the pole anglers will be able to reach our casting limits. In fact, all the anglers could well end up fishing the same line down the river.

This is a problem we shall have to try to resolve in practice. If we find the fish are under our rod tips, then that's where we shall fish.

To be selected to fish for England is a big responsibility, and a great honour. Yet what recognition does the team get in national media?

We're unknown to the general public, unlike the soccer stars who appear daily on the telly and in the papers.

Angling is the biggest participant sport in Britain, yet we're ignored by the publicity machine. Surely the team deserves some spotlight for being chosen to represent its country.

I know I've got a reputation for fooling around, but that little badge that says England makes all the difference. Every team member is an ambassador, and we'll live up to that idea.

Anyway, I've always got big brother Kevin to look after me if I get into a scrape!

JUST ONE MORE HOUR AND WE'D HAVE BEEN ON TOP OF THE WORLD...
[July 27th, 1972]

MY FIRST fish in Czechoslovakia was a 'daddy' ruffe! I caught it from the porthole window of the England team's floating hotel the night we arrived in Prague.

I had taken some casters and a short roach pole in my personal baggage so I could have a quick dabble before our tackle and bait arrived. A great cheer went up as I whipped out the Continental 'cocky' and we all went and celebrated. That was the start of a week which was to end with England nearly becoming champions of the world.

The team got to Prague on the Tuesday evening to give us plenty of time to practice for the world match the following Sunday. The city struck me as austere and sombre, with a lack of bright clothes among its citizens. But the River Vltava looked impressive - wide and deep. The match stretch was 16 miles away on the Berounka, a tributary of the main river. And the following morning we were standing on its banks.

A length of the river had been set aside for practice. But we couldn't believe this was the stretch; it was so shallow and fast moving. We noticed a weir and three of us went in the deeper water above, and four in the fast water below.

It was a struggle for us to catch even a bleak in the slow stretch, yet the banks were lined with anglers patiently legering. Eventually Kevin came along and casually told us he was in double figures at his peg below the weir.

We grabbed our gear, moved down and immediately started to catch fish. Just about everything swam in that river - chub, dace, roach, bream, tench, perch, barbel, rudd, bleak, nase and even carp.

Nase were a new fish to us. We christened them 'silver barbel' due to their weird looks. At a distance they looked like a dace, but they had such a scoop of a mouth that they had to be bottom feeders.

We caught them from around 4oz up to 2lb, and they really shook the rod like a barbel. You could catch them at all depths.

Every member of the English party had double figures that day, and Robin Harris caught around 25lb. Half the local village turned out to watch him.

We didn't bother to restrict ourselves to limited line this time. The object was to find what were the predominant species. The answer was just about everything!

On Thursday we found the match stretch but this was closed to angling. So we joined the other teams practising on the length downstream.

Unfortunately we chose the wrong bank and had to ask two young lads to row us across to the deeper water. Robin stayed where he was and took 25lb while the rest of us took mixed catches up to 20lb.

Here the river was similar to the Trent but wider. Nowhere was there more than four feet of water.

We discovered that casters in the groundbait brought fish on the feed: Howard Robson couldn't catch a fish until he fed with them. So we told team manager Stan Smith we needed more casters for the match. Stan got on the phone to his wife who in turn rang Benny Ashurst at Leigh in Lancashire. Benny did what he could and rang Ken Silcock of Gladdings. Ken got some more casters from Austin Clissett at Birmingham, plus some pinkies from Roy Marlow at Leicester.

It was a great effort by the lads back home. All the bait - including three biscuit tins of hook maggots - were loaded on the plane at Heathrow under the direction of Ken. He even told the pilot to put the bait in the front of the hold so it would be cooled by the cold air.

The team didn't know whether the fresh bait would arrive in time so we spent Friday morning cleaning our remaining bait.

Then it was back to the river to fish under actual match conditions. The five team men - myself, Kevin Ashurst,

Jimmy Randell, Johnny Parsons and Robin Harris - all fished in a line.

Kevin, Robin and Johnny were to go for bigger fish, while Jim and myself went for bleak. Now, normally the bleak anglers would shoot into an early lead, but after five minutes we were struggling to keep pace.

After an hour the men after bigger fish had opened such a gap that it was pointless fishing on for small stuff. At the end of that three-hour practice Robin had 45lb, Johnny Parsons and myself had over 20lb and Jimmy Randell had double figures. Jim would have had more but for two lads falling into his swim.

Johnny Toulson had over 20lb, including an 8lb barbel, and Howard Robson also had a big weight. We tried to keep our catches secret, but other teams came and watched us fish. At this stage we felt we must be favourites for the match!

On Saturday morning we had a team meeting before the draw for the sections. I drew E, Kevin D, Johnny C, Robin B and Jimmy A. We quickly drove off to walk the match stretch and this was when I had my first disappointment. Both A and B sections were faster water and looked the winners, while the other four sections seemed slower and deeper.

All the week we hadn't seen a sign of the French or Belgian teams practising. Now we began to wonder if they knew something we didn't.

Our bait was stored in a rambling outhouse by the river. We dare not leave it outside the hotel for fear of sabotage. But I had smuggled a pigeon from England in my luggage for some on-the-spot gozzers. It was already well blown and provided me with a few maggots for the match. Before the start I gave some to Kevin. He was to put these to good use.

Competitors were allowed to plumb the depth before the whistle and I was amazed to find I had only between five and six feet of water. I had expected more, so things were looking up.

Five minutes before the start, an enormous cannonade of groundbait shook the river. Every competitor seemed bent on outdoing his neighbour and up to 25 balls of solid pudding hit each swim.

Predictably I didn't see a fish caught round me for half an hour as they quickly swam out of range. And when they came back they were...bream!

This was something I had not expected, but I felt the French were already capitalising on their knowledge. I stuck to gozzers and finished with 16 fish for 4lb 2oz – a nase, two roach, one bleak and 12 bream. I caught more fish in the last 20 minutes than I did in the rest of the three hours. And this late feeding was something all our team experienced.

Kevin was going so well at the end that if the match had lasted another hour, I feel sure he would have overtaken the winner. As it was he won his section with 13lb 5oz to finish fourth. Robin Harris absolutely slaughtered his section with 12lb 11oz. He discovered that red pinkies were catching and whispered the word to reserves Howard and Johnny who told Jim and Johnny Parsons.

Both reserves helped the team magnificently throughout the trip. The night before the match they had only a few hours' sleep after they prepared our bait and shared out the groundbait.

I was disappointed with my own performance but highly pleased with the team's position of second. And I know Stan Smith was delighted too.

We were second best on the day, but we would have beaten the French if we hadn't been restricted by the 15-metre line rule. All of us held the end of our rod butt to get an extra foot further out.

As it was, we ran the French very close. At the end we were closing the gap fast and another hour should have seen us take the lead. The French anglers are very, very good, but I believe they must have practised on the actual match length some months before.

On the day we found that loose-feeding was the answer, yet the fish would accept plenty of groundbait during practice. I'd like to have known that before the match!

At least I hope we showed that selection is the best way to form a competitive England team. I only hope I get the opportunity to fish for my country again.

LEAVE THE WORLD TEAM ALONE
[March 8th, 1973]

I THINK it's about time I stepped into the great International team debate. Plenty of words have been thrown around and some anglers - particularly those in the south - have been getting pretty hot under their oilskins.

Well, I've got a message for them...stop beefing and give the chosen team a chance. Every man selected is a top man in his area. When seven men are chosen to represent one-and-a-half million coarse fishermen then there are bound to be disappointments.

There are many top-class anglers with more right to a place in the International squad than Ray Mumford and co. But we've heard no moans from men like Johnny Toulson, John Illingworth, Pete Warren, Roy Marlow, Ron Russell, Bob Tromans and many, many more.

The South has only seen a glimmer of their stardom, and just can't appreciate the depth of ability. Just look at their records. Toulson finished third and fourth in the last two Nationals as well as beating the French in an International match on the Trent. Illingworth is the finest angler in the Bradford and Leeds area - two of our most consistent National teams. Pete Warren is undisputedly the top angler on the Trent this season, while Johnny Rolfe is another grand angler. My mate Roy has already fished one International, finishing fourth overall and second on weight. And both Ron Russell and Bob Tromans are two of the fastest anglers in the country when it comes to small fish.

The point is that all these men have got a right to grumble but sensibly they have kept quiet. The team has been selected and it's up to every angler to back it to the hilt. The time for recriminations - if they are needed - is after the match.

Last year's selected side finished second, England's highest-ever placing. So there's no reason why this year's team shouldn't do even better. These anglers who are crying our team down before it's even fished are putting their own heads on a chopping block.

I know some anglers in the south are saying that we should try to match the Continentals at speed fishing. Well this is a load of rubbish. I've heard that some of the Italian team can knock small fish out at the rate of 600 an hour! No angler in this country is in that class so why bother to try and match them. Let us set the trend by going for sizeable fish - the field where England shines. Pick a team of small fish men and we are beaten before we start. The only way we could pull back the Continentals on small fish would be for the NFA to pick a team of teenage anglers and train them for years at snatching.

I see the south are also demanding a super league, which is nothing more than just a series of trial matches. Well once you start to have trials instead of selection, this is one step backwards. Birmingham, Bradford and Leicester - the top three National teams over the last ten years - choose their teams by selection. Trials give the average angler a chance instead of highlighting your best men.

It's also worth remembering that many of the southern matches are rovers, meaning that an angler can pick his own swim. If some of the Midlands stars fished rovers on their rivers, they would be virtually unbeatable week in, week out. Ran Russell knows the Severn around Bewdley so well that he can virtually tell you how many stones are on the bottom of each swim. If rovers started on this river I don't think he would get anyone to fish against him.

Nothing against Ray Mumford but I read one comment of his: "I was last away, fished a bad peg and won the match." Well if he won the match he was on the best peg on the day, unless the competition was that poor!

The NFA have a hard job in picking the International

squad. Whatever they do is going to be wrong in some people's eyes. I say that if anyone has any grumbles let them take these men on at fishing their own waters.

Stan Smith is as straight as a die and will do everything in his power to make the team work. Do anything wrong and you can expect a roasting, fish well and you will be praised. Once you are in the team you have got to prove yourself. Being the individual winner one year won't guarantee your place the next.

You've got to get used to fishing with up to 1,000 spectators standing behind you. Some anglers might crack under this strain. If I'm picked as a reserve I'll be team runner and glad of it. Stan Smith always has the last say and I respect his judgement. So I say let's give this team a chance. If there's any pulling apart to be done, let it wait until after the match.

OUR TACTICS WERE THE RIGHT ONES
[August 2nd, 1973]

BEFORE the inquest on the World Championships gets too heated, I think England's performance in finishing third should be put into perspective. Remember that 16 teams were fishing, but only two used reels and running lines. The odds favoured a pole team winning, so we did extremely well to finish in the frame.

And four from our side of the Channel fished in the first 18 anglers, including an Irish lad. We were obviously fishing under a handicap from the start, and the applause for England when we mounted the rostrum showed we have earned the respect of Continental anglers.

South Africa used poles and finished last, yet they told me after the match that they wish they had stuck to their normal method of using a rod and reel. They had tried to match the Continentals at their own game and come unstuck. And this is what I believe would have happened to England if we had gone for small fish with poles. Instead of bringing back trophies and a share of the honours, we would have returned to a hostile reception from those critics who slammed the team.

Our plan of attack was to come through from behind, taking a few small fish in the first hour and then larger fish as the match progressed. And the plan worked well for Kenny Giles and myself. Kevin Ashurst raced off to an incredible start but his swim died. Robin Harris had a bad draw on a swim which was even too deep to plummet, while Clive Smith just didn't have any decent fish in front of him.

There's no doubt that if the match had lasted another hour, Kenny Giles would have been World Champion and I would have come second. We were both catching fish at a good rate by the finish. The 20-metre line rule also cost Kenny and myself of the chance of the title. Kenny saw the perch that spat out his hook and it made his 1lb 8oz fish look tiny. And as for that carp that ripped my line straight off my reel, well it must have been in double figures. I've taken four-pounders from my local canal and got them out on two-pound line, but this fish never even stopped.

If Kenny and myself had both won our sections, England still would have finished third. But there was one vital factor which we didn't make allowance for. In practice, everyone caught fish from the word 'go'. Kevin Ashurst took about four pounds of roach on casters in just 40 minutes and then packed up, so the French wouldn't see our tactics. Now, the match stretch, which was a lot different from the practice stretch, had been closed for three weeks prior to the International. Yet the opposite bank had been given a hammering, with the Continentals flinging in groundbait and wheat.

It's my belief that the majority of the bigger fish moved over to this other bank where they knew they could get a free meal, and the fish we expected didn't show.

Clive was pegged on the narrowest part of the lake and could catch only small stuff. Yet 300 yards away on the other side, the practising teams had been piling in the wheat and drawing the better fish. This is why Ray Mumford was able to take 17lb on the far bank, although I don't know how long he sat there.

If more bigger fish had been along the match stretch instead of the tiddlers, England could even have won. Our plan of strategy certainly proved itself, but small fish blunted its edge.

The team instruction was simply fish with bloodworm or maggots for the first 30 minutes or so to take any small fish which might be about, at the same time groundbaiting with hemp and casters further out. The colossal bombardment for five minutes at the start killed any immediate chances of taking good fish, but the small fry don't seem to be scared. This gave the team time to take some small fish, while the bigger fish were moving on to the bait thrown further out. We all expected to take the majority of our fish in that final hour and close fast on the French. And this came true for Kenny Giles and myself, until that irate Gailic carp decided to make its own explosion in my swim.

I was so angry when it broke my line that I flung the rod behind me in fury, and nearly broke it.

WHY WE DIDN'T TRY TO MATCH THE SPEED ACES OF FRANCE
[September 26th, 1973]

MY COMMENTS last week about France having the best international team in the world were still ringing in my ears when I packed up my tackle after the French open match on the River Maine at Angers.

I went for bream and sat through the match without so much as a bite. I was in a bleak area, and every angler round me went for these tiny fish. This was the second hiding the Continentals gave us. The first came in the 10-man international a day earlier. The French wanted to see us perform on big fish and pegged us where they honestly believed we would catch bream.

But they just don't understand the habits of these fish. In

both matches I had at least 15 feet of water in front of me, and no bream. They had moved into shallower water because of the hot weather.

The contest fished by the French against the Belgians - expected to be a high-speed bleak duel - was won with bream because the area fished was much shallower. Robin Harris was the one England man to draw a shallow swim in the open contest, and he finished third again to complete a fabulous weekend. I believe Robin's swim was only three feet deep.

Of course there are going to be people asking why we didn't try to match the French on small fish. My answer is that it would have been a waste of time. We were there to try and show the French our English big-fish methods and they were just as disappointed as we were that the fish didn't co-operate.

We were fishing at least 15 feet above the water, so we couldn't sink our lines if we wanted to. And this made everything twice as awkward.

The French were extremely interested in our long-range casting and distance floats. They also didn't realise that we used such extremely fine lines. Several Continental tackle dealers have since ordered English peacock and cane antennas, soft shot and our groundbait. And if they sell well, I can see a big export trade in our tackle to the Continent.

Robin Harris was undoubtedly the man of the match for the French. He had a large gallery every time he fished and won huge applause when he went to fetch his trophies. The French are much more impressed by someone who can catch sizable fish rather than bleak.

We don't stand a chance with small fish against the Continentals. I rate Ron Russell the fastest angler in England. When he's on top form Ron can knock out 200 bleak in an hour. But he won't go for them unless he thinks he can win. Yet Ron is just a beginner at the game when it comes to the Italians. They can catch up to 600 bleak in an hour, taking up to 100 fish on the same specially-bred maggot. The French use bloodworm or Mystique paste for bleak and don't catch them at quite the same rate. But remember they are just as good at taking big fish on their poles. And this combination makes them such a danger in. internationals.

One French angler told me that if the day ever came when England beat France on small fish, he would break his rods. And I think his tackle is safe. But I still believe that we can beat the French on their home ground. Robin Harris came dangerously close to achieving this, taking the second highest weight in the open contest. But under the French points system, he finished third. Remember that we had only five English anglers against 160, so the odds were all against us drawing a good peg. If we took 30 men over there, we would have stood a better chance of success.

Next year the England-versus-France battle is scheduled for the North Bank. And don't think that the result is already cut and dried. There are plenty of small fish in the Nene which can be caught under the rod tip, and this will suit the French. We have only a fifty-fifty chance of winning.

If they do beat us, then it will prove that English anglers should explore the use of bloodworm and joker a great deal more than is done at present.

I think the French will be pleasantly surprised when they see the river, but we won't give them the match on a plate by pegging it on the bleak swims.

Robin Harris proved in France that maggots will still catch fish in direct opposition to bloodworm. He started off by fishing beyond the line of French floats, but when he saw them catching pulled back on to their line. And then he picked up enough to finish with 36 bream and some roach, for the second highest weight.

The French don't fish for sizable fish from the word go. They start off by putting in an at least a dozen solid balls of groundbait. Then they go for bleak. After an hour they get out their long poles and drop their float tackle on to the baited patch to see if the bream have moved in. If they haven't, then they go back to bleak. They don't put in any more feed during the match, which is often as short as two hours.

In the open contest, I sat next to a Belgian who came second with 235 bleak in two hours. And he didn't regard that as a good performance. The French angler Christian Forestier only managed to catch 123 bleak in the international, because I stopped the bleak moving into his swim. I was pegged next to Forestier and when I saw the bleak moving upstream towards the Frenchman I kept power-housing floating caster into the river to keep the bleak occupied. The scheme worked because otherwise I believe he could have won the contest.

I managed just 40 fish - five little bream and the rest bleak. But I wasn't deliberately trying for bleak. If I'd gone bleaking I should probably have finished seventh instead of ninth.

My draw - peg one - was the furthest away from the sewer discharge, which was where you needed to be to catch bream. In practice Robin had nearly 60lb of bream from the swim one peg below the sewer, while I took 10lb four pegs below him. The last man in the French side, Forestier at peg two, was the Frenchman the furthest away from the sewer while next man Raoul Time was the next furthest away.

Before we left France, the five of us fished outside the hotel where the French told us bream were never caught. Yet we amazed our hosts by taking 100lb of fish between us. John Illingworth had individual fish to 3lb. There are many more bigger fish in France than is realised, because so many of the country's anglers are just content to catch bleak. And remember that any big fish caught are never put back, so they don't have a chance to become hook shy.

THE 1974 WORLD CHAMPS - LADY LUCK WAS ALL WE LACKED
[October 9th, 1974]

IT WAS a good international. You will hear no complaints from the England team, but we didn't get that slice of luck that often makes the difference between winning and getting a middle-of-the-table placing.

Had just two of us – Ken Giles and one other team man

– got his one big fish out, we should have shot up the placings from 8th to 4th. And had we landed the big fish we hooked there's no doubt about it…we should have won.

It's easy to talk of the might-have-beens, but from the tactical point of view we did everything right. We were right to go for the tiddlers and have the occasional dip for something better. Had we fished all out for big fish one of us might well have won the individual championship…but that wasn't what we were there for.

We wanted the team title…and we still do. And we shall get it one of these years - and maybe not so far away at that. But had we all fished for the big fish – as the Germans did – we could easily have finished deep down near the bottom of the league.

The information we were given was right. We knew there were biggish fish in the water but didn't rate them a big enough possibility to justify attacking them. It was just one of those unfortunate things that we should end up being the only team to contact 1lb-plus fish all along the line. The French didn't, the West Germans failed for thinking they could - and the same could be said of the Spaniards.

We all doubled the Irishmen pegged on one side of us on fish count but one Irishman took a point off us by landing a 3lb bream. None of us beat the Dutch anglers on our other flank – but the Dutch are top class speed merchants at pole fishing and we can't really expect to beat them the first year we have a serious crack at them in the way we did.

Daniel Maury, editor of the French angling magazine 'La Peche', paid us a compliment by saying that we fished very well with poles. That's some consolation but we all know that with a little slice of luck we could have finished much higher.

Only ten of my 122 fish topped an ounce. The biggest might have weighed 2oz. I fed between three and four pints of joker and used 2lb of groundbait to help put them in. We all used sand in our groundbait. The wind was a facer, which wasn't bad. There was no problem with drift and I must admit I liked the water as a venue for a world championship. I'm sure there must have been many less capable waters used in the past.

The individual winner, the German, Richter, put two carp on to the scales that gave him the equivalent of 10lb-plus. We dare not use the tackle he did – thick line and big hooks – and his team's placing (13th) proved us right.

No-one should expect instant success for England in world championships. We fish against the best in the world but we still win in the near future. I feel completely certain about that. When we get a real chance to use British national styles we shall do in the world match what we did to the French on the North Bank in the Angling Times International, fished earlier this summer.

The chance could come sooner than is generally realised. Poland is tipped as the likely venue for next year's contest... and that will suit us very nicely. That will be a big fish match if it comes off for the Polish fisheries are well stocked with what I call silver barbel.

The manager of the West German team told us that this year's Polish National Championship was won with a weight of 45 kilos, which, roughly translated, means 100lb. And that lot was caught in just two and a half hours.

We shall have the 20 metre line limit in operation again next year - unless Stan Smith can get us something better when he goes to the CIPS match management meeting later this year. The rules are up for revision on British insistence.

We can expect the French to support us. They are as interested in our styles as we are in theirs. Jacky Morzieres, this year's individual winner, has given me orders for floats, rod rings, swingtips and other British accessories which are not available in European tackle shops.

Many of the top Frenchmen have spent a lot of time practising with swingtips...and they have caught a lot of fish. I doubt if they are doing that to vote against our styles becoming accepted by CIPS.

There's one other rule, one that has never received much,

if any, mention in the angling press, which works against us. When the whistle ends each world championships, that is it completed. There's no fish-playing time left. What's not on the bank doesn't count.

Mendes Gomex, the Spaniard who finished second this year, hooked a carp in the closing minutes of the championship. He played the fish out and netted it half a minute before the end. Had he taken 31 seconds longer the fish would not have counted. This is an anti-big fish rule. Mini-fish are whipped out of the water in a split second so they are unlikely to be excluded by that rule.

How hard did I fish? When I tell you that I had an unlit cigarette dangling from my mouth for an hour you may have some idea. I normally chain-smoke my way through contests. When my fish were coming fast I couldn't spare a split second.

STAN SMITH – THE DON REVIE OF MATCH FISHING
[January 28th, 1976]

SO STAN Smith is now the Don Revie of British match fishing. I'm delighted for both Stan and England. No one need now doubt that our first World Championship team win for England is very close. It would be foolish to make predictions but it could well come this year in Bulgaria.

If we have to wait until the next time the contest is fished in England I am certain we shall see it then. I believe the appointment of a supremo makes that much difference. Stan Smith will be able to pick his own squad, instead of relying on a committee in which he had a voice but from which he couldn't be sure he would get the men he wanted.

We have already come a very long way since the days when the England side was filled by men from the top five teams in the National Championship. If we haven't come far enough that's because miracles cannot always be achieved overnight.

The irrepressible Ivan Marks. During the 1970s his face was the most recognisable in the sport.

Ivan first fished for England in 1972 and went on to collect 12 caps. It was his greatest regret that a silver, taken in 1976, was the closest he got to either individual or team gold.

Above: Ivan in the 1960s. He was the golden boy in a golden age of matchfishing.

Left: Bream were a species that Ivan became synonymous with.

Above: 1977, and the England team gather for a photo call. From left to right is manager Stan Smith, Ivan, Kevin Ashurst, Ian Heaps, Mark Downes, Dickie Carr and Tony Scott.

Left: Ivan was to discover Ireland in its coarse fishing pomp and regularly travelled to enjoy its fish-rich waters.

Ivan fishes from the porthole of the England team's floating hotel in Czechoslovakia, 1972. He taken casters and a pole in his hand luggage to fish before the official bait and tackle arrived.

Above: A master of the tip, Ivan was among the best feeder anglers of his time.

Below: Four members of Leicester AS - or the Likely Lads as they were more famously known - gather at the end of a day's fishing. From left to right is Ivan, Dave Downes, Dave Rossi and Roy Marlow.

Above: Ivan strikes into a bream while fishing on the River Nene in Peterborough. He cut his teeth on the species, learning from a young age their value as weight-builders.

Watching the master at work. Such was the desire to see Ivan in action, people would even pay to get a better vantage point.

Ivan was among the first to realise the importance of groundbait to catching fish.

A young Ivan Marks shows off a small common carp. As a boy he would fish with the seniors - until he was banned for being too successful!

But, just for starters, let's look at England's record since a selection committee picked the team and since Stan has been manager. In Czechoslovakia 2nd, in France 3rd, in Belgium 6th and in Poland 2nd again. As a record for four successive years that makes very good reading, even though that first team win remains elusive.

Stan has had his critics but I am certain he is the man for the job. Let me tell you why. No one wants England to win more than he does. It will mean more to Stan Smith than to anyone else the day it happens.

Most people who know Stan call him a hard man. All right, he is a hard man, but the day England win the world title we may perhaps for the first time see the real Stan Smith - the Stan he has so far kept almost exclusively to himself. I know Stan has a burning ambition to win, for England to win. He also has the knowledge and the ability to make it happen.

Let's look briefly at his credentials. What makes me so sure Stan Smith is the right man? First because he keeps his nose to the ground. He has done a lot of behind the scenes scouting that few people know anything about. He has turned up at all sorts of matches. He has walked the bank and watched. Stan has always had an eye for young talent and he has never neglected that part of a manager's function.

He has to look for much more than a pure ability to fish and to catch fish. He has to find anglers with the big-match temperament.

It may be relatively easy for Joe Soap to win one big match, even three on the trot, but will that man be able to repeat his form when he's fishing in front of a crowd of thousands, all watching critically for mistakes?

Stan has to find anglers who carry on fishing effectively when they have drawn the worst of pegs; men who do not become disheartened.

Without perhaps ever showing it publicly, Stan Smith is proud of his task and of his teams. He doesn't like the Press criticising any member of anyone of them. That's his job.

He does the criticising in his own way.

To some extent Stan has weathered the hard times. Those first four years were the hard ones. He now has experience on his side. I am sure he has learned in the job and is now ready for the real power just given to him.

I don't see why anyone should be at all surprised that Stan is now the England equivalent of Robert Tesse. Tesse is the brains behind a long succession of French wins but let's remember that Tesse had the No.1 team to win with.

So Stan's first task is to build the England team the way he wants it. We already have three World Champions in Billy Lane, Robin Harris and Ian Heaps. With Stan now getting a free hand on team selection the time is very close when we shall have five men capable of taking the world title and, perhaps for the first time, five men all capable of taking individual honours as well.

I suspect that Stan is likely to be paralleled to Don Revie for much more than his title. I think Stan will also select a team pool of anglers out of which future sides will be selected. Don Revie has 30 men. I rather think Stan will settle for around 14 or 15. I would doubt if those anglers will fish together as a group but they will be groomed to fish for England. It is possible Stan's squad could be smaller, even as few as eight or nine, but I've a hunch he will want to include a number of younger anglers in a Revie-type under-23 acknowledgment.

There must be a place for youth. We have an increasing number of experienced matchmen who have been blooded already, some with distinction. But competitive fishing is like football in many ways. If a footballer begins to go over the hill at 30 or thereabouts so the matchman passes his peak in his middle to late forties, with eyesight the key factor.

It remains to be seen if Stan will name his team pool or not, but even if he keeps the names to himself I am sure there will be one. Anyone with real talent will have the chance to get into the reckoning simply because the manager wants to win more than anyone else in the country.

No one can hope to become an effective manager without the full authority. Stan Smith has that now. He has passed through his apprenticeship. Now for the World Championship title...

I WAS SO CLOSE TO WORLD GLORY
[October 6th, 1976]

THREE more fish and I would have been writing this column as World Champion.

That's how close I came to winning that 90-minute small fish sprint. And my England mate Kevin Ashurst could have won it with just half-a-dozen more chub.

After getting so close neither of us can say we're not sore. But someone has got to come second and in this match it was me. That's all there is to it. But I think both Kevin and myself can take a lot of consolation from the fact that there we were against the world's top pole anglers on a venue ideally suited to their methods and we came so close to beating them.

It was a fantastic match. Ian Heaps' three-hour catch record went about ten times. I beat it and I was fifth best weight!

Where we had problems was that we had no idea of the water's potential. In practice just a mile away from the match stretch we had a struggle to total 2lb 8oz between us. Then suddenly we were on, the dam wall with millions of bleak and chub at our feet.

That practice session worried us a lot and I think we recovered quickly on match day. One thing is certain - once we had a look at the water in the morning match we knew just how to fish it.

I'd love to fish it again. England would be certainly in the top three and challenging very strongly. And in a couple of years when the chub have stepped up their growth we would be odds on favourites.

I wanted England to win the team championship and it didn't come off again. But look at it in the cold light of the next morning!

England took on the world's best against the odds and came fifth. When you see that such pole experts as France were 12th and Belgium were tenth it is a measure of how well we did.

For me it was a great match although we came out second. It was a terrific venue which lacked only a 100,000 crowd to make it into one of the best in the championship's history.

WE SHOULD NOT QUIT COMPETING IN THE WORLD CHAMPS

[September 26th, 1979]

THE clamour is under way for a drastic revision of the National Federation's involvement with CIPS, the European organisation, with the World Championship the central issue.

No-one can pretend that all is well. There are serious grounds for complaint about the CIPS' attitude to improving world championships and it certainly seems that we are not getting value for the time and money committed to these annual championships and meetings.

So what's the solution? Some say let's pack it in. What's the use? Everything's stacked against us. There's no way we can hope to win a team event while the rules and venues remain as poor as they have been.

There's a lot of truth in that but one inescapable fact remains: we shall never force change on to CIPS by resigning...by running away. In my view we've just got to stay with it. Let's hang on and keep up the pressure until, point by point, we finally either make them see the logic of our arguments or we see the sense of theirs. It may take ten or 15 years but we must not run away from our responsibilities just because progress seems hard to obtain.

There's nothing easy about World Championships in any sport. We've only won soccer's World Cup once...and that was when it was staged in England. Maybe we shall have to wait for an English venue!

I'm not suggesting we should be complacent about the problems but I'm sure the NFA Contest Committee, and Stan Smith in particular, are quite capable of sorting the mess out. It's just going to take time and perseverance...and we have to accept that. I'm sure Stan won't become discouraged, because he is keen. Despite all the unnecessary aggro that has been heaped on him from time to time, he is a good man for the job. If he did pack it in, or was sacked, his successor wouldn't have instant answers. He'd face the same problems and the same opposition.

In my view we must continue to participate in World Championships. Maybe the long term members of the England squad - Kevin Ashurst, Ian Heaps and I - haven't managed to inspire anything to brag about from the team point of view, but we have learned a very great deal about fishing in Europe. That must be very useful when it comes to blooding the youngsters - lads like Paul and Mark Downes, Tommy Pickering, Steve Gardener and Stu Killen. But surely we can't hope to benefit by denying these up-and-coming anglers the chance of fishing for England in the future.

There won't be instant success. The odds will be stacked against us until rules, conditions and attitudes within CIPS change. But they must have their chance. Remember, no-one sacks the striker if he fails to score in a match in which he's never given the ball!

We knew it would be hard and we planned for each member of the team to get a minimum of 10 to 15 fish weighing 1oz to 2oz each. Our sights weren't set too high. Preparation had at least given us a realistic target. We improved on last year's poor showing. We can't claim any particular credit maybe, but this was very hard...and no-one was water-licked.

Of course we want better venues. So do many other teams, but I feel sorry for the Spaniards. This was, I believe, their first home match and they wanted to do it right. They failed – perhaps because they tried too hard, or maybe because there was no-one in the central administration to help and advise them. But we are not the only team with a gripe. The Italian team manager wasn't overjoyed when we chatted. He told me: "We haven't fished a natural river for seven years" (Czechoslovakia was the last).

The Italian went on to say that recently we had done little more than fish for little fish that might just as well have been carted around from one venue to the next, year after year. He actually wanted to move the venue 36 hours before the event, when he anticipated a flop.

He, obviously, wasn't happy, but the German team manager was a little more hopeful. He told me that it would take good weights of fish to win next year's event in Germany. There's certainly no place for excessive pessimism. The next three years - if events stick to schedule - will see World Championships staged in Germany, England and Ireland. All three ought to be good venues, offering a fair chance to all the contrasting styles.

That's what it's all about. We want to see the best teams winning by methods that prove superior on the day...in a contest where all styles are permitted and where the team that chooses the best one takes the honours. That's match fishing.

All credit to the French for winning once again. Whatever you may say and think, they are dedicated professionals... professional except, of course, that they don't fish for cash prizes as we do in Britain. They used 4oz breaking strain nylon tied to size 24 hooks. If I went into the biggest tackle shop in Britain, or the biggest wholesaler, and asked for 4oz nylon his reply would be: "Pardon?"

We can't take the credit away from the individual winner, either. He weighed in 5lb 10oz. That's a good catch of little fish in three hours...and a rate that would win a fair number of British opens.

I'm disappointed for myself and for England, of course. A hell of a lot of work went into that effort. I had one 22-hour day...and that's a lot of sweat in a country as warm as Spain proved to be.

PICKING THE RIGHT VENUE TO HOST THE WORLD CHAMPS
[April 2nd, 1980]

THE World Championship is expected to take place in Britain in September of next year. Deep thought is already being given to the actual location - coupled, of course, with further thinking on whether or not we shall actually compete!

Leaving aside the second point, as a matter for the officials to deliberate on, I am left pondering...where do we fish it... if we stage it?

I'm glad in most respects that I don't have to make that choice. No doubt that's down to England team manager Stan Smith - but Stan's not let me or anyone else into his thinking on the subject.

There are many suitable venues but, since the World Championships are traditionally September dates, we have to consider what fishes well in September - and the very first requirement has to be a water that is even and will fish well.

I look for one holding a mixed stock of fish and a variety of sizes of fish of each species. I want skill to show through but only after having had to win its spurs against good performances by as many teams as possible.

It is because of the out-and-out need for 'fair' fishing - from one end to the other of the match length - that so many World Championships have been fished on man-made waters. The fact that this hasn't worked out too well is obvious - but can we do any better?

As I say, I haven't a clue what's in Stan's mind. Could be there's a lake at Sandringham or in the backyard at

Buckingham Palace that he could get this once - but there's no doubt he's thinking about every possibility.

Still water though could be dangerous in September. If we have a cold tail to the summer and the first frosts with it, then stillwaters won't fish well and we finish up fishing a poor prospect. On the other hand, suitable rivers - and there are quite a few - could also be out of sorts as the result of heavy rain...so the man who actually makes the final choice has to carry more than his own weight of responsibility.

Which explains why man-made waters have been so popular. Theory at least suggests hat the fish can be contained within a defined area and are therefore available to be caught on the day in question. The central committee of CIPS, the European confederation, has to approve all venues. We can't impose one on them and they have a complete aversion to natural waterways. These, by their reckoning, are too varied, too wild, if you like. The swims are not identical. Depths, widths and flows are not the same for everyone.

What we are looking for is a suitable area of something like 100 pegs. The Huntspill is ideal in make-up...but there are not enough fish in it (on recent showings). If anyone fancies the Trent at Burton Joyce, as I do, bear in mind there's a bloodworm ban on that water - which wouldn't suit the Europeans. Could a ban be relaxed? You tell me!

I summarise our more well-known rivers as venues like this.
- Trent: Yes, in some places.
- Warwicks Avon: Yes, that too is good enough - in parts.
- Severn: Too prone to flooding to be an acceptable risk.
- Wye: Too much of a 'wild', natural river. Not enough 'even' swims.
- Hants Avon: Same snags as the Wye.
- Norfolk Broads area rivers: No chance. Who stops the boat traffic?
- Gloucester Canal: A very good possibility.
- Witham, Welland, Nene, Thames: All good in parts. Can't be dismissed.

What of a traditional canal? There are some good lengths

about that fish well on goodish days. The snag with all of those has to be the inability to provide a stretch which can also accommodate a tremendous number of spectators without loss of 'form'. Other than the Gloucester Canal, I think those available are too narrow and too shallow to be worth considering.

Spectators have to be a very serious consideration indeed I am quite prepared to believe that when this day dawns there will be 20,000 British anglers up early and on the way to see it for themselves. Remember, this is a chance that is unlikely to come again, at least within a decade. Many people will recognise that if they ever want to see a World Championship this is the one. No-one can afford to wait for the next one...

I know of one water that I think could be first class but it would require a lot of effort spent on the water itself...the lake at the National Exhibition Centre, mid-way between Coventry and Birmingham. It's close to a motorway - which means people could get in and out easily. There's plenty of car parking space. The lake has fish in it now but it would need even more. Perhaps many more. But there's plenty of time to get it right...provided the planning starts soon.

There may be other much better waters around. Maybe there's even better water already looming large in Stan Smith's thinking. Many of the country's stately homes have their own lakes and some of these are also, no doubt, well up to scratch. The snag is, of course, getting to know them well enough to be absolutely sure the choice is right.

One thing's for certain we can't just blindly select a water and leave it at that. We have got to do our darndest to have it right on the day - and that's far from easy.

I'm not at all sorry the choice isn't mine. This is one can I wouldn't want to carry!

[Chapter Three]

Ivan Marks on...
TACKLE

> Anglers have a long way to go,
> it seems, before they fully
> understand their tackle. Even today
> experienced men, as well as
> beginners, are failing to balance
> their tackle to their rods.

THE LOW-DOWN ON FLOATS - GOOD AND BAD

[November 11th, 1972]

'VE BEEN sorting out my tackle which usually ends up in a mess half way through the season. Floats are strewn everywhere round the house and I have a hard job rounding them all up...and an even harder job deciding what ones to keep!

Many floats I've made and used in the past are now resigned to the dustbin although they would still catch fish. It's just that the Leicester anglers are always developing their tackle to suit the changing conditions - and keep one jump ahead of the opposition.

Basically I can divide my floats into groups for use on the various rivers where the big matches are fished. Of course I have other specialist floats as well but the floats I'm going to talk about will cope with most situations found in match fishing.

We'll start with the bream floats where long distances have to be cast on lakes or slow-moving waters:

ZOOMERS: These are the floats that conquered the Welland, Nene and Relief Channel five years ago. But they have since been superseded by the peacocks. Peterborough angler Tug Wilson is generally credited with being the first angler to experiment successfully with loaded floats for bream fishing. The Leicester anglers simply borrowed his idea and improved on it.

My zoomers are made from balsa and cane with roughly the equivalent of 1.5 swan shot loaded into the base. On the line they carry anything up to 2.5 swan shot. Length is about 8.5 inches.

Zoomers must be fished with the line attached top and bottom so that they cast long distances correctly. An AAA shot is placed under the float to keep the correct depth. The majority of the shot - say 1.5 swan - is bunched on the line just under half the distance from hook and float (4ft 9in in a 10ft swim). A small shot from a BB to a No 4 is placed 18 inches from the hook.

The art of using a zoomer is telling the bites. With bream fishing you are looking for lifts which may be no more than a quarter of an inch. The fish will take the bait as it drops those last few inches towards the bottom holding up the smallest shot.

PEACOCKS: These are the big-fish floats now in common use on the wide Fenland bream rivers. Kevin Ashurst used a peacock and balsa float to win an AT League final on Ireland's River Suck as long as eight years ago. But they have become popular only in the last two years.

Locked on the line at the bottom end only by two swan shot, they cast long distances with an ease not found in other floats. Shotting further down depends on the water being fished. On the Welland more weight can be put under the float, but on the Nene the weight must be nearer the hook to get the bait past the bleak.

You need a BB shot nearest the hook to show lift bites at 30 to 40 yards out. Length varies from 8in to a foot. We did try using longer floats up to nearly two feet but they were no more successful than shorter floats.

Straight peacocks without a balsa body are used for roach fishing on rivers such as the Nene, Welland and Witham. They don't take so many shot - more like two swan and a BB. The float is locked with a swan and an AAA. The other three BB can be split down to suit yourself, but any bunching must be just under half way from the hook to the float to ensure trouble-free-casting. This rule applies to all floats.

For drain fishing the peacock quill can be locked with two swan shot. The remaining BB is split down into a No 1 shot just below the float and two no 4s near the hook. This rig works well for shallow water up to seven or eight feet deep.

A narrower piece of peacock quill can be inset into the top to make the float more sensitive. I usually paint most of my floats black with an orange or red top.

ANTENNAS: Sometimes you want to fish at distance with the weight on the line and the float held top and bottom, especially when the wind is blowing against the current. This is when the ordinary cane and balsa antenna float comes into its own.

Size can vary from 5.5 inches to 8 inches and shot-carrying capacity from two AAA to five AAA depending on the size of the body.

For close-in fishing they can be locked by two AAA and the line sunk by submerging the rod tip if the wind is bad. Cane tips vary in thickness from 2mm to one-eighth of an inch depending on the sensitivity required.

Remember that if you fish a peacock float top and bottom for distance work, your float will invariably end up bent or even broken.

LINE – THE MOST VITAL LINK IN YOUR TACKLE
[November 30th, 1972]

TOO many anglers expect one spool of line to do everything. They leger, floatfish and trot with the same breaking strain regardless of conditions.

For legering you need a heavy line that sinks quickly and easily to avoid a big bow forming underwater when you tighten to the lead. I use 3lb breaking strain, soaking the spool in liquid detergent if I want it to sink really fast.

Certain makes of line are more suitable for leger fishing. I favour two brands - a new German line and one of the oldest makes on the market.

For floatfishing I use anything from 1b 8oz to 3.7lb. I take five reels with me and you'll find most names of line on the various spools. Different rivers call for different brands as various conditions require various strengths. It's no good using a light 1lb 8oz line when there's a bad downstream wind. For correct tackle control you must go to a 2.7lb or even a 3lb and sink it. And while I might use one make of line on the River Nene, I've found that another brand suits the Severn.

Bait presentation is better when you're using a light line. But you have got to have confidence that you can hold fish with a 1.7lb. I used to successfully fish the Severn this light, but barbel will force me to go heavier.

A light line is all you need when fishing the Trent for roach with a top-and-bottom float. With warm water from the many power stations affecting the river, you can hope to catch your roach 'on the drop' in the first four feet of water. I cast a few yards downstream and tighten up straight away. Bites should come in the first two or three yards down as you check the float from racing away. But a strong downstream wind means you have to sink the line and fish from the bottom of the float. And this is when you need a heavier line. Then I leave as much as an inch of float showing so that when I hold back, the float does not disappear under the surface.

Newcomers to the Trent might like to try a little dodge that has helped me to catch a lot of fish in the past. Pinch a small shot, like a number six, about 18 inches to two feet above the float, fixed top and bottom. This sinks the line from shot to float. The idea is to aim to keep the shot just under the surface with a bit of slack line to the float. This gives the fish more confidence when it bites and teaches you to hold back correctly.

You trot down keeping the line tight to the shot - not the float. If you see the shot coming out of the water you just ease off the line. It's a silly little trick but it works well, even in a downstream wind.

I change my floatfishing lines every three weeks. You would be surprised to learn how much strength they lose through the action of daylight. A loss of a few ounces breaking strain could cost you a match-winning fish. It's as well to cover up your reels with a cloth when they are not in use to prevent the line from becoming brittle. And always remember to use soft split shot which you can slide up and down the line.

The hard stuff pinched on tightly will produce a weak point which could show itself when you are playing a fish.

Some anglers laugh when they see me rolling a zoomer float round my mouth. Well, I'm not trying to eat it...I'm just making sure that it's damp before I fix it to my line with two rubbers. Have you thought of the friction a dry float causes when you move it up the line? If you don't fancy sucking it, you can always drop it in the water.

Line varies from batch to batch. As a tackle dealer I've noticed that as the demand for a certain make of line increases, the quality seems to decline. This is probably because the machines used in the line's manufacture are being overworked and something suffers. If you do buy a good spool of line, rush back and buy the whole box. But make sure to keep it in the dark. You just can't be certain that the next time you buy that particular brand, it will be as good.

In the shop, look to see that the nylon is round and that there are no 'flats'. These are weak points produced in faulty manufacture and give themselves away by reflecting a different colour. Sometimes I find two or three boxes of weak line in a batch.

Even with a good line, many anglers give themselves unnecessary problems by incorrectly winding the line onto the spool. This creates kinks and spirals which can travel right down to the hook length. And by the time the line has straightened out, it's time to buy another new line. Never wind your line onto the reel by sticking a pencil through the hole in the plastic line spool and reeling. The line should be wound off the maker's spool with the broad face upwards so it comes off in coils. And if your reel winds anticlockwise, the line must come clockwise off the spool.

I believe that the line has been put onto the spool this way in its manufacture. So unless it is wound off the same way, it will be permanently twisted and under tension.

Another tip for anglers who use closed face reels. Always wind on the last 40 yards by hand, building up the spool from the middle to the front face. By having the line on the reel built up at a slant like this, I get very few tangles when I'm fishing.

USING A CENTREPIN
[January 4th, 1973]

T HE REVIVAL of roach fishing on the River Trent has meant a renewed interest in centrepin reels. Nottingham anglers swear by them and their success over the years shows that it's hard to beat good centrepin anglers on running water.

I've got a centrepin reel in my basket. It runs on ball races and because its action is so smooth and silent I've christened it the 'Rolls Royce' reel. Before closed-face fixed-spool reels came on to the market my centrepin was in constant use. I won two big Trent opens with the centrepin, one of them with 28lb from the Golden Mile. But nowadays it rarely goes on my rod. I've replaced it with the closed-face fixed spool. I can cast further with the fixed spool, fish further out and control my float just as accurately...because I use it like a centrepin reel!

Let me explain. When you are trotting rivers like the Trent your float tackle needs to travel down at a slower speed than the current. The modern alloy centrepin reel does this for you. The drag of the current pulls line from the reel acting as a brake on the float tackle as it travels downstream.

With the old centrepin reels which weren't so free-running the angler had to feed his line through the rings with his left hand. It was up to him to control his float correctly. If he wanted his float to travel down faster, he had to spin the drum and feed line faster.

This was how I learned to fish running rivers such as the Trent. And I still fish like this today, even though I'm using a fixed-spool reel. My right-hand index finger controls the line leaving the spool of the reel, but I still feed the line through the rod rings with my left hand. This way I remain in complete control of that float. It travels downstream how I want it, not at the whim of the current. My finger is only just touching the line to act as a brake, and there's probably no more than three inches of slack in my left hand. If I want to steady the float I just stop letting line out.

This way I can fish the Trent at two or three rod lengths' distance while the centrepin men have to fish closer in. Mind you, there might still be the odd occasions when I would use a centrepin reel, such as when the river was running faster than normal and I needed to fish near the bank.

Likely Lad Johnny Essex has won a match on the Trent this season using a centrepin reel, and Robin Grouse is practising with one. But nine times out of ten I'll stick to the fixed spool.

There's no reel faster than a centrepin at recovering line. The experts hit the drum hard and skim their fish across the surface, but 'batting' is an art by itself.

I'll use a closed-face reel on running water every time rather than an open-face reel, even though the latter has a faster action. And one of the main reasons for this is the ever-present problem of wind. With an open-face reel, wind will often blow the slack line across the top of the reel so that it wraps round the spool button on the retrieve. Some southern anglers have got around this problem by building up their spools with plastic wood so they are completely flush with the top.

But why go to this trouble when a closed-face reel eliminates the problem? Fish into a facing wind with an open-faced reel and you could crack the line. A breeze makes the line foul round the bale arm where it snaps when you wind in quickly after striking.

On fast-running rivers where bites are quick you just haven't got time to keep glancing at your reel to make sure the line's not fouled. By the time you've checked it, you've missed the bite. This is where the closed-face reel is supreme. I reserve the open face reel for slower rivers such as the

Welland and Nene where I'm casting long distances for big fish. Then I've got time to check the reel.

UNDERSTANDING HOOKS
[January 25th, 1973]

WHEN the water temperature drops, fish become finicky in their feeding habits. Often they will just-suck in a caster and blow it out again without your float moving.

Most anglers completely bury their hook in the caster to fool their quarry. But this can also fool the angler when the fish taste the bait yet decline to accept. I prefer to leave the tip of the point showing - no more than a 32nd of an inch - out of the side of the caster. This sometimes catches the skin inside the mouth of a crafty fish when you reel in your tackle.

I am fishing to win and bonus fish caught this way can make all the difference between success and failure. I will completely bury the hook on a no-hope day when I know I don't stand a chance. And I will also hook them on 'maggot fashion' when fish are coming fast.

Fine-wire long-shank caster hooks are ideal until fish start to feed furiously. Then they soon bend straight under the continual pressure from fighting fish. If I expect to catch a big netful of roach I use a bream hook, a flat-forged reverse. This especially applies in Ireland when you are catching roach at one a minute.

Anglers are often straightened by big bream when they are roach fishing with caster hooks. The answer lies in the strike. Don't hammer the hook home, lean into the fish.

If you try to force out a big bream with a fine-wire hook, of course it will straighten. Be patient. It might take five or six minutes to bring to the net but that fish could win you the match.

Many anglers have criticised me for using a size 20 hook

in last year's Great Ouse Championship. But I proved that you can get big bream out with a hook this small if you play them carefully. A 20 makes a smaller hole in a bream's mouth than say a 16 and so doesn't pull through so easily. Mind you, if I'd known Geoff Bibby was running me so close - he caught 62lb 8oz to my 62lb 10oz - I would probably have put on an 18 and hustled the fish out quicker. The best weight I heard on the bank while I was fishing was only 30lb.

I started off with a size 20 because I didn't fancy the area I drew. This is something I usually do when I'm fishing for a section place or for a team, rather than for a win. My standard hook for bream fishing is a size 18.

In the Relief Channel match I set myself a target weight of 30lb - about 15 fish. Anything over this would be bonus fish. This target weight is an important aspect of match fishing and has a direct bearing on the tackle and hook size used. Non-match anglers laugh at the size of hooks we use for bream fishing, but we have to make sure we are going to get bites.

You haven't got to be fast on a bream water, but rather make sure every bite counts. On the Welland or Witham you usually need only about ten bream to win, so you have plenty of time to play each fish.

On the other hand, if you have set yourself a 20lb target and you catch a bream with just an hour to go, it would be worth slipping on a size 16 or even a 14 to get those bream out quicker. Over the space of 60 minutes you might pinch ten seconds on a fish. If they were coming fast, this gain in time could give you long enough to catch that bonus fish and boost your weight to a winning one.

A lot of my fish are taken on the drop and the slower the bait falls, the better. Now if you drop a size 14 and an 18 in the water, the bigger hook should hit the bottom first. There might be only an inch in it but that could be the difference between getting a bite and not getting one.

It's the weight of the hook that is important rather than

its actual dimensions. Remember it must be pretty murky at the bottom of 12 feet of water, even for a fish's eyes. This is why, once I start changing hook sizes, I never swap makes. Different makes of hooks are forged from different thicknesses of steel. Swap one brand of 16 for another brand of 18 and the smaller hook could weigh more than the larger!

Some anglers go down to books as small as a size 24. My limit is a size 20 although I did once use a size 24 in France and caught a 4lb tench. Yet when the locals saw my tackle they all exclaimed that my hook was far too small! Apparently they use the ultra-tiny hooks just for catching fish two inches long.

I am one of those fortunate people who can tie a hook in a few seconds so I don't whip them until I get to the bank. Then I can choose what length bottom I need. There are only three matches where I tie the hooks beforehand - the National, World Championship and the Woodbine.

I don't bother with eyed books either, using only spade ends. But for rivers like the Severn an eyed hook will hold the bread on better.

One thing anglers should remember when buying loose hooks is to test the temper before parting with their money. Take out a hook from, say, a packet of 100 and make sure it is not too brittle. If it does break under stress, then the whole hatch could be faulty.

FANCY FLOATS DON'T CATCH FISH
[November 11th, 1973]

MANY anglers who look into my float box get the surprise of their lives! Instead of rows of immaculate, highly-varnished jobs, they see a drab, matt black jumble. But those who think: "What a load of old rubbish, I never thought Ivan Mark's floats would look like that," will never cotton on to the fact that it's not fancy floats that catch fish, it's the bloke that uses 'em!

My floats are a bit crude I admit. But they all work on the day and I can read them like a book. I prefer to make all my own. It's dead simple. All you need is several sizes of round balsa, some sarcandas reed, peacock quill, a few eyed hooks, whipping thread, thin cane and a few pots of paint and dope.

With that little lot you can make almost every float you will ever need for any condition. I usually have a float-making session every three weeks and make up to a dozen or so. But I usually end up with one for myself and give the rest away!

You don't need a drill, just an old knitting needle which could have been purpose-made for the job. Getting the body and cane or reed straight is easy. Just push the needle in from either end of the balsa. If you choose five-sixteenth or half-inch wood you won't split it, and with a little practice you will get the hole dead centre eight times out of ten.

For a neat float ring just straighten a hook, dip it in Araldite and push it home into the balsa. The barb makes sure the float won't fly off when you cast.

Typically, I usually have a session a few days before a big match. I make them on Thursday; give them a few coats of dope on Friday and paint them at about 2am on the morning of the match. I hang them up in front of a fire all night and get up at six to finish them off.

If they are not quite dry, I dust them in talcum powder to stop them sticking to each other. So, with luck, I can have the right float ready. I know it sounds a bit rushed but I'm a busy lad.

How do I know when I have made the right float? I'm not scientific in my choice at all and just have that feeling that this is a good 'un. It's like offering a musician two violins, one a Strad and an ordinary one. They may look just the same but somehow that feeling of quality jumps out at you!

After doping, I rub all the rough edges down with really fine wet and dry paper then put on the paint. I prefer Humbrol matt black, but sometimes use dark blue. It all depends what's handy.

Using my simple methods you can make a dozen floats an hour easily. Making stepped sarcandas reed floats obviously takes more time. But it's worth your bother because at present they are expensive to buy in the shops. Again, cutting the right lengths of reed is not a calculated thing.

A good angler just knows what he is setting out to achieve. You might make dozens to get one exactly right. If you do, and it performs really well, make up some more before you lose it.

I never varnish them. Apart from the fact that I never have time, the dope and matt paint keeps the water out, so why bother at all?

Another thing. You won't see many colour-tipped floats in my box. Matt black and a narrow white band is all I ever need. This white band is the secret of all my floats. I paint them in different widths about an eighth or a quarter of an inch from the black tip. Anglers sitting behind me are always baffled at seeing me strike when they haven't seen the float move. But I know for a fact that it has. The little white band has told me that something is happening down below. It also means that I can have quite a bit of float sticking out to give me just the right buoyancy, yet I just have to concentrate on the white band.

I can even fish with a float actually under the surface. Ridiculous? Just think about it. How many times do you strike and get your bait back, untouched but convinced that it was a smashing bite. The simple answer is - it wasn't. When you throw in loose feed, or little fish are charging about, they cause all sorts of underwater disturbances and even collide with your end tackle. This is what often makes you think it was a bite and waste precious time and probably a real chance of a fish.

Let it go under if you know these little fish might be doing this, and only strike when you see it move a second time. This is why some anglers think I'm a slow striker.

LOOKING AT BREAKING STRAINS
[February 5th, 1975]

'VE HIT a snag this year...nylon monofilament. It can be unreliable in the lower breaking strains. We all have our favourite brands of line – but even those well-tried and tested products can vary through the years. I hit my snag - and I wasn't the only one - when I started to tie hooklinks at the start of the season.

Suddenly, it seemed to me, the 1lb breaking strain monofil I was using was much stronger than the same line I had used the previous season. I put it to the test...and 1lb breaking strain actually broke at 1.6lb stress. Now that won't let anyone down in terms of playing fish. The line won't snap. But it meant that I was using a line which was six-tenths of a pound stronger than I needed for my hooklengths.

If I had wanted 1lb 8oz breaking strain that's what I would have bought but I was getting a stronger, and therefore a bigger diameter, line than I needed.

As I have said before, I have proved to my own satisfaction that the finer the monofilament used for hooklengths the greater the number of bites which will follow.

Obviously there's a limit to the finesse anyone can tolerate, for the time comes when the finest of line isn't good enough for the job. Just to prove a point, I once tied hooks to 8oz line on a day when bites were very hard to come by in the Leicester Canal. I got bite after bite while everyone else was failing. The only snag...I was hooking carp weighing anything from 1lb to 4lb and I broke on them - every one.

I believe that for most of our fishing, where there's the chance of the occasional big fish, 1lb breaking strain is the lowest breaking strain usable, consistent with first getting bites and then getting the fish into the keepnet.

But when the 1lb line I am using suddenly becomes 1.6lb, I'm not happy. Fortunately I had another 100 metre spool of that 1lb line left over from the previous year. It was gold dust to me.

Just as there can be poor batches of what had always been good line, so a previously poor line can show improvement and at least for a time becomes as good as the best. For that reason it is important to check what you buy. Don't just take it for granted that the breaking strain and diameter printed on the spools is exact. Test your line and make sure you are getting what you want.

There are countless reasons why a fine diameter and low breaking strain hooklength produces more bites. The nylon is less rigid, it fishes a falling bait better, it settles on to the bottom more lightly. A fish is able to take the hookbait without becoming scared, the bait is waved around more attractively in the flow (if there is any) and when a fish sucks the bait into its mouth that bait is suctioned naturally. It lifts off the bottom and into the fish's mouth in precisely the manner the fish expects it should.

Anglers who have problems using 1lb breaking strain hooklengths must look to the rest of their tackle and the way they handle it for the solution. Rods must be relatively soft so that the tension on the line is cushioned by the yield in the rod top. It's a case of doing everything gently. Control a hooked fish but don't bully it. Make it swim where you want it to go. That can be done with 1lb line in most situations...but take it easy.

Manufacturers should be able to supply us with 1lb line which is exactly that. It's their obligation to provide the goods. The tackle dealer can only sell what's available - so don't blame the tackle dealer if the line isn't exactly right. I can't imagine there will ever be a serious demand for monofil of less than 1lb strain. I suppose customers in our Leicester shop are as discriminating and trendy as anglers in most other shops, but only one in 500 asks for line of less than 1lb.

Most of that demand is to sample the line and to find out what it's capable of, rather than a firm commitment to regular use.

It figures though that if many of the 1lb lines are currently breaking at 1lb 4oz or even more, then some anglers see 12oz line as the solution - hoping it will break at 1lb.

There's room for a lot of research into nylon line. Why can't we buy monofil that sinks at 2lb breaking strain? That would be a very useful asset. Conversely, most 3lb lines sink - so why can't we have one that floats? We need both sinking and floating lines in much the same way as the trout fisherman. He's catered for. Why aren't we?

Research costs money. To market a line precise in all details, with guaranteed properties, manufacturers would have to pass the extra cost on to the consumer. But it would be very useful to be able to buy a line that exactly fits the requirements. That, I believe, would be worth a little bit more cash.

BALANCED TACKLE IS THE KEY
[October 29th, 1975]

ANGLERS have a long way to go, it seems, before they fully understand their tackle.

Even today experienced men, as well as beginners, are failing to balance their tackle to their rods.

The first essential of balanced tackle is matching the line and hooklength to the rod...and remember it isn't the reel line itself that is the crucial factor but the hooklength – since that has the lower breaking strain.

I said last week that for squatt fishing a 13ft rod is far and away the best there is. In my view there just isn't any other length worth considering. So what then is the maximum stress, the greatest power that a tip-actioned 13ft rod can impose on the line? Work it out for yourself as we have done and you'll settle on the surprisingly low level of 12oz.

That's all the pressure you can apply with a 13ft rod when using it correctly. This quickly makes it clear that there is no point, no point at all, in using a 3lb line and a 2lb 8oz hooklength on a tip action match rod. You simply overload the rod with line which gives you next to nothing in return.

It could, I suppose, be argued that if you foul a snag on the river bed you can take the line in your hand and apply greater pressure than is possible with the rod - but that's side-stepping the issue.

A 1lb 4oz breaking strain hooklength balances to a tip-actioned 13ft match rod. The 1lb line has an 8oz safety factor against the 12oz pressure from the rod. If you consider a 2lb breaking strain hooklength is necessary, or if, for example, you tie your hook direct to a 2lb 8oz reel line you have no option but to use a stiffer rod. Without that you achieve nothing.

Some people who have watched me fishing have made the point that I make my rod work, that it bends, that I'm not afraid to make full use of it. Be that as it may, when my rod is under sensible stress it has only an 8oz load on it. We've proved that with a spring balance. The rod isn't, of course, bent to the maximum. That's bad fishing. If it can pull 12oz, and I settle for 8oz, there's reserve power available should it be required.

I don't, of course, consciously think about that when I'm fishing. No one does that. But when you are aware of the limitations of your tackle you can easily develop a subconscious reaction to it.

There are other factors which must be taken into account when considering what constitutes balanced tackle. Nylon has a lower breaking strain when it is wet than when it is dry. And the weakest point on any reel line and hooklength assembly must be a knot.

The amount of breaking strain loss attributable to knots varies with different qualities of line and with the various knots. There's no precise table which can spell this out in line detail. But you must take these losses into account if you attempt to work out a balanced rig mathematically. Most anglers don't do that of course, but so long as you remember the basic points I have listed no one will make king size errors.

But the whole concept of balanced tackle tells us there can never ever be such a thing as a combination rod - a rod for all or at least a number of separate functions. The tackle makers used to shower combination rods on us years ago. They don't make that mistake today.

It was also once fashionable for the makers to offer us roach rods, bream rods, chub rods. That might have helped them to sell their wares but a rod doesn't know what species it is intended to be used for. It only reacts to the amount of load imposed on it.

In other words, from the breaking strain of the line used with it. The biggest risk of breaking a line comes from shock impact. That's easy to prove. Take a length of 6lb monolil, grip it firmly, snatch and the line breaks instantly. Now try again- but gradually increasing the amount of pressure on the line. Don't snatch and the line will be found to be very strong indeed. In fact, it will most likely hurt your hands before it breaks!

This simple little test tells you right away that sudden shock is to be avoided at all costs. Keep your fishing smooth and free from stress. Let's look briefly at three rods, all 13-footers - the CTM, the Mark 6 and the Persuader.

The Persuader is the softest of the three, the CTM the strongest. Allowing for knots and the difference in strength between wet and dry monofil, the Persuader balances best to a 1lb 4oz breaking strain hooklength. The Mark 6 is ideal for 1lb 8oz to 1lb 12oz and finally the CTM relates to 1lb 12oz to 2lb.

I am not trying to tell you that one rod is a better buy than another, simply that no two rods are the same and that these three are typical of the range of good quality float rods currently on sale in tackle shops.

I like a softish rod myself, so I use a Persuader. If you like one that's marginally stiffer, remembering you have to balance it to the water – to the snags and to the fish - you may prefer a Mark 6 or a CTM, or, of course, any from the other ranges available.

THE PROS AND CONS OF MONOFIL
[November 26th, 1975]

I N THE last 20 years the nylon industry has made great advances...yet we are still getting basically the same lines that were available to us all that time ago. There hasn't been much, if any improvement, yet the development of fine, limp monofil with a high breaking strain in relation to its diameter is something every angler wants.

Perhaps the manufacturers are satisfied because they are already selling us lines and don't see the need for much research and improvement. They don't have much incentive maybe, but the first manufacturer to market a truly improved line will make a killing in the market.

Those of us who take the trouble to examine monofil carefully can see flaws which the average man only discovers when his line lets him down with a fish. Some of the flaws are simply packaging problems. For example, every line should break at the strain specified yet very few do and batches of line can vary. It follows, of course, that if breaking strains were constant then diameter would also conform - but it doesn't on many lines.

Let's look at some of the factors which determine whether a line gives a good, bad, or indifferent service. Monofil has a limited fishing life. It reacts to bright sunlight. Some lines absorb ultra violet from sunshine more than others. The less-absorbent have a longer life. In general terms that means that the line needs a matt, not a bright finish. Matt line is also better from a fishing point of view. A bright, shiny line looks thicker than it really is, thicker, for example, than a matt white line.

I have already mentioned the dangers from worn rod rings. It's also worthwhile pointing out the problems arising from worn bale arms and bale pins. Nine out of ten of the fixed spools we get into our shop for servicing have this fault - which, until it is discovered, is damaging to monofil.

The lines we use for match and pleasure fishing are rarely

thicker than 5lb. It's surprising how much damage this fine line does to metal when under tension.

Detergent is another enemy of monofil. We use it to help ensure we can get the line to sink when we want it to but for all of that it does diminish line strength somewhat and this needs watching.

We can criticise some manufacturers for a lack of uniformity in their line. It's quite easy to see the 'flats' in some line - see them with the eye that is. When I'm in doubt I give line what I call the 'tongue test'. The tongue is extremely sensitive and by drawing monofil lightly across the tongue you can discover rough patches if you suspect they are there but cannot see them.

Elasticity and stretch are two important properties of line. First I must make it clear they are not one and the same. Stretch is simply what it implies, whereas elasticity relates to suppleness. A supple, as opposed to a 'stiff' hooklength gives you far more bites. Roach and bream don't grab your bait with their teeth. They simply inhale water into their mouths and this sucking process puts the bait where you want it to go.

The lower breaking strains of nylon succeed as hooklengths because they are finer and because they therefore allow your hookbait to be drawn into the fish's mouth without hindering the process.

Stretch is one of monofil's most important features. It is your defence against shock impact; the line stretches instead of breaks. Manufacturers don't apparently look at it quite like that. Some of them are trying to sell us pre-stretched line - line with the elasticity removed. I can't see they are doing us any sort of service, for we need that elasticity, particularly in the lower breaking strains.

The continual use of a normal monofil line, one with its elasticity remaining, gradually diminishes its ability to stretch. What happens is that line progressively becomes longer and thinner until it reaches the point where it will stretch no more. Once that has happened and the 'stretch' has been removed, the line will snap.

This is one of the reasons why longer hooklengths have become fashionable over recent years. Eighteen inches of fine nylon provides greater stretch than 12 inches of the same line. Thus the safety factor is greater - and there is far less chance that you will be broken while striking or playing a fish.

I mentioned knot strength recently. Monofil is reduced in strength by up to 40 per cent by knots, the amount of loss depending on the knot itself. If you doubt this loss exists try it for yourself - and don't forget to wet the line for there's another loss of strength. There is no point in testing a dry line - after all no-one has so far succeeded in fishing with a dry monofil line!

SWIMFEEDER SECRETS
[December 1st, 1976]

I HAVE always been a little bit anti as far as swimfeeders are concerned. They create a commotion when they hit the surface, take a little bit of the fun out of playing fish and give tackle a cluttered-up feeling.

I rarely use a swimfeeder in the summer. Perhaps prejudice is only one of the reasons. I think I can feed at long range in summer without the need for this sort of feeder. But the case changes drastically in winter. The fish want less food thrown at them. Cereal feed can be positively dangerous and can kill your chances stone dead.

Given the most favourable of all circumstances no-one can throw loose maggots or casters more than 20 yards - either by hand or by catapult - and the big snag is that the greater the distance the greater the tendency for the feed to scatter. In the summer that doesn't matter very much, so long as your feed drops into a 12ft square area there are likely to be enough fish around feeding heavily enough to clean up the area and home in on to your hookbait.

Winter is something quite different. Fish are more lethargic in their movements. They don't seek food quite so eagerly and you need to keep your feed patch very much smaller as a result. How can you do it? Groundbait isn't the answer. You will need to get your loosefed maggots and or casters into a small area - much smaller than you can hope to achieve with a catapult or by hand. The simple answer is a swimfeeder.

You can control the arrival of your loosefeed with a swimfeeder better than with anything else. Bites will be fewer than in summer but they are likely to come from the bigger stamp of roach.

What does that mean? First that you should not use as much feed as you would in summer and secondly that you shouldn't cast so often. In fact in a five-hour contest it shouldn't be necessary to cast more than 50 times - once every five minutes. Unless, of course, you are catching a lot of fish!

There can be up to 75 big maggots in a swimfeeder and it should take no less than five minutes for the fish to clear that lot away. You must give them the time to take your hook maggot.

Many anglers make the mistake of recasting far too frequently in winter. Fifty times is enough when you are hookbaiting with maggots but if you've worm on the hook then the casting rate is even slower. I believe that ten casts in five hours are sufficient if you are baiting with worm.

A lot of anglers are frightened off swimfeeders simply because they believe they have to fish much heavier than they feel is necessary. Let me reassure the doubters. There's no need to use a great thick line. You get twice as many bites on 1lb 8oz line as you can hope to get on 3lb. So why imagine there's any need for heavy line just because you intend to use a swimfeeder?

If you are fishing for roach and bream a 2lb line is adequate – always assuming, as I have stressed before, that the line balances to the test curve of the rod you are using.

I can whack a swimfeeder across on the Welland on a 2lb breaking strain line. Unless I am unlucky I wouldn't lose a single swimfeeder in a full day's fishing. And I certainly would never cast one off.

Remember that a swimfeeder may seem quite heavy when you cast it out but it is nothing like so heavy when you strike. I've never found it gives me tangles. There is a need to give a lot of thought to the distance between feeder and hookbait but I will tell you about this next week when I will also detail the two methods of casting that can be used.

I suppose it is right to say that I regard the swimfeeder first and foremost as an aid to catching more roach than I could otherwise manage on winter days. But I ought to make it clear that it can also help with bonus fish - chub, perch and bream or whatever there happens to be around.

And I tend to go for the block-end feeder rather than the all-through type simply because I much prefer to use the feeder for maggots rather than for casters or groundbait. I'm sure that's right for winter fishing.

As I said comparitively recently, maggots can be every bit as good as casters in the winter - particularly when match fishing. The fish react to maggots much faster. Less time is wasted. That's got to be important in winter simply because the amount of time during which fish are prepared to feed is very much shorter anyway.

POLING CAN WIN ANYTHING
[March 30th, 1977]

THERE'S a common misconception going the rounds that pole fishing means a mad dash for mini-fish and nothing else. So far as British fishing is concerned that's a long, long way from true.

It's easy to see how pole fishing got its reputation for tiddler bashing and nothing else. After all, it is a European method and anglers over there have tended to use the style in its most limited form. Perhaps though it might be more accurate to say that we've heard most about their mini-fishing exploits, for even from over there there have been occasional glimpses of the other side of pole fishing.

The best example we have had here that pole fishing can be used to catch bigger fish was provided by Pierre Michiels in the 1974 Gladding Masters contest at Coombe. Spectators are still talking about Pierre's performance – 17lb of class roach, taken with a big pole. Okay, he got smashed from time to time through the contest. That wasn't really the fault of the method, but simply because he had to fish extra fine to get the roach to feed.

A year later, a Birmingham AA team of stars, Kenny Giles, Kevin Ashurst and Tony Scott, were walloped by three of Europe's best pole anglers, during the Birmingham Parks Festival. Maybe that's where the Starlets realised the style had a future or they've used it well enough since - although even they have tended to go for the small fish with it.

My point, though, is that pole fishing need not be as restrictive as people seem to imagine. And that's a theme I will develop in this continuing series.

At the moment, pole fishing is not so very popular. More and more anglers are starting it every year but the figure doesn't yet run into thousands. Realise, though, that the anglers who might be regarded as the cream of the British open match circuit - the men Stan Smith looks at most regularly for his England team - are all on it to a man: Clive Smith, Scotty, Ian Heaps, Kenny Giles, Kevin Ashurst to name some.

I've had a fourth and sixth in Trent Winter League contests, with a best weight of 11lb, fishing the pole. In addition I've had 30lb of roach from the Welland on it, up to 18lb of bleak and gudgeon from the Trent and other quite notable weights from both the Welland and the Nene, all while pleasure fishing.

All of which leaves me under no illusions: this is a winning style. It will win almost everywhere on its day – and that's the key to the method. It's all a matter of targets.

As I've explained before, in every match I fish I set myself a target weight. Could be a winning or a place weight, but I set myself a total to aim at, confident that if I achieve it then I'm in the money. So if I'm fishing the Great Ouse Championship and the target weight is 40lb, then on all past form I cannot use the pole. There's no chance of 40lb by pole fishing on the Relief Channel.

But if the Nene Championship target weight for a high placing is 10lb, who discounts the pole for that? No-one but an angler who is too hidebound by tradition to recognise that in many circumstances he has a better chance of getting 10lb on the pole than any other way!

I've got to admit that few, if any, British anglers are the complete masters of the style as yet. We're all still learning... and the sooner you start to learn, the less you'll have to make up when the infrequent pole wins develop into a more steady sequence.

It's natural that the method should first show its benefits in team fishing. It brings greater consistency to the weights obtained by any team of 12 anglers. On balance, the improvement with the lower team weights more than cancels out the fact that the method has yet to prove itself with the top weights in mammoth matches.

The National Championship's individual section can be won on the pole, you know, and don't doubt that for a moment. Can't tell you where and when, all depends on the water on the day, but it will happen one day.

I can see the day coming when the pole gets some really big weights of roach and skimmers out of the Fen drains... and from waters as big as the Middle Level. Forty pounds is quite on the cards.

The snag is that the poor old pole angler of today is very much a curiosity. Other competitors see him manhandling a 27ft pole and classify him as an idiot. Later, when they've suddenly realised they are catching nowt, they'll get up from their baskets and walk over to watch him fishing...and scare his fish away! So the style hasn't yet acquired general acceptance. That's coming, but it's slow.

I'm not suggesting for one moment that it will ever replace any other style. But both Kevin Ashurst and I fished the pole in the individual section of last year's World Championship. I think it was generally agreed we put up a fair performance that day, and I managed second place with something like 24lb. I fished conventional British tactics in the team event to finish second in my section. I would have needed another 4lb of fish to have won the section.

Maybe I might have run it close had I used a pole, but remember team fishing demands a team effort. I wasn't, with existing knowledge, prepared to jeopardise the team's chances by poling it. It wouldn't have mattered quite so much if I had blown out using the pole in the individual contest. At that stage I had no-one else to consider.

ROACH POLES
[April 6th, 1977]

WITH so very few people possessing enough knowledge to offer worthwhile advice on the subject, it's no wonder that buying a first roach pole presents all sorts of difficultly to British anglers. They just don't have a clue where to start. How can they? And even the tackle trade isn't as knowledgeable as it really needs to be.

So what then is a good roach pole? What does a good pole look like? What should it do...and, just as important, what does it cost?

Go for a rigid pole – it musn't be sloppy or it won't do the job. I don't rate telescopic poles at all...haven't got one and wouldn't buy one.

Now poles are available in all sizes, from 10ft up to 27ft and more. Maybe you can't ever picture yourself handling a 27ft pole. It's a frightening length at first sight and the average first buyer is happy to settle for a compromise.

As the result bad buys are made. I believe that most anglers who begin by buying a middle-length pole end up regretting their decision.

Remember the crucial points. A 27ft pole has seven joints. Take one off and the pole is a metre shorter. Take two off and you are fishing with around 20ft of pole. Now when you first buy a pole you are bound to reject the idea of using the whole thing...but you can alter your taste as you become more experienced and proficient. It is much cheaper to buy a full-sized pole first off rather than start with a smaller one.

Remember too that, strictly, you need two top joints. One is the joint fitted to take the hook attachment to which the elastic and then the line is fitted. The other needs to be of stiff tip action and is intended for small fish. You won't need a hook attachment for small-fish fishing. So start off by buying the largest pole you can afford. Twenty seven footers are available in the price range £26 to £32.

Which pole do you buy out of the selection on offer? The range of imported poles gets bigger every year but I prefer to settle for something I know, which is perhaps safest in the long run.

Herbert, the two Tesses, Guineneuf, Thime, name who you like, and you can be sure that these men and others like them who are the cream of the French match circuit, use Garbolino poles. What's good enough for them is good enough for me.

Now I suspect you have already been wondering how on earth YOU can expect to handle a king-size pole for the full duration of a typical English fishing match.

Easy. First settle for 22ft - as I do, keeping one joint of the pole in reserve. You may still be shuddering at the thought that a 22ft pole has 9ft in hand on your traditional rod, but it is by no means as unwieldly as you might think.

Instead of sitting square on the river, you have to sit side-saddle when using a big pole. The butt of the pole is then laid across your knees, with a 2ft overhang. Your arms are spread so that when you lift with the left hand you press with the right your knees become the pivot point...the rod reacts - and that's how you strike.

There's no need to suffer the exertions of holding the big pole unassisted for five hours. The French, of course, don't suffer the problem because their contests are shorter than ours; less than three hours as a rule. And in any case their targets are usually different from mine. Out and out speed fishing is only one aspect of poling. I still go for the idea that it's better to get the best of both worlds.

It's all a question of targets...and tactics to achieve those figures. There's little point in using a really long pole to catch tiny fish since the casting and landing operation is much faster with our traditional British tackle. But if you are pecking away at bleak close in to the shore line then a 9ft pole will be admirable...the three top joints from your 27footer.

THE MAGIC OF THE SPRINGTIP
[June 22nd, 1977]

THERE has never until now been such a thing as a universal bite indicator. Every one had its limitations, which make it ineffective in some permutations of fishing conditions. Which make the spring quiver something special, for that works under all conditions. I've used it to fish pulling water that's 15ft deep. I've used it on the Trent and, of course, it's class itself on stillwaters of any depth and width.

It really does knock a quivertip into a cocked hat. The prime disadvantage of the quiver was always that even with parallel glass, the tip provides increasing tension as the fish pulls. In tapered quivers that resistance is so powerful that fish realise something's wrong and drop the bait.

The spring quiver behaves very differently. Once the coil is broken, once it begins to register a fish's movement, there is no build-up. It doesn't stiffen. No extra tension is required to put additional movement into the tip. Which means that bites develop to the full. Fish don't become shy and disappear at speed. And because the resistance is so slight the mini-bites are quite exaggerated and a higher proportion of the bites produce fish.

The spring aspect of the indicator can be used in varied strength - which means you can set it differently in modestly flowing water to counteract the light tension showing on the tip.

It shows a bite quicker than any other indicator, simply because there is less inertia to overcome and less effort is required to get it bending. In fact, once you have cast and then modestly tightened the line, the coil is already semi-broken and is all ready to go.

The advantages are all but endless. There's no longer any need to pore over your indicator watching for the slightest trembles. Movements are so much greater that you can virtually sit back and relax. The spring quiver actually takes the tension out of you as well as out of your bite indicator!

I hadn't won a match with it until the recent Ballinasloe Gala, where I won the first day event with 32lb. I won that by fishing at long range for rudd - although I did get a couple of bream as well. There's nothing half-hearted about rudd when they're having a go, and these fish were no exception. But the difficulty was the long range. The spring quiver was positive enough to help me hit each bite quickly, rather than delay and run the risk that the rudd would quickly burst the maggots and spit out the residue.

It is better in any sort of wind than the swingtip can ever be because the springs housed under the silicone rubber covering make it self-regulating. These things really have been a long time in the proving. A number of well-known anglers have been using them for three years...and some of them are better known now as the result of using spring quivers than they were before they started!

In fact we could already have claimed a first National win with them - by Dave Downes for Leicester AS on the Witham

- were it not for the fact that Dave spent the first 40 minutes of that National fishing for bites on the float. Dave eventually knocked out 40lb of bream but his delayed start at them cost him first place. Roy Marlow and John Castledine have both taken weights comfortably over 30lb, winning big opens in the process and the record is good enough to make me think that swings and quivers are now firmly in the obsolete stage.

Think about it for a moment: you need dozens of floats, perhaps hundreds, some people would say, to be fully equipped on that front. For legering you need an assorted half-dozen quivers and at least a couple of swingtips...or a single spring quiver!

It takes only a split second to alter the indicator to a quivertip for flowing water if conditions change to the point that the spring aspect is no longer functioning adequately.

There's no messing about, no time wasted, no rethreading of the line through the new quiver or what have you. So the device saves fishing time, saves money and gives a far better bite registration than anything currently available.

The springs are non-corrosive, so they won't tighten up with rust as some of the traditional springtips do. It's my opinion that this new device is the best invention in legering for many years...and that opinion is likely to be proved with increasing regularity through this present season.

GO BARBLESS - YOU WON'T REGRET IT
[December 12th, 1979]

THINK I was one of the last, if not the last, of the anglers who might be reckoned to be at or near International class, to switch over to barbless hooks. No misgivings now! I'm sold on barbless hooks all the way - for everything except bream fishing.

More about that particular exception later, but I have no qualms about barbless for roach, chub and barbel.

Barbless have a number of advantages. Number one has to be that the hookbait is left in better condition after it has been placed on the hook.

A barbless hook punctures the bait, but fills the hole it makes. This means that the juices cannot escape. A barbed hook, however, is widest in the metal at the point where the barb is located. Thus, when the hook is mounted in the bait there is slackness around the metal of the hook through which the juices leak out.

Now no-one can convince me that a leaking maggot is as good a bait as a sealed one. The former is badly injured and can't therefore wriggle as well or appear as attractive to the fish as one in full possession of its health and energy.

The barbless hook must be the answer to especially fragile baits, like bloodworm or thin-skinned maggots.

Another key advantage is that a barbless hook is so much better to seal into a good hook hold on the strike. The movement as the hook takes its hold is smooth, whereas a barb creates a 'bump' on the metal shank that must brake the hooking process and hinder penetration.

No, I'm not arguing that an efficient reaction to a good bite doesn't hook fish effectively on barbed hooks. Obviously, it does. The important point relates to difficult bites, the ones we are always likely to miss, the ones we reacted to quickly but late, the ones that were not positive.

I'm sure that many of those bites are lost because the fish was merely pricked...and the prick didn't develop into a good hook hold simply because of the resistance of the barb to further penetration.

The advantages of barbless don't end there. We are not exactly flush with fish these days. It's up to us to minimise wastage and to ensure that we keep accidental mortality as low as possible. A barbless hook is easier to remove. There's no stress, no strain. It comes free under minimal pressure and the fish suffers from little more than a pin prick. There's no unnecessary twisting and turning of the hook needed before it comes out.

On many occasions the barbed hook is also easy to remove but it is undeniable that marginally more force is required to unseat the hook. Now this is insufficient to present any sort of problem with lip-hooked fish. Deeply hooked fish are more difficult and I am sure that casualties are fewer if the hook is barbless.

It's one of those absurdities of conservation that people who actually appear to be taking most trouble to remove the hook in a manner that inflicts less damage usually end up doing the opposite. So far as unhooking fish is concerned the prime needs are speed, a limp but positive hold on the fish (so that it is not squeezed) and a good unhooking technique allied to a barbless hook.

So far as fishing is concerned, confidence is the important factor. For the biggest stumbling block to barbless hooks is fear that they lose their hold while a fish is being played.

Now I still favour my forged reverse size 20 - barbed - for bream fishing. The hook size is small in relation to the size of the fish since I am not talking about skimmer bream but about your genuine 'humphries'. Mind you, Kenny Giles doesn't suffer from inhibitions of that sort. Kenny won the Embassy on the Guden using barbless hooks on a day when his 110lb catch was half roach, half bream. But when I'm fishing somewhere like Coombe, for example, where the fish are big and the range can be more than 50 yards, I like the added security of a barb.

It is by no means as important at short range when you are fishing less line – and having to cope with less stretch. Some anglers feel, too, that if they fish barbless hooks while bream fishing on the bomb they are never completely certain that the bait is still on the hook. There's never that same mental block in float fishing simply because the bait is in the water for shorter periods.

The hook is continually being lifted out of the water and recast so it's then easy to see the bait.

With bream legering the period between casts can be as long as 20 minutes – and that's a long time to be in doubt.

Of course match fishermen are not the only ones currently using barbless. I know that Bob Church and many of his pals use barbless for pike fishing. Even trout anglers could turn to these hooks in time. Some are already experimenting.

I suppose confidence is the key to it all. Once you realise that fish don't drop off - so long as you play them properly - you're halfway there.

There's no need to change your brand. Odds are you can buy barbed and barbless in exactly the same pattern. But if you want to give barbless a trial simply rub the barb off one of your usual hooks with a knife or disgorger. I'm sure you will be pleasantly surprised at the advantages.

One last plus point: we are progressively using finer and finer lines and hooklengths to ensure we get our share of the bites. Anything that reduces the need for even marginally stronger tackle must help that process...and it clearly needs less impact to set a barbless than a barbed hook.

Chapter Four

Ivan Marks on...
TACTICS

> Many anglers lose heart when they draw near a big name. They become nervous and spend precious time watching to see what he is up to instead of concentrating on their swim. They try to copy the crack's method when they would be better off sticking to their own style.

FLOAT CONTROL IS OF VITAL IMPORTANCE
[July 29th, 1972]

WE ALL know the saying 'don't try to run before you can walk.' Well, for anglers I juggle it to read 'don't try to catch before you can control.' Let me explain what I mean. Many anglers sit behind me when I'm fishing well out on the wide rivers and watch me control my float correctly to get bites. But when they come to copy me they fail to catch fish and soon become disheartened. Then they start blaming secret baits or special groundbait. What they don't realise is that it's taken years and years of practice and experience to learn to control a float correctly at distance. How can they hope to do that in just one session?

My advice to anglers who want to master the techniques of float control is to start by fishing under your rod tip. Admittedly there won't be so many fish close in but at least you can draw them to you and present your bait correctly. When you've won confidence in your bait presentation and float control, then try a little farther out. After plenty of practice perhaps you will be able to join the Leicester anglers and fish the middle of those wide Fenland rivers.

We Leicester anglers have been experimenting with some very long peacock quill floats to get our line as much below the surface drift and wind as possible. But we don't think they work as well as the shorter floats we have used for years.

A peacock quill float between ten to 12 inches long with a small cork body is our major weapon. For rivers such as the Nene or Welland we insert a finer piece of quill in the tip to make bite registration more sensitive. The all-important factor in this method of fishing is to sink your line straight after casting. We favour a heavy 3lb line that sinks quickly, but usually use a five-foot hooklength of 1lb 8oz to get the bait fall we favour.

Remember the Leicester anglers' secret when floatfishing is to try to get the fish feeding 'on the drop'. A swan and an AAA shot lock the float on the line, and if the bleak aren't about then just over an AAA is all that's needed further down. If bleak are a pest then go heavier to get the bait past their greedy little mouths. When the float's out there, try to keep the bait moving as slowly as possible. If there's no pull on the river then the bait should be stationary. Fish aren't going to chase a moving bait. Slow the bait's passage down as much as you dare by delicately controlling the line. But be careful when you check the float that you don't pull your bait out of the fish's mouth.

What would you say if just as you were sitting down to supper, your missus moved your plate across the table? Then just as you were ready to tuck in again, away the plate went a second time. You'd either give up the idea of eating, or smack her in the ear!

On days when a strong wind is blowing downstream I usually pinch a shot on the last 18 inches of line to drag the bottom. This steadies up the progress of the bait, and the float rides down in front. I'm not frightened to have an inch of float showing under these conditions, although I can hear anglers behind accusing me of being crude. Well, that float doesn't have to go under for me to see a bite. I get used to the 'bounce' of the float between the waves as it trundles its way downstream.

When it keeps at one height I know that a fish has lifted that bottom shot. Spectators see me hit a fish and think that I'm striking blind. But I know different.

If you find your maggots are being sucked but you haven't seen a bite, pull your shot up and down until the float moves. Don't just sit there hoping for something to happen.

Under conditions of a strong downstream wind on a wide water, many anglers lose fish by incorrect striking.

Don't strike upwards. This puts resistance on the line from the water and the float hardly moves. Strike to the side pulling the line through the water. We call this cutting the water with the line.

All the time you're fishing, keep feeding with a small ball of groundbait on every cast. This keeps the fish interested.

Once you lose them, they may not return.

The two Leicester anglers in the Gladding Final on the River Nene didn't distinguish themselves. Ray Mumford's incredible catch of bleak made everyone look sick.

But this match was between only 33 anglers. If say 400 had been fishing as in an open match, I don't believe Ray would have won. He would have finished high up in the prizes but someone would have caught bream or roach. This is why the Leicester anglers don't fish for bleak. We believe our method is the winning style.

TIPS FOR SWINGERS
[July 13th, 1972]

MOST big open matches on bream waters are won on the leger. Float tackle will score with the smaller fish but to stay in the chase for the bigger bream, you must go on the 'bomb'.

Legering is often criticised for being crude compared to float fishing. But swingtipping Leicester-style is a sensitive art. We 'read' the tip as we would a float. Remember that both give a visual indication of what's happening to your bait.

As when float-fishing we try to take the fish 'on the drop'. We feel that fish are more likely to accept a falling bait than a static one on the bottom.

So to do this we use a long tail or hooklength ranging anywhere between three and six feet. This gives the bait a natural fall. I usually tie the Arlesey bomb at the end of my reel line, using two loops to join the hooklength to the main line in paternoster fashion.

It's very rare for me to use a bomb heavier than three-eighths of an ounce. Sometimes I will go to a smaller bomb when conditions allow. Remember a lighter lead will sink slower and give the fish more time to take the falling bait.

I try to keep to a long swingtip around 12 inches as this is more sensitive than a short one. To protect it from the wind, my umbrella goes in the water while I get cold. There's nothing like a netful of bream to warm you up!

Another essential for the serious swingtipper is a target board. Some bream like the Relief Channel fish will straighten the tip, but others hardly move it a fraction. A quarter-of-an-inch bite is good for Nene bream. And try spotting that without a target board on a windy day.

When you are all set to fish, cast out just beyond your groundbait. Shut the reel's bale arm and put the rod in the rest. But don't tighten up to the bomb. This is a form of slackline legering.

As the bomb travels down through the water, the swingtip is pulled out straight. But it drops when the bomb reaches the bottom. I'm looking for bites as soon as the tip startsits fall. When the tip is limp, I give the reel handle two or three turns. The tip straightens out and then slowly drops back again. I'm searching for a twitch upwards as a fish grabs the falling bait, or a fast drop as a fish takes the bait and swims towards me.

The direction and force of the wind will control how well you are able to fish this style. If it is upstream or behind you, it works well. But a downstream wind is the kiss of death. On a very calm day you can watch the line cutting through the water to get to the swingtip. Then any unusual movement can be struck immediately. If you can't get the bream to take the bait as it is falling, then obviously you are forced to catch them on the bottom.

Now this is where I get impatient, and the reason for those much publicised mid-match strolls. I get restless waiting for a bite, and have a strong job resisting the temptation to reel in the bait. If I'm walking the bank, the bait is lying there waiting for a shoal of feeding fish.

So when I do reel in and I see a chewed maggot, I know that fish have moved into the swim. I believe in searching the swim for fish by casting the bait beyond and also short of the groundbaited area. A float would normally do this for you, but remember that a bomb is static.

However, there are those occasions when the river is running and a still bait would look unnatural to the fish. Then I swap the bomb for a bullet and let it move round the swim.

As the bullet trundles through, the swingtip gets into a rhythm of lifting and dropping. Any sudden change in the pattern could be a feeding fish and warrants a strike. This method of fishing is similar to watching the lift of a float in heavy waves. When it doesn't rise, you strike.

Everyone gets the problems of sucked maggots when you don't see a bite. The fish has beaten you. All you can do is either shorten or lengthen your tail.

Again, striking lets down many swingtip anglers. Leicester anglers have learned to strike along the bank of the river, pulling the line through the water. Many successful anglers strike upwards. Well, good luck to them. But we'll stick to our style.

DON'T COPY THE CRACKS – STICK TO YOUR OWN STYLE
[October 12th, 1972]

HUNDREDS of anglers have the ability to win a big open competition. But their lack of confidence beats them before they start.

These are the Dave Bedfords of the angling world who can't perform on a strange water when the pressure is on them to win. So they make it easy for the cracks to succeed from indifferent pegs.

Many anglers lose heart when they draw near a big name. They become nervous and spend precious time watching to see what he is up to instead of concentrating on their swim. They try to copy the crack's method when they would be better off sticking to their own style.

Remember that it's probably taken 15 to 20 years for the top angler to perfect his fishing. So the other anglers can't hope to beat him at his own game.

It's no good believing that if you can catch 20lb, they can get 40lb. The top anglers are only mortal and have their 'off' days the same as anyone else. And to win, they still need a good peg.

When I first started match fishing I didn't even know who were the cracks of the day. I just sat down and got on with my fishing. There were plenty of surprised faces when I won.

When I'm feeling down and out I'm praying for a bad peg. I dread drawing a corker in case I mess it up. And if I do win on one of these days, it's usually by a small margin. Only I know that I should have caught a lot more.

Luckily these 'off' days are few and far between, and I'm able to shrug them off. Being beaten by the man at the next peg is an upsetting experience but it happens to everyone at some time. I always remember the Welland Championship when Joe Waldron slaughtered me. He took 21lb to my 8lb, but there were no grumbles from me. Joe just had bigger fish.

It's important to forget the bad days otherwise your confidence will slide. And then you could be out of the money for ever.

All sorts of silly things help to give anglers confidence. It could be a lucky float or a certain peg number. My lucky number is 13 so when Leicester drew 67 in the Avon National I was confident we would do well. And so it proved when Phil Coles won the individual title.

The year before, on the Severn, several of the Leicester team went down before the National to an open match at Borley. I drew next to Kevin Ashurst, and if that wasn't threat enough Johnny Toulson was pegged a little further downstream.

At the finish I had 19lb - more than Kevin's and Johnny's weight combined! The rest of the team couldn't believe this and it proved the fillip we needed to help us win the National.

What I knew - and the rest of the team didn't - was that Kevin had lost the first hour practising a secret method which didn't pay off. I kept that dark until after the match.

Spectators behind an angler can do more to ruin his

confidence than anything, unless he steels himself to ignore their remarks. If I'm having a bad competition and I know there people watching me, I'm there to be pulled around.

But it still won't throw me out of my stride. In this year's National my first cast went straight up a tree. I had a big gallery plus the TV cameras behind me, yet I soon got the feel of the match and performed.

I had another tangle later that took a bit of sorting out. And after the match a lad came up to me and said: "I'm glad to see that you are just the same as the rest of us when it comes to tangling."

One lad who suffered from spectator nerves in the Second Division National was Coleshill's Alan Clark. He couldn't settle and this affected his performance.

I felt extremely sorry for him as I had no doubt that on his home river he would have been brilliant. A new water can often upset an angler – and cause unnecessary mistakes.

It would take an atom bomb to blow me off my peg when I'm catching fish. I fish like a machine running at a steady rhythm, cutting down movements to the basics. I'm organised to the point where I know I can lay my hands on everything. The only time my rod leaves my right hand is when I'm unhooking a fish or when I'm groundbaiting. Then I change hands and strike with my left. I can't groundbait with my left hand further than 15 yards, otherwise I feed the whole of the river!

I dislike using a landing net, except when absolutely necessary; it's too easy to tangle the shot. I usually lift fish to 6oz or beach 'em and pick them out by hand.

I go fast without giving the appearance of speed. The man at the next peg could be doing twice as much work, and end up with half my catch. He's like a man about to blowout his big ends.

Benny Ashurst always used to joke: "If you don't see Ivan walking the bank, you're in trouble." He meant that if the fish were feeding at my peg nothing could distract me from the job, except perhaps a blond in a bikini! Mind you, I'd tell her to come back after the match.

Lack of sleep before a match doesn't affect me either, although I might collapse on the bank afterwards. But a little thing like a person standing in the wrong position on a peg can upset me.

But there was one time when I could cheerfully have chucked my rod at the crowd watching me. That was in Prague during the last World Championships when I felt I didn't have a grip on the competition.

Thirty minutes passed without a bite, and for the first time I began to feel desperate. I was pacing myself to the Belgian star Marcel van den Eynde, who won the International in Holland.

As it was, I doubled his weight but the Italian next door beat me by 1lb. Later I didn't feel too guilty about this, as even if I had won my section England would still have finished second.

WINTER BREAM
[November 11th, 1972]

WINTER bream fishing is a waiting game. The first frosts and cold winds send the bream scurrying into deeper water where they form massive shoals.

But trying to persuade them to feed can be more difficult than ending a person's hunger strike. All you can do is cast out and leave your bait alone for as long as 20 minutes at a time, hoping for a fish to pick it up.

Weights in the winter are usually lower than summer catches so you can afford to wait for bites. If you took one fish every half an hour in a five hour match, you could finish up with 25lb – enough to win most winter contests.

Of course you must draw on the fish otherwise you could sit all day without a bite. These bream shoals are massive but one peg away is too far. The fish won't move once they've taken up their winter quarters until spawning time.

Certain areas on the Fenland rivers are noted bream grounds from now until the end of the season. I would always be happy to draw a peg in the 200s on the Welland, particularly just upstream of the noted red barn – now painted green.

Every bite counts in winter so concentration is important. The bream are usually heavier as they've packed on extra weight to combat the colder months.

At this time of year worm fishing becomes a must. But most anglers make the mistake of tackling a contest with just a carton of brandlings. They wouldn't go fishing with just half a pint of maggots!

Heavy goundbaiting is definitely out. About five or six pound is as much as you would want to use. The bait – red worms or brandlings – can be chopped up and mixed with the groundbait.

Remember that fish are moody and will not go head over heels to feed. So bombarding them with heavy balls will kill the swim, as well as frightening off any smaller fish which might be around.

The Leicester lads have noticed on the Welland that they can catch good quality roach by loose feeding at certain pegs in midweek practice sessions. But when they draw the same pegs in a match, anglers after bream 'fill in' the river with the result that not a roach is to be seen.

I usually fish a worm on a small black hook such as a size 18, knocking off the head and threading it on like a caster. The bait is only about an inch and a half long and sometimes I thread on a little pinkie as well.

Legering with either a swing or quivertip rod makes it possible to notice the slightest knock. Rivers in winter can vary so much in speed that I always carry at least five different quivertips with me of various thicknesses. I still use as long a tail as for summer fishing but I keep a careful eye on the anglers around me when they catch a fish to spot the position of their bomb. If it's different to mine I alter it quickly.

Some anglers may think that a size 18 hook is a bit small to fish with worm. But I'm after bites and if the fish are finicky I may get two or three whereas the angler using the larger hook will 'blow out'. If the fish start to come fast I can always change up to a bigger size.

Four years ago bream fishing in the winter was unheard of. The fish have always fed, but in the past the bait has been wrongly presented. Now modern legering methods have changed this.

It's possible to sit on a huge shoal of bream and not get a bite. Then suddenly they start to feed for no apparent reason. Although the angler is unaware, the water temperature may have risen fractionally or the wind direction altered - only small changes but enough to start the bream feeding.

Many bream matches have been won in the last hour so it pays to patiently sit it out and wait. If like me you have trouble leaving your bait alone, smoke a cigarette slowly before reeling in.

Rain will improve sport in most of our rivers, which at present are suffering from drought conditions. Last week I went to the Wye Championship and thanks to an extra eight inches of rainwater in the river all records were broken.

I had never fished the river before and this cost me a place in the prizes. I was told beforehand that dace would win so I planned my match accordingly.

But too late in the match I found that I had drawn a chub swim, and I hadn't the float or the bait to tackle them. I finished third in my section with 24lb of mainly dace, but I could have doubled this weight with chub if I'd had enough bait to feed the dace out of the swim.

As it was, I was casting further across than anyone around me with a four swan shot loaded zoomer, but it wasn't the right float for the job. If I'd known I'd drawn a chub area my whole plan would have been different. But this is where pre-match practice makes perfect.

THE FRUSTRATIONS OF A COLD-WEATHER FISHERMAN
[December 7th, 1972]

TEMPERATURE is the key to winter fishing. A sudden frost can kill sport as sure as if a bottle of cyanide had been tipped into the river.

In winter you've got to sit and wait for bites whether you're after bream or roach. If you treat the water as you would in the summer, I can guarantee that you will catch nothing.

Fast-flowing rivers such as the Trent which are fed by warm water from power stations are the exception. These rivers will often fish better during the winter.

On slow-running rivers such as the Ouse, Cam and Nene the fish become lethargic and reluctant to feed. It's up to the angler to kid 'em into taking his bait. He certainly won't do it by continually throwing in handfuls of casters. If the fish do decide to have a nibble, there will be so many casters on the riverbed that the chances of them picking up his bait will be virtually nil. Half a pint should see you through a match on the day when the fish are dour. Just sprinkle three or four casters round your float every cast.

If you find it hard going in the week on a river, then under match conditions it will be ten times more difficult to catch.

The upper Nene is a good example of this type of fickle water. In mid-week practice you could take 20lb, but on Sunday the same swim could be dead.

The only answer is to fish a crafty style by setting your float overdepth, casting out and waiting for the fish to come along. On a roach water in winter these tactics may bring you only a few fish, but they could well be fish near the pound mark. And you don't need many of those to win a low-weight competition.

Hooks must be small - an 18, 20 or even smaller. And line should be no stronger than 1.8lb.

I often use an inch-long length or peacock quill which lays flat on the surface. When I get a bite it runs along. I shot up with dust or number six shot, stringing them along the line if the current is gentle. A number six shot anchors the bait to the bottom, and I try to fish right underneath my rod end.

Under these conditions a roach pole can give you that extra control and allow you to fish more sensitively further out than your rivals. Try to work out beforehand what you need to win the competition. There are only certain rivers where you can win on roach and on the Welland, Witham and Nene you will usually need somewhere between 15lb to 20lb of bream.

Roach usually just disappear on match days. About five years ago when the Leicester anglers were concentrating on the Relief Channel we used to take between 30lb and 40lb of roach in midweek practice sessions but we never saw them in a competition.

Nothing can be more frustrating than winter fishing. You can draw a good swim where you know the fish are thick, yet they just don't want to know your bait. But it is important never to give up hope. When I was younger I used to leave my peg and stroll the bank if I couldn't get a bite after a couple of hours. Now I tend to stick it out.

A sudden change in water temperature can put the fish bang on the feed. This often happens on the Trent when a power station perhaps five or six miles upstream begins to pump in warm water. In the last two hours it's possible to take ten pounds of roach after a biteless beginning.

Most rivers have power stations somewhere along their length. And if you can fish in the influence of the warm water, you should catch plenty of fish. One of my favourite pleasure fishing spots is the Great Ouse at St Neots. The river here is warmed right through the winter by the Eaton Socon power station. No need for gentle loosefeeding - there are so many bleak on the move, even under the coldest conditions, that I use a ball of groundbait every cast and five AAA shot to get past them down to the roach.

One of the matchman's problems is that the power stations don't operate on a Sunday to the same extent that they do mid-week. I can remember two pound winning a winter match at Trent Lock when the same peg produced 20lb in the week. And the only reason was the lack of warm water in the river.

It's a similar story on the North Bank of the River Nene, which is warmed by the power station at Peterborough. I caught only two pounds in the Nene Championship this winter yet had 20lb from the same area in midweek when the turbines were pumping.

My home water, the Leicester Canal, can produce double figures when it is steaming in the week, yet you can sit there for hours without a bite on a Sunday.

Chub are one of the few fish that seem unaffected by the cold. But coloured water will quickly put them off the feed. I haven't yet got round to taking a thermometer with me in my basket but an appreciation of the effect of low-water temperatures can prevent many blank days.

CHOOSE THE RIGHT ROD FOR TIP FISHING
[December 28th, 1972]

SWINGTIPPING and quivertipping are both similar forms of legering...but that doesn't mean you should use the same rod for both.

My quivertip rod is nine feet long, a foot shorter than my swingtipper and a shade more powerful. It's a tighter, stiffer rod all through.

When you are quivertipping you don't want a rod that bends right round with the tip. It would be too slow on the strike. The bend must be in the top joint and quivertip, which should form a uniform curve. Remember that with a 12-inch quivertip the total length will be much the same as the swingtip rod's ten foot.

The swingtip rod is a much looser rod with a fair bit of give. It has to pick up a long line and at the same time absorb the lunges of a heavy bream without the hooklength breaking. For this reason it should be designed to balance the weakest link in the chain.

Too many swingtip rods on the market are designed to work with heavy lines and anglers' catches suffer as a result. Many anglers favour a short swingtip rod which gives a quick strike. But by using a ten-foot swingtip rod I can comfortably clear any marginal weed and cast with an extra-long tail. The only disadvantage with the longer rod is the 'bounce' in the middle which can reduce the efficiency of the strike. But you've got to strike a happy medium on rod length and I feel that ten feet achieves this.

When you are swingtipping it's as well to remember to use three rod rests. If you use just two, one at either end, then the rod will bow in the middle. When you strike you will have to pick up that bend before the rod is working to hook the fish. This will slow your strike just that fraction of a second, and you could lose the fish.

A rod rest supporting the middle of the rod will help to keep the whole rod straight. It's the same with swingtips. I use a shorter tip of around eight or nine inches in the summer to hit bites quicker. The shorter tip means there's a little less slack line to pick up before you contact the fish.

In the winter I prefer to use a longer swingtip, perhaps up to 15 inches. On rivers like the Welland and the Witham, which have a winter flow, I let my bait roll along the bottom. The swingtip reacts to the current and moves with an up-and-down rhythm. If the rhythm alters it could be a fish... so strike.

You may need to replace your bomb with swan shot to get it moving slowly in an arc through the swim. If it still anchors to the bottom reduce the shot until it shifts, making sure that it moves through slower than the actual current.

Too many anglers put on the same swing or quivertip winter and summer, lake or river. Yet they wouldn't dream of fishing the Severn with an antenna float they used the week before on a lake! Different tips are needed for different waters to match the flow and the bites expected.

Obviously a fairly stiff quivertip works better on a fast flowing river, while a nice 'loose' tip performs on a Fenland drain. But whether you are swingtipping or using a' quivertip, one thing is essential to both - the target board.

When you are looking for bites that may move the tip only one eighth of an inch, a target board is a necessity. With the swingtip a lined board is probably best, but for quivertipping a plain black board with two clear patches will work just as well. Staring at a quivertip against a background of rippling water can play tricks with the best pair of eyes. But a plain dark background will present few problems of eyestrain.

Some anglers persist in holding their rods in the air at a high angle when they are quivertipping. I do this only when the river is running hard and I want to avoid weed fouling the line. Otherwise I fish with my rod parallel to the bank.

WHY TEMPERATURE IS KEY
[February 8th, 1973]

FISH behaviour is not predictable. If it were, I'd be on a certain winner every time I drew on fish. Other factors come into play which the angler can only guess at.

I remember a day on the Relief Channel when we were practising for the Club's National. We all stuck to the float, except Brian Holland. He went on the bomb and started to perform. And by the end of the day had left us all in the dust, winning the sweepstake with 50lb.

Come the day of the match and we had made up our minds to leger. Brian Envis drew a reasonable area near Stow Bridge, groundbaited well out and dropped his bomb on the baited patch. He waited, and waited, but his swingtip refused to budge.

The time ticked away and Brian realised that if he didn't change his tactics he was in danger of returning a nil weight card for the team. So, in desperation, he retackled with a light float to try to catch a few small fish. He miscast and his light float sailed out to the groundbaited area. No sooner had it settled than Brian thought that he had lost a shot. So he started to reel in when he found, to his amazement, that he had booked a bream!

To cut a long story short be finished the match with 44lb - all bream taken high up in the water. The bomb had taken the bait through the water too fast for the cruising bream. But with float tackle the bait fell slowly through the top half of 18 feet of water.

The Relief Channel, along with the Nene, Trent and Middle Level, is one of the waters where it's possible to catch fish in midwater. This was brought home to me during a practice session at Downham Market.

I sat witbout a bite for two hours yet I could see the odd bream rolling on the top. So I changed to a float which disappeared on its first cast. I knew the bait had been taken 'on the drop' so I knocked five feet off my depth, and from then on it was a fish a throw.

The Leicester Canal was a noted water for midwater feeding. Although the depth was around six feet it had a 'false' bottom at about three feet below which fish would not swim.

I first discovered this when I came out of the Forces about 12 years ago. Technicians from the local power station would take a special thermometer down to the canal, throw it in and get a reading of the water's temperature. Then they would operate a valve in the instrument which allowed it to sink to the bottom where they took a second reading. And always the temperature on the canal's bottom was considerably colder than the surface temperature. This difference in the temperature created this 'false' bottom which kept the fish in the top half of the water. The whole canal length had to be extremely warm before you could catch fish on the bottom.

I believe that this temperature factor is the key to finding those Relief Channel bream. Temperature plays a big part in the species' feeding habits, so imagine the difference in degrees between 18 feet and the surface during a hot summer day. Those Channel bream come swimming up from the cold to find the temperature they like.

This is the reason why the Leicester anglers prefer to fish 'on the drop' in the deeper rivers and lakes. Even when we are legering we never tighten up straight to the bomb. This only forces the bait through the water quicker. We like a long, natural fall and the fish prefer it as well.

Many matchmen sit on top of a bream shoal throughout a whole match and perhaps have only two or three bites. If only they realised the fish were shoaling off the bottom they could put themselves in the prizes.

It's the same on the Trent. You can start off catching fish by trotting, then they disappear. A lot of anglers don't realise those roach may have risen a couple of feet off the bottom.

Too many anglers make this mistake of sticking to one method. Just because it brings them a few fish, it doesn't mean to say it's the best one on the day. Altering your tackle might bring you a bream every ten minutes rather than one every 20 minutes – the difference between catching 20lb and finishing 10th or catching 40lb and winning. You've got to work at it.

No angler worked harder in the last Great Ouse Championship than my mate Roy Marlow. He finished with 30lb yet couldn't get those bream feeding - only four of his fish were hooked in the mouth, the rest were foul hooked - some in midwater. Roy tried everything he knew when he realised just how many bream were in front of him. He was gambling all the while. If he had managed to get them feeding for just one hour he would have passed me.

When you sit on fish and catch one in the first five minutes you have got to make them pay. You're either going to break all records or lose them. This happened to me in the Welland Championships. I knew it couldn't last, and had all my bream in the first 90 minutes. Unfortunately I was one fish short and had to be content with second place.

MIND YOUR STEP WHEN IT COMES TO BREAM
[May 3rd, 1973]

THERE'S nothing more choking for a match angler than to arrive at his swim just in time to see a pleasure angler tip back a huge net of bream. Rather than inspire confidence, he knows that the frightened fish will rejoin the shoal, scare them and stop them feeding. But it does give him an indication of the number and size of bream in some of these Fenland rivers - fish that the matchmen rarely sees.

There's no doubt that the biggest bream feed at night, or in the early hours of the morning. By the time the matchmen start they are full of feed and difficult to tempt.

Matchfishing bream waters in the summer is really specimen hunting in daylight. If he takes fish of 4lb he has done well. But if he fished the same swim at night he could be catching fish up to 7lb. This is particularly true of rivers such as the Relief Channel and the Welland. Brian Envis pulled out of two colossal bream in the Welland when the wind put extra pressure on his line. I know they are in there because I saw the River Authority restock with bream of 7lb plus near Crowland bridge about five years ago. I believe they were netted from a small drain near Thorney.

Night fishing is not allowed on the Relief Channel but is on the Welland, and I fancy any competent angler could knock out 100lb-plus of bream there on the right night.

Another water which would provide big bags at night is Coombe Abbey Lake - a famous bream water and the scene of two Woodbine finals. I've sat there for many a biteless evening, even though I've known fish were in the area. Then as soon as it started to get dark the swingtip never hung still - not with bites but with bream hitting the line. They were on the move ready to settle on some grub, but unfortunately we had to pack up because night fishing is banned at Coombe Abbey Lake.

So why do fish feed better at night? Well, I've got my own theory about this and it all comes down to one word...

vibration. Fish feel vibrations through the water by means of their lateral line and if they sense the 'clump, clump' of angler's boots during the day they don't feed. At night, when the banks are silent, the fish relax and get their heads down for a feed.

It's always noticeable that the River Witham fishes much better during the week than it does on Sunday. I put it down to the fact that up to 150 cars probably motor along the bankside road and park after the draw. The fish quickly feel the bank vibrating and lie doggo. Go in the week when the traffic is quiet and you can catch a netful. We say the fish can count up to seven, and stop feeding on Sunday!

Another spot where the vibrations from traffic affect the fishing is the Bedford Gravels on the North Bank of the River Nene. All the cars pack into that little area at the draw and consequently weights suffer as a result.

The effect of footsteps on fish was brought home to me with a jolt during a sweepstake on the Relief Channel. We drew at Downham Market and walked in a line along the bank, dropping in between the pleasure anglers already fishing. Roy, myself and Bryan Lakey sat in a row and never had a bite. Yet the chap who walked the furthest caught the most fish, while the second weight came from the angler with the other end peg. Eventually I moved my gear to the other side of Downham Bridge and caught. So the fish were definitely feeding, except on the pegs where our combined footsteps had scared them. The anglers on the two end pegs could draw on undisturbed areas.

Then there was another day on the Cut-Off Channel when I spotted a huge shoal of bream rolling near my swim. I got up to see the size of the fish, yet as I walked along the bank I never seemed to get any nearer to the shoal. They had "heard" me walking along and kept their distance. But when I returned to my basket, back came the bream. So what is the answer? Start matches earlier and keep away from the water when walking to the pegs? Fine sentiments, but how many anglers would stick to them?

Personally, it doesn't bother me if anglers walk near my peg on the Welland. It drives the fish across to the far side where I'm going to fish for them anyway. The anglers who prefer to fish at shorter range suffer.

I've known matchmen do daft things like drive their cars down to the water's edge on the low numbers of the North Bank and along to their pegs. Then they complain because they haven't caught any fish.

I never complain to spectators who come to watch me fish. This is the price of success and I accept it. Yet they can unwittingly upset the fish. I remember a match on the Severn when I was catching one or two. A small crowd gathered behind to watch. Then a boat ploughed through the swim and the fish went off the feed. I knew they were still in the area but wouldn't return while the spectators stayed on the bank. Rather than ask them to move away, I got off my basket and went for a walk. The crowd gradually dispersed. Ten minutes later I returned and started to catch again. Back came my gallery, but it didn't matter now.

LEARN TO READ THE WATER
[May 10th, 1973]

READING the water is the matchman's most important job before he gets down to the actual business of fishing. If he does it correctly, then he will be putting his tackle where it gives him the best chance of bites.

Swims rarely alter much over the years - unless the river authority starts dredging - so it pays to remember the features of rivers and what pegs provided the fish. I used to write this information down in my early years, but now I just shake my head about and it usually comes out.

I've fished the River Blackwater at Fermoy only twice but what I remembered was borne out by last week's Angling Times Final. The shallows produced the fish as I predicted, although the swims down from the viaduct to the spinney were not pegged. As the river was so low, the organisers thought competitors would not have sufficient water here. But these swims would have been crawling with fish.

The winner came from the spinney which is not normally pegged as higher water cuts off access along the bank. He probably had the best draw on the day and did his job by winning. And you can't say more than that.

If Leicester had been fishing there would have been no team instruction for any man pegged in the trees. It was an unknown quantity. But any man who drew a swim ten pegs further downstream would have known what to do.

A large bed of rushes a third of the way out pushes the current across to the far bank where it runs across shallows. The fish lie across the far side at this time of year to spawn or clean themselves, and this is where you must use the long cast to fish. This is what Rotherham did. They read the water and won the final as a direct result. It's no good putting your bait where there are no fish, just because you think you are using the right method.

I'm sure this is why Roding Valley failed to do well. They are good roach men, used to scratching in the side with delicate tackle. Somehow they can't seem to adapt to use 'crude' gear – big floats and heavy shotting. And this is what was needed to fish at long range.

Of course you can take the Witham lads anywhere and expect them to do well. For my money they're the finest anglers in the country...barring Leicester of course!

Later in the year the fish move off the shallows back into the deeper water and this applies to many rivers as well as the Blackwater. I just wonder how many anglers pegged in the unproductive deeps at Fermoy bothered to put on a quivertip and fish right across under the trees. This is where the dace lie.

The point I'm making is that Leicester know all about the Blackwater although we've matchfished it only twice. We collect and store the information gathered from matches for future use. As a group we have no secrets from each other.

When we are fishing a match on the Welland or the Nene we know as soon as we draw whether we stand a chance or not. Last season, peg 50 performed several times in Welland opens. So if any of our party drew that swim, they were confident they were on fish. And that man would also know just where to put his bomb. There would be no time wasted trying different areas. He would know what distance the bream would be lying from the bank. This is the sort of information that has helped the Likely Lads to be so consistently successful.

For the newcomer, it's as well to keep some sort of diary of which areas produce fish at different times of the year. This knowledge can save valuable time when matchfishing. Look down the results of open matches published in Angling Times and make a note of the winning peg numbers. You'll be surprised at the patterns that emerge. For example, on the Nene you'll notice that more winners of the Peterborough Hospital Cup come from the South Bank to the Café stretch than from the other way. Whereas the Nene Championship is either won from those 40 pegs on the South Bank, or the big numbers down towards the Sluice. Those permanent pegs one-to-170 just don't get a look in.

As I said, we have no secrets from each other when it comes to swim knowledge. If any of us ever gets the chance to go back to Denmark for the Woodbine Final, there'll be a little map drawn with the best areas marked on it. Don't think that all the swims on the Guden hold huge, unlimited shoals of fish.

Ray Marlow, Jim Todd and myself practised on the Guden before one of the finals. Jim and Ray put me in a swim where I had only about 4lb in an hour-and-a-half. Ray beat me in 20 minutes and Toddy was going even faster. But we had proved the point that some swims were no use. So I moved a few yards and caught a fish a throw.

All this information is stored for future use. Dave Downes does a bit of writing, while I'm fortunate that I can remember these sort of facts. When Ray Marlow first started match fishing he was another Dick Walker, taking notes of the water temperature, wind direction and everything. Now he's got the confidence of knowing that he can read the water.

TOUCH LEGERING ISN'T FOR MATCHMEN
[May 24th, 1973]

MOST specimen hunters seem to advocate feeling the line for bites when legering, rather than rely on visual aids such as swingtips or butt indicators.

In his article two weeks ago, Dick Walker wrote that he doubted if many matchmen realised how much more effective touch legering was, once it had been mastered. Well, I believe in making angling easier for people - not harder. No doubt years of experience have given Dick 'educated fingers', but the chances of an average angler feeling a shy-biting bream by holding the line must be virtually nil.

I don't know if all Dick's fishing is done on private waters, but I would think that even he might be struggling to feel bites on the Witham. Here you can often expect the swingtip to move only a sixteenth of an inch.

The only practical way to compare the two styles for sensitivity - my eye against Dick's touch - would be under laboratory conditions.

The point I'm making is that Dick is at the very top of the tree when it comes to specimen hunting. Along with Fred J Taylor, he has perfected touch legering to a very fine art. No doubt they are years ahead of the field with this technique. But I don't believe they can expect the ordinary angler to pick it up after a few outings. That's why you have got to translate the bites into visual form with the aid of swingtips, quivertips and other forms of bite indicators.

My fingers are so rough and horny that it's doubtful whether I would even feel a bite from a 20lb carp! Dick would probably grab my line and say 'bite' while I was just sitting there.

Freddie Foster is the country's number one swingtip angler, but I bet that if you asked him to feel a bite by holding the line, he couldn't - like 95 per cent of the country's anglers.

Every sport throws up its supermen. With cricket it's names like Bradman - one of the world's finest batsmen - and Larwood - the exceptionally fast bowler. With English soccer it's men like Bobby Charlton and Stanley Matthews. Now, there's only one Matthews and there's only one Dick Walker. And in his theory and his fishing he is so far advanced of the normal angler that they cannot hope to copy his exploits.

Fred J Taylor has explained to me how he feels these bites, and I'm certain that I couldn't master the technique to his high degree. If it were that easy to do, I'm sure that many ordinary specimen hunters would be entering open matches and making a fair bit of money.

One thing I should like to know is how Dick detects 'drop back' bites when touch legering. When I'm swingtipping I don't tighten up to my bomb until it has reached the bottom. A fish will often take the bait during its descent and swim towards you. The fall of the swingtip then quickens and you know it's a bite.

It must also be difficult when touch-legering to tell the difference between a fish swimming into the line and fish taking the bait. When you are swingtipping, it becomes relatively easy to detect this type of bite and leave your bait in the water. The tip usually moves very fast in one pull and then drops back to its original position.

I always remember a match at Marco Lakes in Middlesex, when Phil Coles had his swim bubbling with bream. He had all the Likely Lads standing behind him giving advice on when to strike and when not to strike. His tip was moving anything from one inch to six inches and local anglers nearby were saying that he should have caught a hundredweight. But in actual fact Phil had only eight genuine bites that day and caught six fish - enough to win.

It's not always easy for the untrained eye to detect a bite on a swingtip. There was one match I fished - again at Marco

Lakes - when an angler sat a few feet away from my tip. Every time I struck and caught a fish, this man would look at me in disbelief. He was nearer my tip than I was, yet he never even saw a bite. In the end, he accused me of striking 'on the clock.' So next time I saw the tip move, I said 'bite.' He still claimed not to see any movement. So when I saw the tip move again I repeated the word 'bite', struck and landed a bream. And this was the only way I was able to convince him.

At the time, I had my swingtip just above the surface of the lake and was using the water as a target board. One little wave would hit the tip, then the next one wouldn't. So that was a bite. Other times every wave would hit the tip - a dropback bite. I'm always looking for a change in the rythmn and that is the secret of swingtipping.

MY FLOAT TACTICS FOR THE WELLAND
[July 12th, 1973]

IT'S no good looking good on the river bank if you can't catch fish. There are thousands of matchmen in this country who've got the smooth style when they're in action, but they just don't get the results.

To succeed at match fishing you've often got to be slightly crude in your technique, but still have the finesse to use the style. It's like horse racing. The most brilliant-looking horse on the course can run like a cart horse, but a terrible-looking-animal may be the best in the country.

I'm often accused of being crude, and so is Kevin Ashurst, but we both get results because we understand why we are fishing in a certain way. Kevin's like me. If he's fishing with a float and finds it's too long, he's not frightened to break a piece off to get it right. This may look crude to the spectator but we are doing it for a reason.

I first met Kevin 12 years ago on the lower Great Ouse. I had just won a match at Ten Mile Bank using a sliding float and Kevin came running along the bank to have a look at my float. Then he went home and made some like it. Since then we've been the best of friends...even when he beat me in the Gladding final last month.

This Saturday is another big match that I've got my eye on. That's the Welland Championship. I should have won it last year, but one bream cost me the match. I prefer to floatfish the Welland rather than leger nine times out of ten. And as I've been fairly successful on this river I get plenty of anglers watching me who then try and copy my style.

Now to the spectator, my style must look as crude as hell with anything up to two and a half inches of float clearing the water. They go away, try to copy me and blow out completely, because they don't know why I allow so much float to clear the water. I like to get everyone on my style, because then I've got more chance of winning. I've got 15 years' experience of float fishing for bream behind me, so if anyone is prepared to take me on, then fair enough. It's the bomb anglers who represent the threat.

I'll briefly run down my style for the Welland, but it's one of those things that's almost impossible to put into words. You've got to see it for yourself. Early in the season, the main concentrations of bream are above Crowland Bridge. So this is where you want to draw. But a weedbed runs right down the centre of the river, which helps the Leicester anglers no end.

Try putting a bomb across the far side and all you'll do is foul your bait and terminal tackle with this weed. So the leger anglers are beaten before they start.

To floatfish the Welland with a loaded float there must be no downstream wind otherwise you can't control your tackle correctly. Under ideal conditions with little or no wind, use a zoomer float fished top and bottom. The float is loaded with the equivalent of one and a half swan, while it takes about two and a half swan shot on the line.

By fishing the float top and bottom I have perfect control over that float and the bait. I can hold back, lift the bait or let it run through. Even a slight breeze won't blow the heavy float out of position.

If the fish are feeding on the drop, the float will lift as a fish stops the bait from reaching the bottom. Then you've got to play around with the shot so that the float gives you the best indication. If there is a slight run on the water and the fish stay on the bottom, then I fish a foot overdepth, pinching a small shot near the hook, its size dependent on the flow. This is my tell-tale shot as I inch my float through the swim. When a fish picks up the bait the float lifts and I strike.

It all sounds very simple in print. But making it work is another matter. And picking out the bites is the hardest part. When light conditions make it difficult to see the float, Iswap to a different colour plastic float cap. Or I'll even bite off shot so that more of the float sticks up out of the water.

When the wind gets very bad, and I still want to floatfish, I'll use a peacock fished bottom end only and sink my line. But you must have plenty of shot down to get past the bleak.

Odd pegs above Crowland Bridge will produce on the bomb when an angler casts out and finds a weed-free patch. But this is the exception rather than the rule.

Incidentally, although I regard Roger Firth's 21lb of bleak from the Welland as a fine achievement, don't expect to see the river dominated now by the bleak men. The Welland bleak feed like this only when the river is in flood and running. Under normal conditions, bream will still win every time.

THE ART OF GOOD CASTING
[July 19th, 1973]

THE ABILITY to cast long distances with float and leger tackle is an absolute necessity for the modern matchman. But distance isn't the only answer - you've got to be accurate as well.

The secret of long-distance casting is to do everything with ease, and not to force the cast.

I always follow through with my rod to the eight or nine o'clock position so that it finishes the cast in front of me. But many anglers make the mistake of straining the rod by using a lot of power to cast, and then suddenly stopping the rod at ten or 11 o'clock.

Watch a golfer take a swing. After he whacks the ball he follows the stroke through with the club. If he stopped the stroke a foot after he hit the ball, he would risk breaking the club!

The other important point of casting is to toss your bomb or float high into the air, so that it falls in an arc to that far bank. A bad caster will always aim his tackle down on the water instead of up, and so lose distance. Aim very high when you are casting, letting the line go when the rod is behind you at around two o'clock. This way your bomb or float will go up 20 or 30 feet.

Many anglers let their line go too late at around 12 o'clock cutting their distance. I always watch my bomb or float through the air, just as a golfer tries to keep his eye on the ball. I aim for the far bank but check my tackle so that it falls lightly on the water in the groundbaited area.

Different floats need different methods to cast them. With a stick float and closed-face reel, I cast underhand for maximum distance. It's more of a flick than a cast. Sometimes I need to cast a float fixed at 16 or 17 feet deep without tangling the line on the cast. There's an art in this which involves copying the fly fisherman.

Lay your line on the water between float and hook, and then pick it up to whip behind you. When the line is at its furthest point behind, start to come forward with the cast.

The taller you are, the easier it is to cast with a float fixed deeper than the rod. Roy Marlow is a good six-footer, so with a 13-foot rod he can cast a float fixed at up to 20 feet deep. The smaller you are, the harder its gets.

A zoomer float travels through the air in front of your bait but when you check it, try to avoid making a big splash. Don't put your finger straight on the reel, but rather slow the line down when the float approaches the baited patch. Many anglers blame their float when they fail to reach the distance. But it's usually the person casting who is to blame, or the wrong shotting pattern.

I don't want to cast to the end of the world - the far bank of the Welland is far enough for me. It's no good casting your float miles if you can't spot bites. The angler's eyesight is the limiting factor at distance float fishing. If you set a float to show half an inch, it's easy to put it out of sight.

These days, everyone should be able to get their float and groundbait to the far side of a river like the Welland, which means casting a good 35 yards. Catapults can get your stuff further than you can cast, which means a great evening up of skills. Fifteen years ago, there were only a few matchmen in the country capable of fishing at these distances. Now the majority can do it.

When you're fishing at these distances, you need a rod that's capable of hitting a fish without breaking on the strike. This means a soft rod with plenty of give. If you use a rod that's too 'tight', then you could be in trouble if it picks up the line too fast. Too many anglers buy a rod and use it with any breaking strain of line. Match rods today are designed to work with light lines, and a bottom of 1.7lb breaking strain. And the same applies to swing and quivertip rods. If you use them with a heavy line, all the action goes out of them and they become sloppy. It's like a fly man using a heavy No 10 line on a rod designed to cast a No 6.

When you're after small fish, there's little point in distance fishing. It just makes things more difficult. Bleak can be a nuisance when you're fishing a slowly-falling bait well out if your float is too light. But you can beat these fish close in by dropping your float and bait in the swim, rather than casting at them. This way the bait falls quickly and unattractively through the water, eliminating that slow enticing fall which makes the bleak zoom in.

The trick in doing this is to let your float land in front of your bait, rather than the other way round.

HOW I MADE MY NAME AS A BLEAK-SNATCHER
[January 2nd, 1974]

FEW ANGLERS realise that I made my name as a bleak snatcher, and not with the bream. Bleaking is the one aspect of our sport certain to arouse either gasps of admiration or just sneers. But whatever you may think, the ability to catch bleak is a weapon which every serious matchman should possess.

I became known in this tricky game in Leicester's club matches in my pre-army days on the Great Ouse at St Neots, Offord, and Paxton, and would probably have gone on as a small fish man, but for Eddie Allen, who taught me all the basic bream fishing skills.

I'm not saying I'm the fastest bleak man in the world. That title could go to the Belgian who whipped out 423 bleak against the stopwatch. But I'm quick enough to help the lads to a winning team weight. We all are.

I could usually knock out 200 plus an hour, but that was before I picked up some tricks from the bleak hot-shots both here and on the Continent. And let's face it, the ability to snatch at a fair rate will come in handy if Nationals go on to a points for fish basis.

Time is the bleaker's enemy. But a blind obsession for just speed should never be sacrificed for a simple, smooth technique. Bleak snatching is one game where the older you get, the better you become. This is because the old hands can shut off from things going on around them, and settle quickly into a killing rhythm.

Don't use spade-end hooks unless the bleak are really finicky. Eyed 16's or 18's are much better. With a big eye the maggot won't be blown up the line, forcing you to change bait so often.

Most bleak speed kings use line which is far too thin. Ron Russell taught me that, and he's one of the best snatchers in the business. The heavier line - I use 2lb 8oz to 3lb - gives me something to look at and more importantly, it lets me flick the bleak into the net without being frightened of breaking the line.

Notice how I keep on about technique and not speed – that follows just naturally.

Taking the hook out of each bleak is a waste of time, and that's something you're short of. Use this trick and it's foot-down all the way! As each fish swings in towards you, hold your hand ready with the back towards you and the thumb pointing down. As the line just above the fish hits your hand, turn it over into the normal position with the palm towards you and thumb upwards. Give it a sharp half turn, and with a little practice, hey presto, the bleak is in the net and the maggot back into the water.

The only problem comes when you hook them in the bottom lip. Then you have to take the hook out normally. In the South they just shake the bleak off. Try it my way, it's faster.

Something I am going to try next year is to half-sink an umbrella into the water and flick 'em off into that. Some Continentals do it, to add those odd ones that miss the smaller keepnet to the score!

It's very important to get organised. There's no time to squander looking down to see if your hand's gone into the right tin.

I rarely sit on a basket, and prefer to squat right down on the water's edge. Again it's simple technique, not speed.

A trick which does work is to splash your tackle into the water. That way, the bleak, competing like mad for those titbits, think it's another goodie and dart for it. Bingo, that's another one in the net. To get this splash, cast overhead, never underhand.

A maggot should never stay still. Sometimes troll it through the water. That way bleak hook themselves by darting at it like a pike at a spinner. And never strike upwards. That's a very common time waster. Just jag it sideways. This way you get three or four strikes every cast. And that really saves time.

Again it's just technique, and does make up for those lost seconds when you snag your jumper or keepnet.

Correct feeding for bleak is not simply a matter of chucking stuff in. They may be small and numerous, but they're not daft. Feed lightly in a smallish circle, and fish in the centre.

And keep ringing the changes with both hookbait and free offerings. Even bleak can get used to one bait. Casters, pinkies, squatts and big maggots in all colours of the rainbow. Take them all with you, you will need them.

The right feed will bring 'em right to your feet. That's just where you want bleak if you are going to crack double figures. The closer you can bring bleak to the surface, the faster you can whip them out.

That's where a floating maggot comes into its own. There's no magic is getting maggots to float either. Just put them in a thin layer of water. The greedy beggars sup it up and get lighter and float. This is something that bream men could do well to latch on to.

Before the whistle, never add a lot of feed into the groundbait bowl. Maggots squirm their way down to the bottom and take up the moisture. So by the time you get down to them, they are floaters, which, if thrown in, will drift down into the next peg, taking all the bleak with them.

If the next peg man has the sense to twig on to this at a time when the other fish are slow in coming, you have given him the perfect opportunity to slaughter you with your own bleak! To prevent this happening, add your feed into the groundbait as you need it, and not before.

Now to floats. I can buy mine in three colours for one and a half pence for about 50. I'm not joking. For surface feeding bleak, a matchstick, attached with valve rubber, takes some beating. After all a float's only there to add a little bit of casting weight.

As I have already said, I don't bleak for first places any more, just for a backing weights for the lads. Murky water can make spotting bites a bit difficult, but not if you use this dodge. Run part of the hooklength between your nails so it curls into a tight spring for an inch or so. Cast out normally and watch that spring like a hawk. When it straightens, it's a bleak. It does straighten with continuous tension after 30 mins or so, so then just repeat the operation and you're back in business.

All these things are simple basics which everyone can pick up. But how many believe what I say when I keep it simple. It would be a different story if a tried to explain the impossible. Then I would be believed straight away. It's funny, but some anglers can't see further than the end of their noses!

FLOAT-LEGERING IS THE METHOD OF THE MOMENT
[December 25th, 1974]

I'VE got news for the match angling enthusiasts. There's a 'new' style of fishing winning money this year - and to judge from the amount of rain we have had this winter it's likely to win a lot more before March 14.

Of course there's nothing new about the style. It's float-legering, a style practised for countless years but never popular with match anglers. Mind you, the present style is very, very different indeed to the popular conception of float-legering.

It's only the principle that's the same. I won £100 last year with it, mostly on the Trent, and although it has only won me around £20 so far this season that total is due to rise... given the chance.

Float-legering on the Trent? I can see some heads shaking at that one. But it's right. When the Trent is a foot or more above normal level I think it's the method most likely to give the best return.

The first essential is a long rod. The popular 13-footer in general use today just isn't long enough - particularly since 2ft of it is used to take the reel and balance the rod.

This is one job the roach pole can do very well. It has the length to provide complete control over the float - and that is vital. I rate an 18ft pole the best length. This is long enough to allow the float to be held still out on the natural bed of the river and away from the inshore weed beds - or their remnants.

This is tight line fishing, of course, and I use an 18-inch length of elastic at the tip of the pole in much the same way as the French - but my elastic serves a different purpose.

The French never fish the bottom. I do of course. That's the basis of this style. My line is held tight to the top of the float – so that I can keep it in position despite the flow of the river. Now, when a fish takes the bait the elastic yields as the fish pulls - which is far better than the fish pulling direct to the rod top and, feeling resistance, quickly blowing out of the bait. The elastic behaves like a quivertip - only more so. It yields to the pull from a fish.

It has other advantages, of course. The elastic can stretch from 18 inches to 6ft under pressure from a running fish and it provides that necessary margin by which biggish fish can be played on a tight line.

Remembering that this method is used in flowing water at times when the river is extra high, the float needs to be a thin one. A balsa and cane stick float is ideal.

It is fished with from one to three swan shot on the paternoster dropper - which should be from five to nine inches long. The hook should have a tail anything from 18 inches to 2ft 6in long. Its exact length is determined by the strength of the flow.

The bait should rub the bottom - but if the flow is strong then the tail can rise up away from the riverbed. To offset this I always use either a micro-dust or No 8 shot on the tail when fishing the Trent - where the flow is greater than on the Nene. That small shot helps hold the bait down in the place where the fish are more likely to find it.

Ideally, the float will be positioned six inches inside the tip of the rod so that you have maximum control. The float can then be moved around in the flow - in any direction.

Plumbing the depth is absolutely crucial. The setting

between the swan shot on the paternoster dropper and the tip of the float must be accurate to half an inch.

What, by now, you will be asking, are the advantages of the method? Firstly your tackle from rod top to hookbait is descending through the water almost vertically. This makes the line a very small target from weed and rubbish being carried away downstream with the flow. You can fish for longer periods before it becomes necessary to lift out and clear the line.

In such situations quivertipping - where the line passes through a greater area of water - picks up too much rubbish to be anything better than marginally effective.

Fishing the float-leger, the tackle can remain in the water for long periods...and I am sure that the longer the hookbait can stay in one place, yet remain an effective bait, the better the chances are of catching fish.

The style calls for a very positive method of swimfeeding. Loose feeding is out. Since the hookbait is fished stationary, the feed must be concentrated into the place where it does the maximum amount of good. So I feed with small but hard nuts of groundbait - not as big as a walnut - laced with casters or whatever is on the hook at a rate of one ball every 10 minutes.

The feeding rate is quite slow. In a five-hour match I would be stretched to use a pint of casters or maggots in the groundbait, but remember waste is non-existent. Every grain of cereal and each caster drops to a point within very few inches of the hook.

There's really no limit to the species of fish which can be caught by this method. I can't see any reason why I shouldn't pick up as many as six good bream off the shelf along the River Nene's North Bank, along with the occasional chub, plenty of roach and whatever else happens to be around.

FEEDING ACCURATELY IS KID'S STUFF
[May 21st, 1975]

THERE are two problems to be overcome when throwing groundbait - getting the right distance and being accurate at the same time. I suppose I'm lucky, I could always throw groundbait exactly where I wanted it. I don't mean I've never ever been off-target.

But, for instance, I can pitch successive balls across the Welland and get them to drop where I want them.

There are others like me who have that happy knack. Phil Coles is one. I could name others. It wasn't that easy for Dave Downes. Dave could throw all right. No problems with distance, but when he first started match fishing in earnest his accuracy left rather a lot to be desired. Now accuracy can be acquired and Dave set out to teach himself, with the help of a little Leicester tuition. He worked hard at it for the biggest part of a close season and he did it with tennis balls. Dave had a long garden. He got himself a target to aim at - a bucket. He gradually lengthened the distance as accuracy developed and he literally threw thousands of times until those balls were dropping into the bucket with remarkable regularity.

He had to be accurate for unless the balls dropped into the bucket he had to scurry across the muddy, freshly dug garden every time to retrieve them.

You don't need to use groundbait. Take my word for it, tennis balls are just as good - and cheaper too. It may seem rather like a kiddies game to throw tennis balls to and fro for hours on end, but two people can learn to swim-feed accurately by doing just that.

Remember though that it must be learned under all conditions. It is important to develop the ability to remain accurate in spite of wind and rain.

And there are other difficulties you must learn to cope with. It is relatively easy for two men standing in the comfort of their local park to throw a ball to and fro accurately.

Now try it sitting down with your feet just 18 inches apart - as they would be if you were sitting at the water's edge.

I prefer to throw off my left foot - with my right foot two feet back, it's more comfortable that way - but river banks make their own demands on the comfort you are permitted.

Learn to throw from uncomfortable positions - once you can throw from a position that suits you best of course.

Dave Downes now throws like a robot. He seems to wind himself up like a spring, whether he is casting or throwing.

It is quite easy really, once you know what to look for, to see that Dave actually taught himself to throw. The natural throwers are less machine-like but Dave's results are now as good as anyone's.

Other people are not so fortunate. Tom Bedder is a good example. Tom is a big bloke. Give him a glance and you immediately think that Tom must be a natural – but he's not. He still can't throw groundbait either a distance or accurately. He misses out on both counts. Jim Todd is another big fellow but he really is good. He's the best thrower of groundbait I know. He's immaculate.

Tom Bedder was saved by the catapult. So there's your answer. If you are a natural, you've nothing to worry about. If you can throw a distance but are inaccurate then practise until you get it right. But if you have neither distance nor accuracy then you are in trouble.

Forget all about throwing by hand and concentrate your efforts into learning to use a catapult. That's of course what Tom did. The catapult is also a useful tool for people who lose the ability to throw. That happens with age, through illness or as the result of a loss of physical fitness. So the catapult is a godsend.

I throw by hand usually although I am useful enough with a catapult. But there are times when I prefer to use the catapult. You see, groundbait projected via a catapult need not be so firm as that thrown by hand. It is retained within the cup. There's no finger or palm pressure on it. At the moment of propulsion it flies cleanly out of the cup and is less likely to break in the air.

For extreme range, too, the catapult is very useful. There have been occasions when I have needed to feed 50 yards out from the bank. The Wraysbury lake contests were one example and it could also be necessary under certain conditions in waters like Coombe Abbey lake.

Give the catapult a good test. You should be able to master it both for feeding loose casters, pinkies and maggots, as well as for really long-range work with cereal groundbait.

HAS THE WORLD GONE WAGGLER CRAZY?
[July 28th, 1976]

AT TIMES, it seems to me that the match anglers have gone waggler crazy. The waggler is a good float, and it takes some whacking when there are problems from a downstream wind. But that's no reason to use it day-in and day-out without giving thought to the conditions the float is designed to combat.

Look at it this way: I reckon that in one in three of the bigger Welland open matches I fish there is a good chance of getting into the money with roach. That's too big a proportion to ignore, so, on the days when there's a chance with roach, tackle up to get the best out of your peg.

And bear in mind that conditions can change during a contest or day's fishing. What is right at the start can create difficulties later on.

Here's an example. Roy Marlow finished fourth at Adelaide on the Ouse earlier in the season with 14lb 4oz. He wasted the first two hours going for bream, although he hadn't much option since odd ones were caught left and right.

Anyway, with the wind coming upstream and into his face he settled for a waggler, fishing just over the lily fringe on the near side. In three hours Roy got 45 roach at 15 an hour.

Had the wind been better - so that Roy could have made his bait presentation perfect - he reckons he could have caught twice as fast. When the contest ended Roy weighed in and then carried on fishing after collecting his winnings. He immediately discovered the wind had changed, to upstream and behind. Off came the waggler. On went a Marksman, one of our all-balsa floats with a fined down tip. His rate of catching increased enormously to 30 an hour...and these were bigger fish, fewer of which were missed on the strike.

Whereas the roach had previously been in the 2oz to 10oz bracket, a number of 12oz to 14oz roach showed. Roy hadn't changed his shotting. It was simply a difference between using the right and wrong float to changed circumstances that increased his scoring rate.

So why does an all-balsa float make so much difference? The bait presentation, instead of near-perfect, became perfect - and that's why the bigger roach become active.

The Marksman was fished double rubber (top and bottom) and the fined-down tip allowed it to be sunk to a dimple. The fish had no resistance by way of buoyance to combat and the bites became unmissable. The float went down and kept going. As we say: 'You could see the line going down the hole.'

Why should that happen, you may ask? Simple really. A waggler doesn't run away smoothly. It can't since it is fastened bottom-end only, whereas the Marksman provides much less drag as the fish runs. So the all-balsa (with that fine tip) gives you time. And although it is highly efficient on the right day, it is just about the cheapest float on the market. I have a range of five, taking from two to four SS through the range.

Obviously the feed rate has to be right to take maximum advantage but at Adelaide, for example, Roy all but tripled his weight rate to 13lb to 14lb an hour from just under 5lb.

The bigger roach don't suddenly move into the swim. More often than not they are there all the time but that small difference leading to prefect bait presentation gets them feeding. They've probably already had half-hearted goes at your bait. The float appears to dither, to be on the brink of submerging, but nothing happens. That's because the bigger roach simply sucks it in and blows it out again almost as quickly. Give the bigger roach credit for a bit of sense. They're clever. They've learned. Most of them have probably already been caught a couple of times.

Look closely at a caster after fish have played around with the bait and you'll find sometimes it's dented. Roach are not the only fish to do that. Skimmers do it too, but if you are not caching skimmers then it's 99 per cent certain it's roach that are buckling the caster shell.

As I say, the bigger roach are never easy to catch in quantity but if your caster comes back dented you can be sure there are some around.

THINK LIKE A FISH
[August 18th, 1976]

I HAVE often said that if you want to be a successful angler - pleasure man or matchman - you must think like a fish. Put yourself, mentally that is, in the position of the fish.

Fish have four basic requirements: adequate food, a suitable spawning ground, and a home which is both comfortable and safe. As far as the smaller fish are concerned, safety may be the number one factor but I reckon that with middleweight fish all four factors are more or less equal.

If fish are creatures of habit - and I go along with that point of view - this has to be habit based on reason, and the reasons can be found in those four important points already listed.

So a fish's habits are based on satisfying its four main requirements - and if you understand that you have something to begin thinking out when you stand on the bank of any strange water.

You have also to think about the way the primary species feed and what they need to fill their bellies every day when they are feeding. Make no mistake about it, a single 3lb bream eats an enormous amount of food in a day. And if a bream shoal contains 500 fish it seems likely that they will eat almost a hundredweight of natural food in a single day.

Tench and bream have a similar food intake but by and large the primary species are interested in different aspects of the food chain. Although there is inevitably some overlap, roach and bream, for instance, don't eat the same food. Roach feed mainly on food found in the water itself. Bream prefer to find their intake within the bed of the river itself. Small bream may compete with roach for daphnia but once the bream weigh a pound or more the bulk of their food comes out of the bottom. Hence the stained appearance of their lower lips and the lower section of their mouths.

Daphnia are, of course, a clue to the presence of roach - although this summer, with the water so warm, the daphnia have multiplied at an astounding rate and there's more than ever before. One of the secrets of locating rainbow trout on Grafham is to first find the daphnia - tiny pin-head sized water insects that move quite fast for their size.

In every fishery there are inevitably some swims that can always be classed as good ones. That's not to say they will always produce the best results. And there are, equally, other swims which are never worth very much at all - although these may sometimes give a better performance. But the bad swims will seldom give better results than the good ones.

In between the two there are others which are never consistently good or bad but which give extreme performances in both directions as circumstances dictate.

So if we can work out why a good swim is likely to fail or why an average peg is likely to fish above its normal self, we are well equipped to make the best of it.

What makes a good swim? There are so many ingredients it is impossible to spell them all out or even to list all the permutations necessary to ensure a peg fishes well.

Could be that a spring in the riverbed will provide water which is superior to that already within the river - it can be warmer, or colder, cleaner or contain a higher dissolved oxygen content. It therefore either attracts or repels fish, according to the time of the year.

Food availability is a key factor and for the answers in that direction we have to look at the nature of the riverbed in relation to the needs of each species and at the existence or otherwise of weedbeds.

Bream anglers will readily acknowledge that the presence of weed in their swims is a near cast-iron guarantee that they are in with a chance if the weed exists in only smallish patches and other swims are therefore barren.

So why then, we must ask, have the bream moved out of Welland permanent pegs 830 to 840? That area has a super weed growth…but the bream have moved out. They were there when the season started but the water cleared and the bream left. Perhaps the water became clear because the bream left.

Or is it that the cooler nights have adversely affected the water temperature in the now shallow river. With 3ft of normal level missing it figures that the few deeper areas will maintain their temperature better than the shallow ones.

And when sussing out the prospects at individual swims it is also necessary to consider the amount of hammer the pegs have had. The 500s in the Welland, for example, have taken an enormous amount of fishing. Everyone who fishes that river has known that's where the feeding bream have been. So pleasure anglers have fished most of the crack swims every day of the week.

So now the bream begin to show in the 400s. It could be that some of the fish in the 500s moved downstream to produce better sport in the 400s. Or are fish that were sluggish at the start of the season now beginning to show up whereas the fish that fed hard and long earlier are now playing hard to get?

If we think deeply about what fish do and why they do it, some aspects of the puzzle are unravelled. If we ever reach the stage where we know exactly what will happen, the fun will have gone out. Fortunately, we're a long way from that stage yet.

BALANCED TACKLE IS ALWAYS THE ANSWER
[May 1st, 1977]

PEOPLE who read Dick Walker's recent article in Angling Times would imagine there is a world of difference in the way Dick and I fish, simply because Dick went to some lengths to criticise the use of fine lines and small hooks.

The use of 1lb 8oz line and size 20 to 22 hooks was criticised, and Dick mentioned that many anglers would be smashed up on this tackle. But, of course, Dick didn't say that with his strong lines and bigger hooks he would be using a stiffer, stronger and heavier rod.

Dick expressed a preference for lines of not less than 2lb 8oz and for hooks never smaller than size 16...and admitted that he seldom uses hooks and lines that fine.

He is quite right when he says that no one can lay down correct line strengths and hooks sizes for any size or species of fish. But we can and we should stipulate the right breaking strain of line to be used with any given rod...and that is the point Dick left out.

A rod knows only that it balances to a specific breaking strain of line. Anything stronger is completely superfluous since the rod can never utilise additional line strength. It doesn't matter whether the angler has hooked a chub or a crocodile, the rod can't tell the difference.

Most anglers fail to appreciate which breaking strain of line balances to a particular rod. Every time I attend an Angling Times forum the topic comes up - which at least suggests interest is growing and that we are beginning to make some progress.

I prove just how little anglers know about this with my simple spring balance test. I ask to them to guess how much pressure I am applying to the tip of my 13ft match rod when its tip appears to be under maximum tension. Answers are inevitably varied but some have ranged as high as 20lb, would you believe? In point of fact I am usually 'pulling' around 12oz and that's enough to impose a formidable bend in my top section.

So how can I justify using 2lb 8oz line when the rod top is already well bent to 12oz of pressure? One pound yes, 2lb 8oz never – not unless I use another rod, of course. Facts are that when I am actually fishing, and that's a lot different to bending rods around in demonstration, my match rod is rarely subjected to more than 5oz of tension, regardless of the size and species of the fish I am catching.

So long as I can avoid the dangers of shock impact, there's not the slightest danger of my line snapping. How can 5oz of tension break a 1lb breaking strain hooklength? If you are still in doubt, do the spring balance test on a 13ft match rod, first with 5oz of tension, then with 10oz, and you will be surprised at the difference in the amount of bend.

Dick said that if you are getting broken, presumably on balanced tackle, you should change to a heavier line. It is, of course, also fundamental to use that stronger rod. If you have been fishing with a 1lb 8oz breaking strain hooklength and the rod balances to it, don't imagine for one moment that a change to 2lb 8oz line will give you an additional 1lb in strength effectiveness, because it won't.

Shock impact is the danger with any line, regardless of its breaking strain. Do a simple test with a length of 10lb monofilament and this becomes much clearer. First stretch a length of 10lb line between your two hands, gradually increasing the load placed on the line. You will find it is extremely difficult to break.

Then, instead of increasing pressure gradually, snatch at it, building up the pressure very quickly and the line snaps easily. That's shock impact. Don't forget that on low breaking strains of nylon the line's ability to stretch is your greatest ally. It helps beat shock impact by minimising the effect of intense pressure - something the tackle trade seems to have overlooked with its new pre-shrunk line. The safety factor has been removed.

Perhaps the best example I can give you of shock impact happens in trout fishing, often with relatively small fish weighing as little as 2lb. A 2lb trout can smash a 6lb point with ease. This is because the length of 6lb line in the point is relatively short. There's only about 9ft of it - and the pukka fly line to which the nylon point is tied doesn't stretch at all.

There is, therefore, no stretch factor worth mentioning to counter the shock impact imposed by a hard-running fish and the result is a break-off. That's another good reason why coarse fishermen's hooklengths should be as long as is practically possible.

Dick made the point that the Americans are promoting the use of finer and finer lines to increase their sales of terminal tackle on the basis that fine line snaps and an increased amount of terminal tackle is therefore lost. I think Dick is doing the Americans an injustice. I believe, like the Americans, that fine lines allied to the correct rods give better sport and bigger catches. On our hard-fished rivers the fish aren't stupid!

There's a great deal more fun and satisfaction in playing a fish on fine tackle and beating it intelligently, rather than in skull-dragging it ashore with heavier gear.

Clearly there is a risk to beginners, as Dick said, but I believe it is better to learn the refinements of hooking, playing and landing a fish early on in one's angling experience.

Except in special circumstances, there is little demand for this heavier tackle Dick has traditionally used. Okay, it is needed on barbel and in heavy-water for chub and for tench and carp from weeded locations. But many more anglers fish for roach and bream in open water where strong tackle is not only unnecessary, but also a positive deterrent to feeding fish.

THE MEN WHO CAN CATCH 1,600 FISH IN THREE HOURS
[May 11th, 1977]

THE SHEER speed of Continentals when pole fishing is staggering. It's obviously a match-winning quality but if we are realistic about it there's little chance of us ever rivalling the fastest rods in Europe. The Belgians and the French don't regard themselves as the fastest. They admit that at the speed game there's only one team – Italy.

Star Italian match anglers are quite capable of 1,600 fish in three hours...that's roughly nine a minute. Which is as near to perpetual motion as we shall ever get in angling.

But speed isn't necessarily something the spectator can gauge simply by watching men fishing. Rhythm is as important as speed. A smooth, rhythmic style beats a jerky action every time. And it is vital that the man aiming for speed should get his targets right. In the last World Championship, in the match where I finished second, I caught one bleak that must have weighed 1oz 12drm. It was a real whopper as bleak go.

I told the Italian team manager that I might have taken the individual honours from his man had I been able to stay catching bleak of around that weight.

"No Ivan," said the Italian, "it isn't possible!" He explained that my 1oz-plus bleak was a fat and none too healthy fish, and he was right. It looked spawn-bound. In fact he said it had a worm infection. And he explained that fish in that condition are not fit fish. They don't move to the bait fast enough - even if there are enough of them - to allow true speed fishing. Which helps explain just how deeply the Italians have delved into this type of fishing.

I know I can catch 300 fish an hour. I never want to prove it because the moment I do then someone else will catch 301 and so it will go on - moving further and further away from the real objective. Speed is important but it isn't the beginning and end of pole fishing European style.

People have said I'm not fast. Fair enough, they're entitled to their opinion. But I've tried to get a flowing style of speed fishing. A jerky angler may look faster but I doubt if he is.

When bleak fishing, for example, I always strike sideways, not upwards. You may not think this means much but think about it. If you strike upwards your bait leaves the water and has to re-enter and settle again. If you strike sideways your hook stays in the water if you missed out on the strike and the next bite comes that much sooner.

Maybe that gives me a gain of two seconds every three casts. If that doesn't sound much, work it out through a five hour contest and see the difference. It could amount to ten minutes fishing time - that's anything from 30 to 50 bleak; at least a pound of fish.

If it's your aim to catch fish fast there are a number of points you must bear in mind. The first is that you need a number of different feed baits; different colours and different baits. The object is to give the fish something different from time to time. A change can prolong their interest. And when using a variety of baits, each possessing different attractions via colour and fall rates, it is possible to lead fish around the swim, keeping them at a required depth.

Fish behave like an army...when you've got them properly drilled. You can get them exactly where you want them in the water – at whatever level suits your fishing tactics...and move them up and down in tune with their actual mood. If they become shy then regroup them lower down in the water by using a faster sinking feed.

My line is never less than 2lb breaking strain for bleak fishing. There'd really be no point at all in using 12oz stuff... and even my hooks are different. I use eyed hooks - so that the bleak can't blow the maggot up the line. That means the same bait can be used a time or two without any need for adjustment. And because they're little fish don't assume the hook is also small. Bleak have large mouths and they feed so fast that an 18 or even a size 16 hook is perfectly acceptable.

Let's never get carried away by this speed fishing concept. As I've said many times, speed times the weight of each fish gives you your match weight. If you know the weight of the average bleak in a particular river and you know what weight you are aiming at to either win or get a high placing then you know roughly how many fish you need... and how fast you need to catch them!

You must set yourself a target weight...and if there's no

chance of getting that weight one way then you must try another and change styles during the contest if others fail to give you the needed scoring rate.

The size of the bleak varies with different rivers. The Welland's are good and big - but they take some catching. The Coronation Channel, the Thames and Severn, they've all got big bleak in them, whereas those in the Great Ouse and the Nene are small by comparison.

Part of the logic of speed fishing comes with realising exactly what you can do...and the days on which you can do it. So speed practice doesn't just tell you how fast you can catch fish - it also tells you that on some days you can catch faster than on others. It is as important to know which conditions are favourable and which are not as it is to be able to catch them!

It's a question of doing the right thing at the right time. Use one style all the time and you're dead in match fishing terms.

Chapter Five

Ivan Marks on...

BAIT

"
I'm sure many anglers believe my tackle basket is a conjuror's box of tricks. Open the lid, sprinkle 'magic' potion in the groundbait, and abracadabra...bream appear.
Of course, this is just a load of eyewash. The Likely Lads use no secret baits or additives. Yet try telling anglers that!
"

CASTER POWER!
[April 13th, 1972]

CASTERS, how I love 'em. I've caught every freshwater fish - barring a few rarities - on those brown pearls. Many anglers don't realise that they are a marvellous bait for trout. I've had as many as 10 at a sitting from the upper Wensum, mixed in with 80lb or 90lb of roach!

Mind you, that catch was nothing compared to the haul I shared with Roy Marlow on a remote Welsh reservoir. There the trout were queuing up to gobble those genuine Leicester casters.

It was last April. Roy and I had been trying unsuccessfully to catch mullet and trout from the River Towy. Then we heard about this huge lake in the north where bait fishing was allowed. The following day we found the water. The towering mountains overshadowed the power station on its desolate banks. I was in half a mind not to bother, but then we found some anglers with nets in the water.

Roy bought the permits while I mixed up the groundbait. The water was huge but I meant to tackle it Marks-fashion. We introduced casters into the groundbait and fished well out with big peacock sliders. We just couldn't go wrong. It was a perch or trout at every chuck. I reckon I must have caught at least 40 trout alone that day. Local anglers said they had never seen anything like it. They were waiting to drop into our swims when we packed up. That's caster power for you!

I believe that all fish will take casters. I've had carp, tench and even eels on them. Now I'm just waiting to hook a salmon. Last summer some of you may remember I went specimen-hunting for Angling Times. But no floppy hat and carp rod for me - just some good zoomers and several pints of casters. The water was Hatchet Pond, a shallow lake in Hampshire reputed to hold some huge bream. I motored down with Howard Humphrey during the night, and at first light inspected the swims.

Two of the big-fish lads had already sat themselves by the deepest water, so I walked round the lake plumbing the depth. I settled for some open water about five feet deep beyond a jungle of thick weed. In went three or four pints of casters and after an hour's wait my 11-inch peacock and balsa float 40 yards away rose out of the water. I struck and found I was playing no Welland bream. It weighed 5lb 8oz and was the smallest of the six fish I was to catch on consecutive casts. The heaviest two weighed 7Ib apiece, and the total catch went 40lb…just six fish.

Those bream couldn't resist casters. I may have been in line for the bream catch of a lifetime if two huge bream hadn't pulled off in the clogging weed. As it was, I had time to put down my rod for a smoke or a chat while waiting for each bream to cautiously back out of the holes they smashed in those underwater "hedges".

I'm not insistent about the size or colour of a caster. But I do make sure they are as fresh as they can possibly be. There is no better way to ruin a swim than by throwing in bad casters. The fish don't stay around. You can draw a parallel with humans. If you walked into a swishy restaurant, ordered a rump steak and then found it tasted bad, you would leave pretty sharply. Well it's the same with fish. I'm sure that many anglers unwittingly buy bad casters and then stop using them when they find they can't catch fish. They blame casters for their poor catches and go back to maggots.

I do use casters two to three days old, especially when I go fishing midweek. Wednesdays are always set aside for practice, but they turn out to be more like parties. Sometimes as many as 20 anglers turn-up to come out with us. But I look after my casters by keeping them in the fridge. Once they are kept in water they sour very quickly. Put them in water only just before you are going to use them. Then you can discard the floaters.

I'll feed with casters of any colour, but I do prefer a really dark-coloured caster for the hook. These are extremely light in weight and nicely counteract the weight of the hook. This all helps to present the bait more naturally to the cautious fish. Casters will consistently pick out the better fish, especially when you are roach fishing. The smaller fish are curious of a caster and just knock it, leaving time for the bigger fish to swoop in and grab. If you are feeding in casters and swap to a maggot on the hook, you will usually start to take smaller fish.

Remember, too, that casters can't crawl away like maggots. So you won't need to feed so many in a river or lake. A pint and a half should do for a pleasure session. But throw in no more than a dozen every two or three casts. I've seen anglers get rid of a quarter of a pint every 15 minutes or so. Have you ever counted how many casters make up a quarter of a pint? I have. It's about 700, so the odds against a fish taking your hooked one are very great.

If you are using groundbait as well, some 50 per cent of your casters will be crushed and float to the surface. So you'll need to double the amount you introduce. In the last Severn National, for example, I got rid of seven pints.

YOU MUST BE ON THE BALL
[May 11th, 1972]

MANY anglers must wonder how a small chap like me can put a big ball of groundbait across the River Welland. Well, I'll let you into a secret. As a cricketer I was frequently banished to the boundary so I soon developed a long and accurate throw.

In those days, I was keener on cricket and soccer than matchfishing. I usually opened the batting for one of the Leicester's top amateur teams, where I gained a reputation as a bit of a joker. I can recall one occasion while I was fielding in the slips when the umpire threatened to send me off for carrying on a conversation with the wicketkeeper!

Soccer also claimed a lot of my time. I was given trials by Aston Villa, Notts Forest and Shrewsbury. But two broken ankles ended what might have been a promising career as a football player.

I tell you all this to point out that I went training two or three nights a week. This helped to keep me in top physical condition. Since I stopped ball sports, I suppose I must have put on two stone in weight. But the muscles I developed are still there. They've helped me to out-throw many other anglers and get the bream feeding at long distance.

All of the Leicester anglers have developed their throwing skills to an extent where they can hit the far bank of a river like the lower Welland with a ball of groundbait. And I'm not talking about using rockhard stuff. Yet I'm prepared to bet that no more than half the anglers fishing this year's second division National on that river will be able to throw across. And remember that if the river is slow and sluggish, the ball will want to break on impact.

Dave Downes used to practise his throwing with tennis balls. His garden was a convenient 40 yards long, so by consistently reaching the end helped him to develop accuracy. I remember reading that Geoff Kirk, the Witham float star, trained with a cricket club to develop his throw. And the Likely Lads usually end a day's pleasure fishing with a throwing match. The one who loses buys the beer.

Two men who can really hurl a ball of groundbait are Big Jim Todd and Kevin Ashurst. Toddy was an athletics star in his younger days and I suppose Kevin gives his right arm plenty of exercise lifting those pint glasses!

The ability to out-throw the opposition might pay-off in a match only once every two or three years. But Kevin used his big throw to win £2,000 at Coombe Abbey lake in the NFA Knock-out. By putting his groundbait an extra 15 yards Kevin made his peg the best on the lake. Other anglers who fished there would probably have failed to win.

Of course next season will see a great evening-up of groundbaiting ability. The change in NFA rules allows the use of catapults and throwing sticks. At the moment I'm practising very, very hard with the catapult. I don't need to use one, but I've got to think of the future. None of us are getting younger. In ten years' time, perhaps, I will be unable to throw as far as I can now. Then I will have to rely on the catapult to help me keep on winning matches.

Physical fitness is important for a matchman. You can't fish efficiently if you feel tired or strained. But I don't believe that matchfishing is purely a young man's sport. Look at Freddy Foster, Billy Lane and Benny Ashurst. They are all in their fifties, but I rate them as good as ever. Unfortunately Billy had to give up the open-match circuit two years ago because of a heart attack. The day before he had walked two difficult miles along the banks of the River Cam carrying all his tackle.

As long as a man's eyesight is good, he can stay at the top. If that goes, he's off the scene. When I worked in an engineering shop, a piece of metal flew into my eye the day before a match on the Middle Level. The hospital removed it, but my eye kept running during the contest. I could watch my float land, but couldn't see it well enough to notice any bites. I just relied on counting and striking blind to finish up with a pathetic 4lb of fish.

Every close season I worry whether my eyesight will let me down the following season. So far it hasn' t. But if you see me staring at a hoarding with one eye closed, you'll know what I'm up to.

KNOWLEDGE – THAT'S THE SECRET INGREDIENT
[May 25th, 1972]

I'M SURE many anglers believe my tackle basket is a conjuror's box of tricks. Open the lid, sprinkle 'magic' potion in the groundbait, and abracadabra...bream appear. Of course, this is a load of eyewash. The Likely Lads use no secret baits or additives. Yet try telling anglers that!

Strangers have often sidled up to me on the river bank,

nudged me in the ribs and whispered a request for "some of that secret stuff I use". I've one answer to this type of inquiry. I ask the angler what river he's going to fish and then tell him that it will take a few days to get the ingredients he wants. When he asks why, I tell him that I mix my groundbait only with water from the river I'm fishing. That usually stuns 'em into silence.

I used to put sugar in my groundbait in common with many other matchmen. But I stopped the practice after reading that sugar takes oxygen out of the water. Since then I've tried adding all sorts of silly things to my groundbait. I've had success with them, too, but it doesn't prove anything. The swim might have been just as productive if I'd used my groundbait straight.

Knowledge of a water is of far more importance. Anglers often ask me what colour groundbait I prefer. Well, I've tried every colour of the rainbow. I've used red groundbait and even vivid orange. They've all caught fish, so what do the different colours prove? I've won a big match using yellow groundbait. You could put it down to that. But then how many other anglers were also using yellow groundbait?

Stick to white or brown pure breadcrumbs and you won't go far wrong. And mix it up in a shallow washing bowl rather than a bucket. You can work your fingers right round the edges of a bowl and mix it properly. In a bucket you're always left with unmixed groundbait at the bottom.

I usually take 20lb of groundbait with me to a match, but how much I use depends upon conditions. If a river is running after heavy rain, groundbait must be more solid to keep the fish feeding on the bottom. If conditions are still and fish are moving off the bottom, then cloud groundbait is better.

Groundbait should be used to get the fish feeding where you want them. Learning how to groundbait correctly comes only through experience. It's something you just can't put down on paper. Remember the fish are the 'governors' and they decide how we feed. All I can try and do is give you some tips.

When the whistle goes at the start of the match, you may have fish in front of you. And if they are there, you can bet your life that there's a reason, such as a good supply of natural food. One ball of groundbait should be enough to start them feeding on your hookbait, which you have introduced with the groundbait. Don't make the mistake of cannonading ball after ball at them. They will soon flick their tails in disgust and disappear into the next man's swim.

Just imagine a hotel restaurant where people are tucking into rump steaks. Suddenly the ceiling cracks, and bombs and debris start to fall all around them. Well, they' re not going to return to that restaurant in a hurry, except back to pick up their coats. So apply the same logic to fish and groundbait.

Once you have got your fish shoaled, and you've caught a few, keep feeding nice and steadily. A golf ball-sized lump introduced at regular intervals should keep them happy. There are times when you can use groundbait and lose fish and vice-versa. Only knowledge gained through a great deal of bank practice will help you here. If the fish do suddenly go off when you've been catching, try loose-feeding. It may be the answer.

One of the problems of loose-feeding on big match waters such as the Witham and Welland is that it attracts small fish. And on these rivers you must have big fish to win. So we use groundbait to get our feeder bait through the smaller fish.

It's a fallacy to say that fish ignore the groundbait and eat only the squatts or casters in it. I've often unhooked bream that have 'spat' groundbait all over my hand. Other times I've been loosefeeding and the fish have disappeared. I've dropped in a single ball of groundbait and back they've come! I do this sort of thing instinctively without realizing what I've done until after the match. There's no set pattern in my groundbaiting.

I've got a reputation for leaving my peg in a match and disappearing for an hour or so. Well, I can't leave my line in the water without catching a fish for any length of time.

I get jumpy and irritable. Five minutes without a bite seems like a year to me. So when the swim goes dead I throw in a bomb and go for a chat with a mate. This gives any fish that might be in the swim the chance to inspect my bait at leisure, and perhaps take it. When I come back I reel in and hope that I've had a bite. This is the encouragement I need to start fishing again in earnest. I haven't been disqualified yet for leaving my peg. But, if I was, there would be no moaning from me. It would just be unfortunate.

MIXING GROUNDBAIT
[June 18th, 1975]

THERE are two ways of mixing groundbait. Both are good, but one is far more demanding than the other. I go for what I call the 'dry mix'. Water is added to the cereal groundbait until it is an adequate mix.

The cereal has never been soaked with water, but enough has been added to ensure that the mixture binds sufficiently to be thrown and is wet enough to sink as required.

But the success of this type of mix is, in the end, dependent on the squeezing ability of the angler. He has to know his groundbait to the extent that he is precisely aware of the pressure he must apply for it to do its job.

If a dry mix is under-squeezed it is likely to float but, conversely, if it is squeezed too hard it will go in like a ball of concrete.

Billy Lane always made a fetish of mixing his groundbait at home before he went to a match. He put it through a sieve to remove the larger, clogging particles. I used to do it too but under the revised NFA match rules I no longer feel it necessary.

Provided you get to your peg with time to spare – and that's always important – there's time to mix. That is my first job once I get to the waterside.

The groundbait is dampened and then allowed to stand

for as long as possible to allow the moisture to be absorbed, Then, once I have tackled up and made other necessary preparations I take another look at the feed. If it isn't right, either too wet or too dry, there's time to put it right before the whistle.

Catapulted groundbait does not need to be so firm as feed to be thrown in by hand. That's a point worth stressing.

Roy Marlow mixes his groundbait another way. He insists this is not only best for him but best for beginners and those in difficulty. I believe he's right, although I'm satisfied with my own method for my own fishing.

Roy over-wets his groundbait. He literally soaks it in water so all the particles are thoroughly wetted. Obviously it cannot be thrown or catapulted very far in that state.

But having done that, Roy then balances it off with additional dry cereal until his feed is of the right consistency to do its work. As a result he has groundbait which incorporates the maximum amount of water whereas mine often has little more than the minimum of water in it.

The difference should be obvious. Roy relies on the weight of the water to help him get maximum range, whereas I rely on the power of my squeeze, as well as the water.

Roy's method has to be the best for anglers who have failed with my method. Make a mistake my way and you will pay for it. Make a mistake with Roy's and you will probably do very little, if any, damage.

His mix, incidentally, is roughly three or four parts of wet cereal to one of dry when he concludes the mix – although the amount of dry has to vary with the distance the feed is thrown. But the dry cereal simply soaks up the surplus moisture and itself becomes thoroughly saturated.

Bear in mind that the groundbait performs a different function for different species. All I have said in this series has been designed to help you get your feed out for long range fishing on wide, still and sometimes deep waters.

For bleak, and sometimes for roach, you hope to catch off the bottom. Then the feed needs to be soggy. A soggy, slow-sinking cereal feed can provide a diversion for the bleak. It gets them out of your swim to allow loose casters or maggots to be put in while the bleak are absent.

At least that helps you get the bulk of your loose feed through the upper half of the depth without bleak scoffing most of it.

I have experimented with additives, of course, but that was a phase I passed through. Nothing except water goes into my cereal.

There's no secret potion, no chemical attractor that gets the fish feeding. It's simply a matter of feeding good quality, well-mixed feed with the right regularity to ensure the fish stay with you once they show up.

In the end your groundbait is as good as you make it. Dickie Bowker has the ability to make his balls of cereal explode under water – literally like a shell-burst.

Once you understand that you can make cereal behave in different ways by the amount of water and pressure you give it then you are half-way to getting it right.

BELIEF IN YOUR BAIT IS THE BEST BOOST TO CONFIDENCE
[September 7th, 1972]

TO SUCCEED in match fishing you must have confidence. And nothing gives me more faith before the whistle than a bait tin full of soft, clean maggots.

Some anglers take pride in their tackle. The Leicester anglers take pride in their bait. We spend hours preparing our maggots and casters to the point where bream can't refuse them.

Ray Mumford works on improving his tackle from the float upwards. I work from the float downwards. Perhaps if we got together we might work out something fantastic!

Hook maggots used straight from the shop are too tough

for the discerning bream. The shy fish tastes the hard outside skin and spits it out before you can strike. My maggots have got to be soft...the softer the better. That's why I never keep them in sawdust. Instead I use bran which protects the outside skins.

It's not easy to get a blow from the right type of fly. I usually put a piece of chicken - a frozen portion from the supermarket will do - among some trees, and leave it alone for about two days. If a fly has laid its eggs on the meat.you will see a small white patch about the size of a cigarette end. Cover the meat with newspaper and keep it somewhere warm. After about four or five days the maggots should be ready to pick from the meat. If you want extra large ones, then leave them alone to feed for longer.

Some waters demand a small maggot, while other venues perform on big maggots. So the water you intend to fish controls how long you leave the maggot on the feed. Sometimes the maggots won't even grow to their full size if the blow is too big for the food available.

Leave the maggots for at least 24 hours before you use them. This clears the feed from their bodies. But make sure you use them within two days.

So you see, breeding maggots for the hook is a carefully-timed operation if you want to take full advantage of top-class bait.

Squatts and pinkies will look after themselves so long as they are kept cool, preferably in a fridge. I just sieve out as much rough stuff as I can.

A peg stuffed with fish will produce a good weight whether you use shop or home-bred maggots. But gozzers can turn an indifferent peg into a winning one. Gozzers really come into their own when fish are finicky, such as on the Witham.

Freddy Foster is unquestionably the most successful angler on that hard-fished river. But his hookbait is said by many to be the finest in England. Would he be so consistent if he relied on run-of-the-mill maggots?

Extra-soft maggots will also tell you when you have missed

a bite. If a bream has mouthed a gozzer and you have seen no movement of the swingtip, the maggot will be crushed and stretched when you reel in. An ordinary shop maggot with its tough skin may show no signs of a bite.

You can often kid a bream into taking properly by slowly twitching the bait along the bottom. It's the dog-in-the-manger attitude. The fish is not really hungry but it takes the maggot rather than let it escape.

TAKING A CHANCE WITH HEMP
[February 22nd, 1973]

ANGLERS are always searching for a secret bait. Well, if one exists I have yet to discover what it is. Mind you, it's true that certain baits such as hemp and wasp grub have an almost magical power to draw fish into the swim. But then you still have to catch them.

Hempseed is proving an increasingly popular bait, especially for roach fishing when used in conjunction with casters. But it becomes hard work when you have to use hemp on the hook.

I often take a couple of pints with me to matches on the Middle Severn. If sport is a bit slow on casters I try to jolly things along by feeding it into the swim, keeping caster on the hook. This usually attracts a better class of fish and dace, chub and roach settle on the hemp and start to feed. You can tell when this happens because the fish start to 'play football' with the shot. Then it's time to knock off a shot so that about three-eighths of an inch of your float is showing. This way the float won't disappear every time a hungry fish hits a shot in mistake for a spare seed of hemp. And you won't waste time striking false bites.

Once I know there are plenty of fish in the swim, I stop feeding hemp and concentrate on casters, hoping to wean the fish back on to that bait. This is when you find out whether or not you have ruined the swim - a chance you take with hemp.

If you can't persuade the fish to change their feeding habits then you are up a gum tree. You'll have to swap to hemp on the hook instead of casters. And hitting fast hemp bites at four rod lengths in fast water is no joke. I don't say it can't be done…it's just that you will miss a high percentage of bites as well as fishing under strain.

I always remember one match on the Severn when an angler came up to me afterwards and asked if I needed glasses. He told me I was getting a bite every put in, yet wasn't bothering to strike. What he didn't realise was that those hemp-crazy fish were literally biting chunks out of my shot. To answer him I pulled up my net as the scales came along and weighed in 19lb. That weight beat everyone except my old mate Roy Marlow. He weighed in 20lb to pip me for top prize.

You have to be extremely careful to which matches you take hemp. Many clubs and associations - particularly those with waters on the Trent - ban the use of the bait.

I rarely use it on the hook, except when I'm fishing our local stretch of the River Soar. Then I can fish under my rod tip and be certain of hitting those lightning bites.

But you can forget the bait in winter. Why do fish become so preoccupied with hemp? Only a biologist could tell us for certain, but it could be that they look like small snails when cooked, or some other natural food. Also there are a number of bushes along the banks of the Severn, so perhaps the chub think they are some type of berry.

I've caught gudgeon, roach, dace and chub – all species that roam through the water in search of food - when feeding with hempseed, but no bream. Hemp would not work in drawing bream into the swim because they only move in a match when an angler makes a mistake.

Every angler has his own particular fad or fancy about bait, but if it gives him confidence then he will have that little bit of edge over the next man. Jackie Charlton is always the last player out of the tunnel when he plays for Leeds. It's his good-luck charm, like my lucky scarf.

And the same applies to unusual baits and additives in the

groundbait. But there is one bait that you will need more than good luck to beat...and I will tell you about that next week.

THE DEADLIEST CHUB BAIT KNOWN
[March 1st, 1973]

I F YOU see Roy Marlow chasing across a field this summer, screaming "This way," don't call for the men in the white coats! Roy's probably just spotted a wasp making its way home during one of our weekly nest-hunting expeditions.

Wasp grub is the deadliest chub bait known and unbeatable on rivers such as the Severn. So the Likely lads have to get this bait if we want to challenge the Birmingham anglers on their doorstep. The Birmingham AA has banned the bait in its competitions giving those anglers who can't get hold of the grub a chance. But this has cut down match weights from the Severn. If wasp grub had been allowed in the 1971 National, there would have been many more weights over the 20lb mark.

But all-in-all I'm in favour of the ban. We have enough trouble getting hold of sufficient nests for a day's chubbing. This is why I've stopped fishing the Severn mid-week matches. Wasp grub will beat caster every time.

I'm a coward when it comes to dealing with wasps. If I see one coming I run a mile, consequently it takes me hours instead of minutes to dig out a nest. So this is where young Phil comes in handy...

If you haven't used wasp grub you can't imagine the effect it has on a patrol of feeding chub. They go crazy for it, cake and all. You can probably pull them from a hundred yards away right through other anglers' swims. No need to worry about fine float tackle either - grubbing chub will pull a battleship under. They will come right off the bottom and attack the balls of groundbait as you throw them in. It becomes more like bleak fishing.

When I'm on the grub I will cheerfully use a hook as big as

a size six and load it up with five grubs. Look at the size of a chub's mouth and you will see why you can get away with such a big hook. It's a crude way of fishing but you just can't put the chub off.

For hookbait I pick out the queens. They are bigger than the usual grubs and more succulent to the fish. But as soon as the hook goes in they die, yet this doesn't reduce the bait's effectiveness. This is strange because you wouldn't expect to catch much on a dead maggot. There again, you don't get many wasp nests floating down rivers. So the fish can't be used to the bait...even though they snap it up like fury.

Always fish wasp grub heavy. This way the bait won't fly off the hook when you cast across to the far side. I use a balsa float taking up to four swan shot and try to just drop the bait in the water. Line breaking strain can be up to 5lb. If you do a strong cast, the bait just tears off. This is another reason why I use so many grubs on the hook. If two or three do flyaway I've still got some left on. You usually have to rebait every other cast anyway.

You can also use the actual cake on the hook, and it doesn't seem to matter whether it contains any grub or not. But the main use of the cake is for groundbait. You can either take the cakes to the match and mash them up with damp groundbait, or pour boiling water on them the night before to mash them up. This last method ensures most of it sinks, otherwise floating cake could take your chub out of the swim.

Pick your grubs out of the cake the night before and put them in bran like maggots. One cake should supply enough for the hook, but I want four whole nests for a day's chubbing.

You've got to be careful how you use it, because it can fill the fish up and ruin the swim. But if you draw a chub area and you've got the grub, then mentally you can start counting the winnings.

The first time I used it was on the Warwickshire Avon at Evesham - the venue for next year's Second Division National. Roy Marlow and myself drew next to each other, and it was an hour before either of us even had a bite. We had spent more than ten quid on nests at thirty bob each, so we were hoping on some return for our money. Suddenly a shoal of chub moved into our swims. I had 11lb in a frantic half hour, while Roy caught some odd ones. But the point was that we didn't have enough nests to hold those chub for long enough. Just round the corner sat another angler with more grub than us, and he won the match with 25lb. I finished third.

Wasp grub has only been exploited by the Severn and Yorkshire anglers, but there are other rivers holding chub where it would work. The other week a big match on the Trent was won with wasp grub, while Geoff Bibby used grub to finish third in last summer's Middle Ouse Championships.

It's a bait that needs a good trial on a 'new' water. Don't dismiss it if you fail to catch the first time. You might have chosen an area with few chub, so give it a number of tries.

One river where it must work is the River Nene. Leicester anglers regularly take large hauls of chub while pleasure fishing at Milton Ferry, near Peterborough, while a match was won at Nassington this season with 12 fish for 30lb.

These are the stamp of fish that will slaughter a match if you can keep them coming. But just one word of warning... it's better to win by a pound than twenty pounds it you are using wasp grub. Otherwise the organisers will just go and ban the bait as they already do in some parts of the country.

WHY BAIT ISN'T CHEAP
[August 30th, 1973]

THE RECENT rise in the price of maggots was inevitable. The food we eat in the shops now costs more, and so does the food needed to breed the bait.

The price of bread has risen, along with other baits like worms and wasps grubs. And in some towns, dealers are charging up to 60 pence a pint for maggots.

Take it from me, the new prices are here to stay. But I think that they have reached a peak...at least for a couple of years.

When maggots are in short supply from the breeder, I often have to drive up to 300 miles to fetch them. You use up ten gallons of petrol doing this, so of course you have to pass this extra expense on to the customer, who must have his weekend bait at all costs.

But running-off casters presents bait dealers with their biggest problems. You never know from week to week just how many pints you will need. You can prepare 40 gallons one week, and end up with 10 gallons left in the fridge.

If I had put in the hours at the factory where I used to work that I now do as a bait dealer, I reckon I'd be a rich man.

Take the weekend of the Second Division National. On Friday morning I was up at 5am running-off casters. And I didn't get to bed until 3am the next day. After just two-and-a-half hours sleep, I was up again loading our van to take the bait to Downham Market. And after a full day at the National, got back to Leicester at midnight. Head down on the pillow at 2.30am, and up again at 6am to run off some more bait for the Peterborough Hospital Cup.

So you see why bait dealers haven't got much time for anglers who moan about the price of a pint. To get 50 or 60 gallons of casters, you need about 100 gallons of maggots. Maggots shrink when they get older, so the casters are smaller. Plus the fact that you've also got to allow for dead skins.

You've got to run off the casters every six hours, which means coming back at midnight if you've left the shop at six. If you miss a run-off, then you can kiss goodbye to four gallons of casters.

Caster production for me starts on Wednesday evening and carries right through until Sunday morning. But the weather can be your biggest enemy. If the climate's wrong, the maggots just don't turn. Then it's midnight driving to Nottingham or Coventry to rustle-up as many casters as you can.

Anglers believe that the hotter it is, the easier maggots turn. Yet this couldn't be further from the truth. A heat wave is as bad for caster production as a cold snap. When it gets very hot, maggots wriggle themselves to a standstill until they are

indswept but happy, Ivan shows off a brace of Irish bream. Back then sport was plentiful.

It's hard to imagine in the current era, but Ivan would regularly fish in front of galleries that were hundreds in number. Typically, he always had a word and smile for all those who came to watch him.

The Likely Lads in their youthful pomp. Left to right is Dave Downes, Brian Holland, Brian Envis Dave Rossi (held aloft), Ivan and Roy Marlow.

Above: Ivan looks to the Gods for inspiration. "If I drew on fish, nine times out of 10 I'd win," he once commented.

Below: A proud Ivan with the spoils of another successful year.

Above: Ivan, flanked by ATV fishing presenter Terry Thomas (left) and then Angling Times editor Bob Feetham, collects his Angler of the Year award in 1977. Voted by readers of Angling Times, it was the third year in succession that he had finished on top.

Right: The master at work. Accurate baiting, Ivan proved, was key to catching big weights.

Right: On international duty with England. His career at the very highest level was relatively short-lived.

Below: In rain, shine - or snow - Ivan would find somewhere to fish. Competing was in his blood.

Below: The eyes that struck at a million bites. Ivan Marks, portrait of a matchfishing legend.

Ivan (inset) when he bestrode the matchfishing world as a giant and (main) just months before he died in 2004. "At the end of the day, I was just an ordinary bloke who could fish a bit," he was to say of himself.

too exhausted to turn. This is why you should never keep a gallon of maggots in a gallon tin. Overcrowded, hot conditions produce health problems for maggots just as they do for human beings.

The energy they use in continually moving gives off heat which eventually kills them. Four pints in a gallon tin is about right. That's still about 18,000 maggots crammed together.

For good caster production, it's better for the weather to be on the cool side. Then you can build up the room temperature to 60 degrees farenheit and bring the maggots inside to turn.

A maggot has to lose that black feed spot before it will turn, and this could take four days. I always damp their sawdust after they are taken off the feed, as this tends to keep them all a similar size.

I don't believe that it's worth an angler turning his own casters. For a start he will need four pints of maggots just to produce a couple of pints of casters, and they could be turning all week. To get enough casters at any given time, you need one heck of a lot of maggots.

Casters should be fridged immediately they turn, but not in the deep-freeze compartment. This just kills them stone dead. Casters are best kept in a maggot container with a plastic sheet between the casters and the lid. This way any unturned maggots will slowly wriggle their way to the top where you can pick them out with ease. If you keep your casters in an air-tight bag, the half-turned maggots will die and foul the casters.

Casters will keep up to three days kept correctly in the fridge. If you put them in water, then you're killing them straight away. Any casters I have left over after a match which have been kept in water, I give to the birds. I'd only use them the next day if I was desperate for bait.

Just because they don't smell, does not mean to say that they are not off. You can't always smell meat that's going bad. But as soon as you've tasted it, you spit it out. And it's the same with fish. Throw in bad casters and the fish vanish.

HEMP MEANS GLORY OR SUDDEN DEATH
[October 3rd, 1973]

THE MODERN matchman now has such a wide choice of baits that it becomes easy to waste time going through the range. A man who tries bread, maggots, worms, casters, hemp and wheat in the same match could lose a couple of hours before settling down to one method. Far better to have confidence in one proven bait and give it a thorough chance to work. Let the anglers on the pegs either side do the experimenting for you with the more unusual baits. If they start to catch more fish than you, then think about switching.

But there again, don't spend all the match watching the men next to you. There's nothing worse. I believe that some anglers should be fitted with blinkers before a match. They waste so much time glancing from side to side.

The angler who throws in half-a-dozen different baits is just confusing the fish as well as himself. If you walked into a pub and ordered whisky, Guinness, vodka, gin and lager you'd soon feel dizzy, and end up being carried home. Well, I believe that fish prefer a choice of a couple of baits rather than having to swim around not knowing what to feed on.

Our recent battles with the Continentals have focussed attention on the more unusual baits, with which they seem preoccupied. The French spend so much effort bringing the fish into their swims that in the end they forget what they were after.

One bait which the Continentals use crushed in their groundbait is hempseed. Of course there's nothing new about hempseed. It was introduced to this country after the first world war by Belgian anglers, and widely accepted in the South. But this season, a hemp craze has been sweeping the country and some rivers have seen more seeds than come out of a combine harvester.

There's no doubt that hemp can be deadly in drawing fish into the swim, particularly roach, but there are other times when it will kill the swim stone dead. I never use it actually on the hook, preferring to bait with casters. This way it's easier to hook the fish.

It's important to let your hemp soak for at least 24 hours before you actually boil it. This gives the hemp time to absorb the water and swell up. I boil for about 15 minutes to make it split, and a touch of bicarbonate of soda will help blacken the husks.

If I believe that there are bream about, I never throw in hemp as I've found that it puts them off the feed. But on a river such as the middle Severn where bream are rare I will always use hemp to draw fish into the swim.

Severn anglers are now using tares on the hook in conjunction with hemp feed, and the big roach are putting in a welcome reappearance.

Weights of 20lb plus have been taken from areas such as Bewdley and Stourport where previously roach have been scarce for years.

Other rivers where I will feed with hemp if the rules allow are the Witham and the Trent. I will also use it on the Welland and the North Bank, but only if I think that there's no chance of catching bream.

Sometimes I also add aniseed to my groundbait, but whether it makes any difference is difficult to prove. If unusual baits and additives give you confidence in your fishing, then all well and good. There's certainly no harm in anglers experimenting with different hook and groundbaits, because it's surprising what fish will eat under certain conditions.

One of the most effective baits in our local canal is chips… yes those yellow greasy things you buy wrapped in newspaper. So many lads toss them over the bridges into the water that the carp, chub and roach have grown to accept them as part of their diet.

The Leicester anglers have spent hours trying out different baits and methods because the man who is first with something new, is the angler who is likely to win. If his method is right, then he has no-one else to defeat. This is why I always try to fish differently from the rest of the field. If 400 men are legering and 50 floatfishing, I'd rather use a float. Because if that's the right method I've fewer men to beat.

At one time we even tried injecting maggots with air to make them sink slower. It worked, but we got such funny looks from anglers who saw hyperdermic syringes in our baskets that we packed it in.

Another good bait which anglers are using more these days is wheat. During harvest time it's an absolute killer for roach on waters such as the Upper Ouse and Nene. You've got to have the confidence to wait for it to work, but your fish will be anything from 8 ounces to more than a pound.

I've heard anglers talking about pinkie casters, saying how effective they can be. Well they probably are, but I should think that if we ever did them commercially they would cost a pound a pint. Pinkie casters sink only for a very short period, and if you were an hour late on the run, you'd end up with a pint of floaters.

The thing to remember is not to get too bogged down with all these different baits. Stick to the basic ones and learn how to use them properly for best results. Save the experimenting for practice sessions when you can afford to fail.

LIGHTING THE FUSE OF A GROUNDBAIT BOMB
[February 15th, 1973]

GROUNDBAIT, like gelignite, should be handled with care. Use too little and you'll just titillate the shoal. Use too much and you'll blow them apart!

I see that Clive Smith - writing on this page two weeks ago - reckons to put in at least eight pounds of groundbait in the first ten minutes. Well, that may work for Clive on the lower Sevem but if I carried out such a bombardment in the Fens I would guarantee to be out of the prizes.

The lower Great Ouse from Ten Mile Bank to Denver Sluice is a wide, deep water somewhat similar to the lower

Severn. It has a strong pull and in places is 20 feet deep. But if you groundbait here in any quantity the bream just disappear. You need to loose feed for any degree of success.

Matchmen who fish the lower Severn Birmingham Welfare matches invariably go for bream. The match starts and the water erupts to a cannonade of groundbait. Any chub that might be about are immediately scared away. Most matches on this water are won with a top weight of less than 20lb. But a lot of chub are never caught because the anglers are preoccupied with bream. If 400 men fished for chub and 100 for bream, instead of vice-versa, chub would win. And I believe some big weights would be caught.

Another rarity on the lower Severn is the angler who plummets his swim before he starts. The competitors hurl in so much stuff that some of it must land on the shelves and ledges where the bream feed. Eight pounds of dry ground bait would cover a mighty big area, as well as shocking the fish! This Severn style of bream fishing is like going on the Welland and fishing the far bank at every peg. At some swims you would succeed - but at others you would fail.

Like Clive I take 20lb of dry groundbait with me to a match in case I sit on one of these 'bonanza' bream shoals that show up from time to time. When bream really get their heads down they feed like pigs. The water changes colour as they stir up the bottom and they need plenty of stuff to hold 'em. An angler probably only sits on one of these shoals twice in a lifetime. But it would be foolish not to have the stuff just in case.

I drew a big shoal in the last Great Ouse Championships but I probably got through only ten pounds of dry for a total weight of 62lb 10oz. If I had used 20lb of groundbait I may have caught a hundredweight....or just double-figures. I took a chance and it paid off for me. I was top weight on the day and that's what counted.

If Geoff Bibby, who finished only two ounces behind, had been fishing within sight I may have used a lot more groundbait to match him. But I couldn't even see the angler to my left as he was hidden in a bed of rushes. All I could see was the angler opposite and I knew that I was way in front of him.

There was about 6lb in the water when the bream moved in. I was a bit wary of scaring them so I fed a ball every so often. Once I was past 20 fish I knew I was in the reckoning. After I had weighed-in my fish, a young angler picked up my kit to fish the hot swim. Another angler moved opposite and filled it in, casting right across. The result was that neither angler even had a bite....

Groundbait can be used to draw an opponent's fish. We call it 'bream stealing'. If I'm catching nothing and I notice an angler three or four pegs away taking bream I left fly with two or three balls to try to panic him into making a mistake. If I'm lucky he will retaliate by bombarding his swim as well. Now there's a 50-50 chance that he will scare his shoal into moving my way. My groundbait has already settled on the bottom so the frightened shoal could stop in my swim. It's an old trick but it often works.

When I'm catching bream my rivals will have to wait for me to make a mistake. If they keep putting in groundbait the only affect will be to tighten my shoal.

Groundbait certainly kept the bream on the move in the last Welland Championship. I caught a fish first cast so this was the signal for the angler at the next peg to toss in a few heavy balls. But instead of pleasing the fish they scooted upstream a couple of pegs. The angler here caught a bream, and lashed in some stuff. What did the bream do? They came straight back to Uncle Ivan.

One trick to remember when your maggots are untouched and you are getting line bites is to put a piece of groundbait on the hook. The bream are eating the groundbait rather than just picking out the feed.

WINTER GROUNDBAITING

[December 5th, 1973]

YOU CAN get away with less than perfect groundbaiting in summer, but it's a different story altogether in winter. There's so much that you can do wrong, it's no wonder that many anglers kill what could be a good swim in the first few minutes.

Take colour for instance. Brown groundbait is fine for the summer, but it won't get to the bottom quickly enough in the winter, so I harden it off with about half the quantity of white.

Where to place it? This is where most anglers go completely wrong. What's the use of chucking it in unless it's hitting the fish, which are in small tight shoals anyway, right on the nose?

Freddy Foster and Benny Ashurst are the absolute masters at accurate groundbaiting and use their skill to perfection in the gruelling winter months. Don't feed at all unless you are sure where it is going to settle. After all, what's the use of feeding up the next man's swim?

If I'm fishing close in, I usually throw in a few maggots and watch them like a hawk. Depending on the speed at which they fall and travel, I decide where I put my groundbait, if I use any at all. This is where that careful mixing comes in. If you draw a roach swim at this time of year, never use more than 4lb. If you are sure that bream should be in front of you, put in a little more laced with worms. But don't overdo it.

On the Welland or Witham I would add casters and a few worms, but only casters on the Trent. But I will always loose feed wherever I can, depending on the flow and depth. The Nene is a caster-only water, as are most Fen waters, but for some reason the Cam is a maggot water.

Knowing your river in winter is half the battle. This is why the locals stick to their home patch when the weather turns cold. When I fish either the Severn or Trent, or any moving water, I always spend a little time looking for boils and swirls, or anything which can influence the consistency and way I should put groundbait in. These disturbances are usually caused by underwater obstructions, and it's either behind, or smack in them, that the winter fish are living. This is where accuracy and correct water reading can make a winning peg. Throw your groundbait in the wrong place, and it will either feed the man downstream or get swept towards you.

This is where the swimfeeder really comes into its own. Swimfeeders place the feed in exactly the right spot, assuming of course that you have discovered where the fish are in the first place!

It's on the likely bream swims that, even if you don't ruin a pitch, someone else will. How many times do you get drawn next to the man who just can't help filling it in? You can't change their ideas either. I usually have a little word and try to convince them where they are going wrong. But more often than not, they think: "Hello, he's trying to kid me on."

Get that sort of angler next to you, and it's home time for both of you. At least 50 per cent of anglers are panicked into this fatal mistake when they see other people catching. If groundbaiting had been the right thing to do, I would have been doing it myself earlier on. But they never learn.

Deciding on when to groundbait or loose feed is always a gamble. I usually put in one or two tiny caster-filled balls straight away, which won't get me into serious trouble, andthen see what happens.

For instance: in a Trent match I had taken 5lb, but realising this was not good enough I took a chance and started feeding groundbait and out came a second place 14lb. Groundbait puts your feed into a small area while loose feeding with a catapult scatters it over a wide area.

Watch Benny Ashurst. He can put his feed onto a sixpence every time. This deadly accuracy scores on every winter water, the Witham especially. Don't forget. You must not panic and fool yourself into believing that the more stuff you throw in, the more fish will come out. All you will do, is ruin your own swim and do the chap a few pegs away the world of good.

Just watch the big names in winter. The only mistake they

will make is drop off the odd fish and we all do that. If you do draw next to a big name, keep calm. They've only got two arms like you. If you do go wrong, don't be bashful. Ask them what you did wrong. They've nothing to hide, and will explain just where you made a mistake.

It's only the moderate match anglers, who think they know it all, who will tell you to clear off. If they do, don't worry. Anything they are likely to tell you will be rubbish anyway!

When you do use casters in groundbait, use the sinkers. Keep the floaters for the hook. They can easily make the difference between catching the odd few fish and perhaps make a winning peg. The minute weight of a hook makes sure that the floating caster falls at the same rate as the sinking kind. The best ones to use are those which have almost turned into a fly. They may look really dark and nasty, but they will score over those lovely golden ones every time! Most anglers turn their noses up at them but that's their bad luck. Just how many people throw their floaters away? Nearly everybody, except the few that have thought this one out.

What would happen if someone came into my shop and I sold him floating casters? That would be the last I would see of him. One of these days they are going to crack on, and actually start asking for floaters for the hook.

We used them to get our second place in last week's Angling Times League match on the Trent. Put it like this. I have used floaters in six Trent matches this season, and I haven't come away with empty pockets!

END OF THE CASTER – AND THE RETURN OF THE PINKIE
[December 18th, 1974]

THE DECLINE of the caster has begun. It is not now so effective as it has been, particularly on the Nene and the Witham, and this is bound to spread. Why these rivers first? The answer is simple. These are the waters which have consistently been subjected to the greatest weight of caster fishing.

I can't say I'm surprised. Every bait has its cycle, rising from nowhere to become a top quality match-winning bait and then slipping back. The caster won't slip back to complete obscurity. It's too good a bait for that but we are heading into the time when it won't be the consistent winner it has been through the last five seasons.

It will come back again. It's a question of waiting for the time when the fish tire of whatever replaces caster…and whatever subsequently replaces the replacement.

Anglers who continue to fish with casters won't be out and out failures all the time on the Witham and Nene but their chances will be much more slim until the revival comes.

Anglers who stand still on the circle instead of following the fashion, can wait for the wheel to complete its turn and they will be back in full business but they will have lean days while they wait.

It's a miracle that caster saturation hasn't shown yet on the Welland. That river has been loaded with casters for each of the past three seasons but I suspect it will be next to follow the Nene and the Witham.

Why has it happened? It's not as though anglers are ladling in equally attractive, certainly not better, baits to make the fish switch. Neither can it be that roach and bream have become over-fed with casters to the extent they become sick of them.

This year has seen progressively heavier caster-feeding. Many is the matchman who has fed four and five pints into his swim in a five-hour contest. But this amounts to very little quantity in terms of solid food. Crush a pint of casters into a bowl, subtract the husk, and there's only half a pint of juice remaining. Fish can soon consume that lot and never know they've had it.

It is my opinion that one 3lb bream is quite capable of eating a pint of casters on its own when it is feeding heavily. Which makes five pints into bream swims not very much at all in relation to the numbers of bream in the area.

So casters haven't lain on the river bed and gone sour. Much more likely that they have been fed into the river sour and I think that's what has induced the fish to change their minds.

Dry casters can be kept fresh in a fridge for a week. Once they are wetted they soon sour. Casters kept in water for 24 hours won't suffer too much provided they are used soon afterwards. But if casters are kept in water for 48 hours they're not much good as feed and it's odds on that the rejection rate by the fish is high.

But to reject a caster a fish must first break its shell – and a sour caster must taste foul. Imagine yourself eating a raw egg that's bad. How long before you eat another? Years, in all likelihood.

The Nene had fished particularly badly this year as the result of the caster failure. I have even reached the stage where I've chosen the Trent rather than the Nene simply because the Trent will give me a better day's fishing. And it's saying a lot that I should leave the river which has consistently given me a good time.

So what's the form from now on? Robin Harris pointed the way when he took a 20lb maggot-fed and maggot-caught catch from the Welland to finish fourth in a Dave Downes open in late October.

And the same is showing in the Witham. Leeds anglers have been consistently putting up a good show with yellow maggots while the River Witham regulars have been left wondering what's happening.

It's my opinion that these sequences of domination by one bait last from three to five years. It was four years ago wasn't it, when casters first became the top bait on the Witham and Nene? Casters will still catch fish – there's no doubt about that. But the best returns will fall to the pleasure anglers who won't be affected by counter baits offered by other anglers.

So the big question. What's to be the top bait next year when the fish resume heavy feeding? It isn't possible to gauge the caster's successor in winter for there's too much fluctuation of conditions for us to see the answer.

Next year's bait could be the pinkie. That's the one which has been longest out of favour. It was a key bait 15 years ago but was knocked out of fashion by the squatt.

The squatt and gozzer combination reigned until the caster broke through. First it was the caster on its own, then the caster-redworm combination. That's the sequence as we have known it through the last 15 years. It doesn't follow, of course, that the sequence will continue in that order but I do have the feeling that pinkies are set for a return to favour.

The bloodworm-joker combination isn't with us in full flow yet. This may come, but it is an extremely expensive bait combination to use in a well-stocked river. Lancashire canal anglers may be able to manage very well with small quantities of bait in fish-starved swims but my thinking suggests that it might cost as much as £8 to joker-feed a Fenland bream swim to the point where it becomes effective with the bigger fish. The head of mini-fish is so high that if jokers are introduced other than in solid balls of groundbait most of them are consumed by tiddlers before they can settle to the bottom.

Although bloodworms are now available in commercial quantities - and are advertised weekly in Angling Times – I can't see many anglers being prepared to pay the price I think necessary to overcome the small fish domination of bream river swims.

MOLE HILL SOIL IS MY SECRET GROUNDBAIT ADDITIVE
[January 15th, 1975]

EVERY time I make a trip to Europe I am on a spying expedition. I'm out to learn all I can about the tackle they use on the other side of the channel. The French tackle shops, in particular, have to be paid a visit and I go into every one possible. Let's face it, the French are currently the best in the world when it comes to match fishing so there must be a lot to learn from them.

During the Angling Times International in France in 1973 a king-size tackle shop at Angers was thrown open to us. We could inspect everything in the shop and were told just as much as the language barrier allowed. What impressed me most of all – and this is in the department where the French are furthest ahead of us - was the wide assortment of additives which go into the French match anglers' groundbait. Nothing chemical, nothing secret, but common-sense ingredients all intended to fulfil a particular function.

Everyone who has seen the French in action is struck by the cannonball behaviour of their groundbait. It goes in with a real whallop - yet, immediately afterwards the French are catching fish.

I have been doing some experiments of my own, not entirely based on the French concept of groundbaiting but involving the addition of various types of soil to the cereal groundbait. That, in itself, is nothing new. A number of top-flight matchmen here have used and still use soil, sand and other 'heavies' as part of their mix.

I'm not too keen on sand scraped off the shoreline of a river simply because this is exposed to all the scum, grease, oil and any other harmful substance which chooses to settle on to it. I go for mole hills, those neat little mountains of soil the industrious mole throws to the surface in its hunt for food and as it extends its underground tunnel system.

The soil is clean, it is fresh and comes from only a few inches below the surface. I have three main collecting centres: The Coronation Channel, the Welland and the Fen drains. Those three localities each give me a different coloured soil. Coronation Channel mole hills are sandish, a sort of biscuit colour, whwreas the Welland much more black and the Fen soil ultra black.

I make a habit of collecting a bag full at each centre when my stocks are running low. The first job when I get it home is to dry it. Once the moisture has been removed the soil is then riddled through a fine sieve - a squatt sieve is about right.

221

All roots, small stones and miscellaneous odds and ends are removed and I am left with soil which when completely dry crumbles into the finest of particles - yes, dust almost.

It's obvious when you think about it that the finest soil additive for the Welland must be Welland soil. That is the natural colour and when it settles on to the river-bed it just disappears. There's no contrasting colour patch on the bottom to make fish edgy.

The soil serves many functions. Its first has to be to provide a muddy cloud closely resembling the colour the water becomes after heavy rain. It is completely natural. Fish are used to picking food out of muddy water so they expect to find food in my mud cloud...and, of course, they are not disappointed.

A soil and cereal groundbait can be mixed to any consistency. It can be modelled on those French cannonballs, or it can be extremely mushy. Whether it is sloppy or firm in no way depends on variations of the ratio of groundbait to soil but on the amount of water added during mixing. I can mix up a super slop sufficient to carry casters three or four rods lengths out and plop them all in a heap on the surface.

There are other advantages. With a soil additive, the groundbait will carry between five and 10 per cent more casters, squatts, pinkies, worms or what you like. And, to answer an immediate reservation you may have, it doesn't burst casters as much as compressed cereal groundbait.

Cereal groundbait needs to be firmly moulded into balls before it can be thrown any distance. So caster shells are inevitably crushed. But soil is heavier. It moulds under less finger and palm pressure and throws that much better too.

My current mix is a pound to a pound for the Trent. A pound of my brown cereal to a pound of soil. That's about a teacupful of soil. The Welland is one of soil to two parts of groundbait.

Economically it is right. It saves you money. I estimate that soil can save as much as £10 a season for anglers who fish every weekend.

I don't pretend for a minute that I have all the answers. I'm still trying to sort out some aspects of this type of feed.

Eventually I will get it absolutely right...I think. At the moment soil has done me most good on flowing rivers: the Trent and Severn mainly. If you draw a whirly swim, where the water boils and there's no steady movement, soil can help you get all your feed down into a limited area where it will concentrate the fish and do the most good. But I am convinced it will also work on the Welland – despite the fact that the Welland is a relatively shallow water.

For long range feeding there is bound to be rather more surface impact than with our conventional feed, but if the colour cloud is right then that must be more than ample compensation.

At the moment I'm inclined to the view that the Coronation Channel (Spalding) mole hills are the best. They come closest in colour and consistency to the yellowish additive the French use so successfully. I used this stuff in a Trent Winter league match when I filled it with jokers, fished bloodworm on the hook, and caught 400 mini-fish for 11lb 9oz...from 2ft of water. In that instance I was in need of a groundbait that would get the jokers down to the river bed quickly. The colour factor was less important, but, nevertheless, blending the colour to the river must be an advantage.

Bream eat groundbait, so some readers may question the worth of inedible matter in groundbait. Is this at all off putting? I don't think so. After all, bream are accustomed to delving into the bottom when they feed.

DO YOU SABOTAGE YOUR OWN SWIM?
[April 30th, 1975]

IT'S QUITE remarkable. Lots of otherwise sound, intelligent anglers, masters of the techniques for fishing wherever they go, fail to become truly competent in the use of groundbait.

Watch any contest, anywhere where cereal groundbait is used, and you won't be long concluding with me that there's a hefty gap in feeding-ability. And that gap is such that it can cancel out all the technical application that a match angler - or any other angler for that matter - has at his command.

I've seen it - you've seen it - balls of groundbait breaking up in mid-air, and landing anywhere other than the spot intended. Other groundbait hits the surface with a sickening clonk. It sounds more like depth-charging than swim-feeding. And there's the other by no means unusual occurrence...the balls of groundbait that sink temporarily below the surface on impact but which rise to the top seconds later to go bobbing merrily away wherever wind and current take them.

My first two examples will literally drive the fish away. In some instances anglers are aware of that possibility but believe that after the initial shock the fish will return to begin feeding on that heavily fed patch. Not on your Nellie!

If there's one angler sitting among a bunch of the heave-it-in brigade who feeds quietly and well, he's the chap who should finish up catching most. If he doesn't catch the greatest weight of fish then more often than not it's because he has made a mistake of another kind himself.

Floating groundbait is easy to see. The mistake is obvious and when balls of feed floating out of the swim, probably releasing their contents as they go before the remainder sinks in one lump, they inevitably take the fish away with them. They then act as a feed barrier that fish moving upstream are unlikely to pass.

On the other hand, groundbait can break too easily and be moved away downstream too quickly. It's all a matter of relating your groundbait to the swim being fished, taking in depth, flow, the distance to be thrown and the fish you hope to catch.

All of this sounds very simple. It is simple...so why do so many people get it wrong? They actually sabotage their own swims, most of them without ever realising what they've done.

Most failures are caused by poor groundbait. Remember, if you can't throw accurately or to a distance, there are ways you can conquer your own short comings - but you will never succeed as long as your cereal feed is inferior.

I've gone through the range. I've tried everything and I suppose I always will. I've got to. But in the end I always come back to the same thing....bread, pure bread, clean, finely ground and the highest quality I can get. It isn't cheap. At the end of last season top grade pure bread groundbait was retailing at between £9 and £10 a hundredweight. It won't be any cheaper on June 16, that's for sure. The price per cwt could have risen another £2 by then.

I look at it this way. Cheap groundbait is cheap groundbait. It can never be a substitute for the best. And I reckon that groundbait is just one of many things you buy where the best proves the cheapest in the end. Buy it in bulk and you save a few bob. But if you can't afford a half-hundredweight then pay top whack for smaller quantities.

So insist on bread and reject what's offered to you if it looks dull in colour. You want your groundbait clean. If you later decide to put sand, soil or whatever else in with it that's your privilege. But see it's clean when you buy it.

I don't sieve my groundbait by the half-hundredweight but it is important to bear in mind that with even the best quality feed there will be a certain amount of larger crumbs in the bag. If I intend fishing a slow-flowing or stillwater bream fishery the groundbait is put through a squatt riddle. This removes roughly a cupful from each 10lb riddled. These larger crumbs are the pieces that cause groundbait to clog. They prevent it breaking up exactly as it should at the right depth to get your feed into the right area in the way that it will be most effective.

My own groundbait is either pure brown bread or a mixture of brown and white, the ratio of the 'mix' depending on the water to be fished and the distance and the manner in which the groundbait is to fed to the swim.

We have gone all through the colour craze at Leicester. But I don't rate colour that important. It could be argued that my general mix – brown and white - isn't too far removed from yellow anyway, but we don't mess around with dyes anymore.

I don't like white on its own. Never use it. Brown without white can be very good. In fact it is the best in the situations where it can be used to full advantage.

YOU MUST BREAK FROM THE NORM
[July 2nd, 1975]

IF I COULD only do it, I would love to be able to loosefeed every swim I ever fish. Small quantities of feed put in regularly must be more effective than the more occasional dollups we put into most swims. The snag is, of course, that it isn't physically possible to propel casters or maggots any real distance.

Under normal conditions no one can loosefeed by hand more than 10 to 12 yards. I've heard anglers claim to be able to do much better than that. I can only say, not under normal conditions you can't! With a gale-force wind blowing from behind you can naturally throw further, but even that isn't all bonus. The feed scatters terribly when it's wind-aided and no one can be certain - even if the wind is giving a range as high as 30 yards - that the casters or whatever will land in the right place.

A catapult does increase your range. No doubt about that. But even a catapult has its limitations. It will certainly add another 7-8 yards to your distance, but no more.

It is important to remember that distance is not the sole objective when feeding. On a bream river it may at times be important, but on a flowing river when you're after roach or dace you pick your swim in relation to the river itself.

Anglers who automatically opt for distance fishing each and every time will be creating problems for themselves... frequently unnecessarily.

The real secret with loosefeeding is regularity. It's not a bit of use feeding a handful of casters or maggots every few minutes. The fish are into your swim, scoff that lot and are gone again.

The secret is to keep them searching for food in your patch. They don't need always to find it but so long as they can be educated to believe there's a constant supply of manna dropping from heaven every minute or so they will hang around the edges of the swim. But even fish soon lose interest in miracles if these occur only every 10 minutes! They soon move out once they've given the swim a thorough searching and can find nothing of interest.

Watch a shoal of swimming fish. Better still give them loosefeed in situations where you can actually watch what happens. They're always darting about. You can throw in a dozen maggots and watch fish glide in and scoff the lot. They move quickly. They don't hang about. Sometimes you don't even see the fish take the maggot. One moment you are looking at a maggot and a split second later it has gone.

Fish like dace and roach don't stay around in one place for hours on end of their own accord when they are hungry. They will literally be searching for food in places they believe give them a chance. How long would you hang around an empty pantry if your inside was rumbling!

There will always be times when loosefeeding is the best method simply because it helps keep the fish concentrated. But the top man is the one who knows when to use cereal and when to manage without it.

The Ivan Marks calculations in that respect are, I suppose, based largely on instinct. I decide to do something and it comes off. I can't always give a precise reason for everything I do. Neither, I suspect, could many - if any - of the other match anglers who win more than their share.

Look at it this way. I'm a gambling man, always have been, always will be. So I want a situation where the odds are in my favour. I think it's up to me to create a favourable situation by the way I feed and fish which gives me those odds.

Take the Trent. Loosefeeding has been all the rage. The cracks do it. Everyone else does it, sometimes slavishly. My instincts are all to break the sequence. Let everyone else loosefeed. I'll use groundbait. Not because it is necessarily the best style of feeding but simply because I shall be doing something different to everyone, or almost everyone, else.

If there are 300 fishing a Trent contest, and only ten in every hundred use groundbait, that means, in my way of working things out, that if my feeding style is right on the day I have only 29 anglers to beat. If I join the masses and loosefeed then I have 270 to beat. It's obviously easier to beat 29 anglers than 270 so, by my assessment, I've got the odds in my favour.

That really explains why the first people to use a particular bait or style are the ones who score consistently. It's only if you are doing something different to the majority that you can expect to win consistently.

I have always believed that fish can, from a feeding point of view, be related to human beings. Sounds daft maybe, but we eat, they eat and I think we can often parallel behaviour.

You like a T-bone steak. So do I. Maybe we could eat four or five a week - if the wife's housekeeping money allows. But if you were obliged to eat a T-bone every day the time would come when you would be sick of the sight of steak...and want something else.

So it is with fish - which to me explains why breaking the sequence is so important. Of course at this early stage in the present season there's not much sequence to break.

So there will come a time when it will be invaluable to put variation in the feed or the bait you offer fish. The one thing that remains unchanging for me is the rate of feed. That, in my view, needs to be constant. A feeding rhythm is vital.

BAIT COLOUR IS A CONUNDRUM
[July 17th, 1975]

THERE'S little doubt that fish don't see colours as we see them but they do have colour preferences. And that preference is ever-changing - so the angler who is first on to the coloured bait the fish accept most readily is the chap most likely to succeed.

Unfortunately there's no instant calculator which provides the information for us. We've got to work it our ourselves and it is, and always will be, a matter of trial and error. One day the fish want the white natural maggot, the next yellow or red, or shades of those two colours.

Of course it frequently happens that two anglers, not necessarily fishing far apart, finish first and second using different coloured hook maggots. Which leads some people to assume that colour isn't really important. That is a dangerous assumption, for I am sure that on any one day, with its varied ingredients - water colour, sunshine, cloud, gales, flat, calm or something in between – helps prejudice fish towards certain colours.

Other factors also come into the reckoning such as the amount of hammer a particular water has had. The flow-rate, depth, size and species being sought, all of these points have some application. In fact the ingredients are so diverse that, as I said earlier, we are left with a trial and error probe before we get the answer.

At least we know fish do have this colour preference - and for the purpose of this article I am assuming white can be classified as a colour. You see fish can build up a prejudice against a particular colour. That has been proved scientifically. Tanked fish have been fed yellow maggots and given an electric shock every time they made a move to eat one. The same fish were fed white maggots and allowed to take what they liked without interference. Later, when those same fish were fed mixed yellow and whites they wouldn't look at the yellows - and can you blame them?

We don't give fish that sort of shock treatment, but they do get a shock of sorts when they a re-hauled out of the water after taking food of a particular colour. So, naturally, they build up their prejudices based on past experience.

That experiment I've just mentioned proves that fish can learn. There's no point in attempting to overcome a mental reaction that the fish may have. It's far better to take advantage of it by realising that one colour will do you a better job than any other.

There are some basic clues which can be of help but these must never be taken to be hard and fast rules. Pink, for instance, comes into its own when a river has been flogged to death. Pink hook maggots and pinkies have sometimes done good work in the Nene, for example, and in the Fen drains in the autumn, after a period when the fish have taken a hiding.

Yellow often comes into its own either when the water is coloured, or when insects are dropping in from overhanging trees, bushes and vegetation. Many anglers believe that casters are a flop in coloured water. What they really mean is that fish have some difficulty locating casters when the water is muddy - so that mahogany caster colour is to be avoided at such times. Not, I hasten to add, that I necessarily agree with that last piece of thinking , but it could certainly apply in some waters I don't fish.

Casters can, of course, be made to be effective on days when fish can't see them so well simply by putting a maggot on the hook with the caster. It could be a yellow or a white for best effect, but that you'll have to find out on the day. The maggot, both by its colour and its movement, helps make that caster easier for fish to locate.

As I said recently, I equate fish to people when it comes to food. They react in the same way that we do over quantity and quality. White has to be a food colour to fish as it is to human beings. We generally regard anything white as clean, pure and wholesome. So do fish, when they find maggots dropping out of dead fish rotting by the water's edge, when they find a milk or creamery outfall or when they chance on slices or loaves of bread. So white will always be the most important colour.

In any 20 matches I fish I estimate that white is the best colour 11 times, yellow ranks top six times and pink or red scores three times. Which at least means that if you always fish with white maggots you will be right more than half the time! But that, of course, isn't enough. You've got to get it right all the time.

When I was first learning about match fishing there was a

time when yellow paste was a killing bait on the Nene. I haven't known it to do anything like so well since, but it is important to remember that colour preference applies to all hookbaits and not just maggots.

There are days when freshly turned casters are superior, others when a really dark caster is tops. You've got to find out what's right on the day.

EASY UP ON THE FEED
[November 12th, 1975]

PERHAPS it's the increasing cost of fishing, in line with everything else, that has inspired the question - "should there be a limit on the amount of bait permitted to be used in contests?"

That's a question being put to me quite regularly these days, particularly at the numerous Angling Times Forums I have attended recently.

If you are prepared to be physically searched every time you fish a contest you may think a restriction would be useful; useful because it reduces the cost of participating.

But it can't really be a logical move. Far better, I think, for the match angler to become more educated in the use of bait. Let's face it huge quantities are wasted. A lot of bait is taken to the waterside just in case it's needed...and rarely is. Sunday's casters are useless for the following weekend. So money goes down the drain.

There's no obligation for every matchman to equip himself with four pints of casters, plus squatts or pinkies, pints of worms and maggots. It's just that those who can afford it don't care to take a risk of fishing with a limited range and quantity of bait and feed.

It was once said that a National champion used 13 pints of casters to feed his swim. I reckon there are 3,000 casters in every pint so if the suggestion was accurate he used 39,000 casters...to catch 15 bream. Now I know some fish have enormous appetites. A 4lb chub will eat a half-pint of casters. A sizable trout will eat two casters as regularly as you care to throw them in – until it has consumed a full pint. But neither the chub nor the trout wants a solid half-pint or pint thrown at it in one go.

Feed that way and much will be wasted. Those whose pocket won't stretch to a heavy outlay each weekend shouldn't sweat about it. It doesn't mean they've forfeited their chances. Far from it. Look at the simple arithmetic. I say there are 3,000 casters in a pint. Let's see how those casters can be used through a five-hour contest for maximum effect.

Assume you make a cast every minute through those five hours - and in the majority of instances casting is much less frequent than that. So that allows 300 casts during the contest - which allows you ten casters for each chuck in if you use up the full 3,000. And that's a rate of feed to be recommended in a great many situations.

It may not be enough to divert swarms of bleak. It won't be sufficient to feed a Severn chub swim. But in 90 per cent of situations it is a quite adequate feeding rate, particularly in the depths of winter.

In fact, if all anglers disciplined themselves to that level of caster feeding the aggregate catches would be much higher. Winning weights would perhaps be lower than they sometimes are, but fewer swims would be busted.

Benny Ashurst was one man who rode to fame on a minimum of bait. He never threw in huge quantities. Benny used the best, yes - there's no substitute for quality - but his maxim was always to keep the fish feeding for as long as you possibly can.

We've passed through the time when anglers traditionally thought it necessary to use a stone or more of groundbait - dry weight at that - at every match they fished. Nowadays the average could be, less than 4lb for each five-hour contest. In my view it can afford to drop lower yet without serious consequences.

The same applies to casters. I think we've seen the peak.

Anglers are beginning to realise, if only because of the cost, that they can sensibly manage with less.

As I've said, there are times when more feed is desirable. A bream swim on the River Welland can take a lot of caster feed. Sometimes six pints isn't too much. But only sometimes... and even then in only a proportion of the swims along the match length.

There's a case for even more discipline with groundbait. The catapult has helped to reduce consumption. Anglers can send small balls further these days - and more accurately - than they could by hand.

The cereal can be reduced still further as more and more anglers realise how concentrated casters can be in cereal. Let's look briefly at a big Welland summer contest...800 pegs with cereal used at the rate of 5lb a man. That's a grand total of 4,000lb of DRY cereal - nearly two tons.

When wetted it would fill 35 domestic baths to the brim. That's got to be too much. The bream will scoff it within 24 hours maybe, but it's too much for a five-hour contest.

Look at it another way. A full-sized loaf, dried and ground, makes no more than 1lb of cereal feed. Can there really be any need for the equivalent of FIVE loaves of bread to be thrown into every swim on the Welland in five hours?

I believe that education is the answer. Self-education, maybe, for this is a lesson anglers are unlikely to accept from me or anyone else. It's a question basically of anglers knowing more about the swims they have to fish. With better knowledge comes better understanding.

A lot of groundbait is bunged into swims that would produce a lot more fish if they were lightly fed. The snag is, you'll say, how can anyone tell in advance? Frankly it isn't easy. I'll admit there are times when the big feed pays off. But I doubt if many Fenland anglers, for example, draw swims demanding more than 5lb of groundbait once in every season.

Fish have reacted against heavy groundbaiting. It was a winning style in the Coventry era of the early 1960s when those anglers were some of the few who fished the float at long range before swingtips caught on. It lost its magic once everyone got on to the band-wagon.

An out-and-out limit would do more harm than good. It would lead to even greater bureaucracy in contests. To resentment. Perhaps even to breakaway elements.

The answer is moderation. Never, ever, buy more bait than you can afford. That's plain daft. A lot more contests are won with a pint of squats and one and a half pints of casters than are won with massive amounts.

MAGGOT DYING MADE SIMPLE
[June 9th, 1976]

IT'S AMAZING what a mess you can make of yourself when colouring maggots. I used to manage to get myself well and truly plastered with dye...and it takes some getting off afterwards. It's no fun looking like a sort of permanent red-nosed reindeer.

There had to be an easier way – and now I have it. I keep my maggot dyes, already diluted in water, in those plastic squeegee containers. It is a simple matter to apply the necessary number of squirts to the maggots without having to touch the dye at all.

There is, of course, the problem of mixing and getting the solution into the container but once that's done the process then becomes clean. A full container will last for many weeks even at the rate I use maggot dye - and I suspect that I use rather more than most anglers.

I go for four separate containers - one for red, one of yellow and two for the two different chrysodines. I mix each solution to the strength that suits my purpose, and you must find your own mix that suits you.

But applying the dye is simplicity itself, whether you are colour-feeding or simply staining your bait. By trial and error you will soon discover that the amount of the solution to be used each time, remembering that in most instances the smallest amount of moisture you can get away with, then the better the results.

I told you last week how I breed my hook maggots. There's no getting away from the fact that these are invaluable and, as I suggested at the time, they need to be dyed in a variety of different colours.

No need to dye massive quantities. Two hundred of each is usually more than ample, but colour variety is important. There are four basic dyes for the job. Rhodamine for all shades from light pink to deep red. Auromine for lemon yellow. Chrysodine R for orange or red and finally Chrysodine Y for reddish yellow.

All are powders which are highly soluble in water and I believe every angler who colours his maggots needs quantities of each. The dyes are squirted on to the food provided for maggots when they reached approximately half-size - if the maggots are to be colour-fed. This simply means they eat the dye every time they tuck into the food.

Staining maggots that are already at full size (and may have been bought from a tackle shop) is simply dying their skins, since they have ceased feeding and there is then no way of inducing the colour into them internally.

Colour-feeding has got to be best. The maggots retain their full colour, whereas stain tends to fade, particularly red and pink. And colour-fed maggots can be more thoroughly cleaned without in any way diminishing the colour.

The more stained maggots are cleaned, the more colour is lost from their skins – although I freely concede that chrysodine hangs on pretty hard!

As I've said before though, none of the maggot dyes we use is particularly pleasant. They have been designed to dye, not to impart a pleasing flavour to the bait. Pity the two can't be done in harmony, but at least up till now we have to realise that maggot dyes don't taste too good.

They tend to be bitter. I know, I've had some! And while there's no certainty that the human palate is exactly the same as that sort of a fish, we are wise to assume that dyes can put fish off - if the maggots are not properly cleaned up afterwards.

So far as staining is concerned, maggots, of course, also need to be cleaned before they are coloured. The bigger hook maggots should be dropped into lukewarm water. This makes them sweat and removes the fat from their skins and the filth from their pores. Then the dye takes much better, the warm water having softened them up and paved the way for the dye to soak in.

Make sure to keep the lid on maggots being dyed. They will try to get out and there's no prize for the angler who produces the longest colour trail from a dyed maggot...especially across the carpet!

As a general rule, keep the maggots as dry as possible - or, as I told you last year, they are likely to float. They can also suffocate if they are made too wet.

Since the season is almost on us, it is also useful for me to mention the dying of feeder maggots. Squatts take chrysodine very well. Simply scatter some of the dry powder into the squatts while they are resident in the damp, red foundry sand in which you buy them. The moisture in the sand causes the powder to dissolve and the squatts soon soak the colour into their skins.

Pinkies are more trouble. They need to be washed in warm water and dried off with dry cereal before they are coloured. A minimum of moisture is essential or the little perishers will climb everywhere and will even bung up the bigger airholes in your tins if you give them the chance.

Chrysodine takes quickly, but yellow and red need rather more time to become absorbed. And once you take the maggots out of the dye, dry them quickly with sawdust, sieve them out and add fresh sawdust. You may need to do this as many as three times to get it absolutely right.

CHOOSING THE RIGHT BAITS FOR WINTER
[December 21st, 1977]

THIS is the time of the year when little things can make a lot of difference to the day's results. Past results confirm time and again, for instance, that the bronzed chrysodine maggot is the best winter hook maggot – and is frequently the top feeder too.

As I have said in past stories, I have unwittingly tasted chrysodine when it has somehow got on to my lips when I have been dying maggots. It isn't at all pleasant to look at but it tastes even worse!

I have always previously made the point, that because I don't care for the flavour myself then it follows that the fish don't like it either…and my chrysodine-dyed maggots have nearly always been very extensively cleaned before use. But does it follow that a fish's tastes are the same as ours? We are none too keen on live water snails and the like - but fish love water insects to eat!

I've thought about this a bit and I conclude there is no identifiable difference between my catches with ancient and with newly chrysodined maggots. The only advantage with the former is that I seem to stay a little cleaner myself! Perhaps the fish actually like the taste!

The one most important point about chrysodine maggots, especially at this time of the year, is that they must sink well when rivers are flowing.

Now most bigger tackle shops stock bronze maggots and it's a simple matter to buy what you need. But many tackle shops are quite small businesses and there are many instances where the choice is limited simply to whites and mixed coloureds - dictating that anglers have to dye their own.

There are two ways to dye maggots bronze. That's because the colour takes very well. Much better than red and pink, for example. You either do it with the dye dissolved in a modest amount of water or with neat, dry dye.

There are pros and cons either way but the main consideration has to be what's best for the bait. So using dye chrysodine has to be the favoured method. The snag - it requires rather more dye. The great advantage is that the maggots are not wetted. They do not therefore absorb moisture and therefore neither float nor sink slowly.

There are, of course, times of the year when the facility to make maggots sink at a reduced rate of fall is a great advantage, especially in still water. It's a question of knowing when to use it. If maggots are allowed to dye themselves in even modest amounts of liquid they absorb water and must therefore be allowed to dry out afterwards...unless they are required to float or sink slowly. That takes two or three days, depending on which way the maggots move in the bait tin. Simply give them dry bran to work in and the moisture leaves the maggots and saturates into the bran.

Swimfeeders are working well at this time so I'll pass over a tip about loading them now. When fishing with an open-ended feeder, first of all bung up one end with a plug of your normal, wetted groundbait. Now almost fill it with groundbait that's absolutely dry... and top it off by adding a second plug of moist cereal. You then have, in effect, a dry groundbait sandwich.

Drop it under water and watch what happens. As the water seeps into the dry cereal, the equivalent of an explosion takes place and the groundbait is ejected from the swimfeeder in a most attracative manner. Well, I think it looks attractive, and this is one instance where that should also appeal to the fish.

There are a number of occasions when loading feeders in this way does a good job. You can create a cloud down on the river bed without the disadvantage of that cloud having to fall through the depth of the river or whatever it is.

The cloud is therefore quite concentrated...and keeps the fish in a heap, and away from the worst effects of the current. It is important to realise that the swimfeeder is a device which can be used to perform a number of functions in different ways.

There is no reason why the existing feeder should not be modified. If, for example, you are using neat casters, there can be a problem of speed of escape through the holes, simply because they are inert. So join two holes up in a number of places so that in effect the outside shell is slotted, and you will find the casters leave the feeder much faster. The real advantage with a feeder that empties fast has to be that the feed stays concentrated. Imagine what happens if the feed leaves slowly and you get a bite when the shell is half-full.

You strike to hook the fish and reel in...showering feed behind the feeder as you retrieve it. That way your swim area can progressively get bigger and bigger.

Water temperature has a great effect on your bait. Think of the difference between both cheese and luncheon meat fished summer and winter. In winter the bait is very much harder because of the low water temperature. You have to combat that somehow.

First point: make sure that the hook point protrudes from the bait. That way it is easier for the bait to break free from the hook and take a good hold in the fish. The other important point is that there is really no necessity to use either cheese or luncheon meat exclusively. Make both into paste baits combined with bread and you'll create a softer bait.

Chapter Six

Ivan Marks on...
IRELAND

" I've just returned from a 12-day
holiday in Ireland - the Promised
Land for anglers. And I can
truthfully say it's one of the best
I've ever taken. "

THE IRISH BREAM ARE SO PROLIFIC
[May 10th, 1972]

IRISH bream are like English bream....only there's more of 'em. I've just returned from a week on the Shannon at Limerick where I witnessed the most incredible catches ever made. And Leicester anglers were taking them!

Four of us - Ray Elkington, Garry Swallow, Tom Bedder and myself - went across for the gala angling week to take a rest from the English match scene. But sport was so fast and furious that we will need another holiday to recover.

As you probably read elsewhere in the paper Tom broke all records with an absolutely unbelievable 161lb 14oz 8drm. And our team, the Shannonside Likely Lads, shared a place in the record books with a three-day aggregate of 431lb.

Unfortunately for the organisers, only 45 anglers turned up for the three match series. I explained to the match committee that the week clashed with several big competitions back in England. But everyone realised that the Ulster troubles kept the majority at home.

This was a big shame as we met great hospitality wherever we travelled. We played cards, drank and joked with the locals. They even insisted on carrying our tackle down to the riverbank.

When it comes to tackle and technique, the Irish anglers are back in the Stone Age. One chap inquired whether I had broken my rod when I was simply swingtipping. And they didn't believe we could groundbait as far out as we were fishing...not until we produced a number of catapults from our baskets. Now, unsurprisingly, they all want to get their hands on some!

But they're a great bunch of lads and I'm sorry that there's no one to teach them in Ireland. Because they've certainly got waters which make our match venues look silly. I can see 200lb being taken in a five-hour match from the Plassey stretch of the Shannon. It just needs the right angler, someone who is young and fit.

Tom, who is only 26, was physically shattered at the finish of his marathon session. He estimated that his two nets held about 70 fish. The secret behind his mammoth haul was the speed with which he beat his fish, often taking no longer than a minute.

Of course, Irish bream aren't very sophisticated. Tom used a size 10 hook tied direct to 5lb line on swingtip tackle. And, for a change, the bait was maggots.

Before the matches we heard that maggots were producing rather than the traditional worms and bread. So we picked up a few gallons from an Irish breeder, who rears some really top-class bait. I shouldn't like to use his groundbait on the Welland, but it works with the Irish bream.

Tom got through a gallon-and-a-half of bait to keep those bream feeding, and this is the sort of quantity necessary to make a big haul. Incidentally, look out for Tom's name in the open match results in the weeks to come. Now that he's had to close his fruit stall at Leicester racecourse on a Sunday, he's coming out with the rest of the lads.

Of the 45 swims pegged, a dozen were the really hot draw. You needed to pick one of these pegs on at least one day to build up a good aggregate.

When my chance came I took 68lb 10oz, but I caught fish on both of the other two days. The main shoals were lying in 14 feet of water - right smack between some four-foot shallows and a 25 feet deep hole. Bream often position themselves in this sort of area, a shelf between two extremes of depth.

Ledges of this nature occur on the North Bank of the Nene and on the Great Ouse at Ten Mile Bank. The Leicester anglers find them by casting out a bomb and counting the seconds until the swingtip drops back. Then we feed them and wait for the bream.

This type of area was where we made the big hauls on the Shannon but Alan Smith bumped into a shoal of four to five pounders in just five feet of water. And in the final 90 minutes of one contest he took out 68lb.

Tom took home a total of £230 for his efforts - very good going for a match between 45 anglers. But I was told that next year sponsorship will pour in a lot more money. So you can pretty well guarantee that we shall be back.

I missed the Middle Ouse Championships by going to Ireland, but the second Likely Lads team kept the Leicester flag flying high. It's going to take some pretty remarkable anglers to pull it down.

IRELAND IS THE PROMISED LAND FOR ANGLERS
[June 1st, 1972]

CATCHES unlimited! That slogan should be in neon lights over the main street of Ballinasloe, the sleepy town on Southern Ireland's River Suck.

I've just returned from a 12-day holiday in Ireland - the Promised Land for anglers. And I can truthfully say it's one of the best I've ever taken.

Everywhere I travelled I found nothing but goodwill and friendship. The Irish people made me more than welcome. And the fishing was just out of this world.

The River Suck must be the finest bream river in Ireland. You probably read in last week's paper how Gerry Colver crashed out 111lb of bream on the last day of the Ballinastoe angling gala week. It has everything bream need - deeps, shallows, bends and reedbeds. There's no river to compare with it in this country...even my beloved Nene.

An angler is spoilt for choice of swim. But it's the deeper water that holds the fish. Some swims are 40 feet deep, but find between 12 and 20 feet of water off a reedbed and you should catch bream.

In six hours' fishing, myself and four other anglers took 182 bream between 2lb 8oz and 6lb 8oz from the same swim. We estimated the catch to weigh in the region of 600lb.

Most of the fish were caught on the bomb. We used maggots or worms, it made no difference to the result Hook sizes ranged from a size 12 to a 6, and lines went up to 5lb. These bream aren't fussy.

We let one man feed the swim and all moved in around him. At one time four rods were bent into bream at once.

Unfortunately this swim wasn't included in the three matches, as we had to wade through a rush bed to fish it. I failed miserably in the contests. I drew peg numbers 2 and 3 on two consecutive days and the highest weight recorded from pegs 1-8 was only 6lb. If the fish had been at these pegs it would have been a different story.

Roy Marlow did well, winning his section one day and finishing third overall. But I'm glad Gerry won. He's been fishing the River Suck for many years now and knows what it's all about.

The Suck gives everyone a chance of a big weight. Trevor Bennett has been fishing with the Leicester anglers for just over a year. Yet he sat on the right peg in one of the matches and pulled out 41lb.

The Suck bream were covered in big spawning warts, and were probably cleaning themselves But you could catch them any time during the summer. You may have to cut your own swim out of a rush bed to get the pitch you want. And don't give up if you catch only six or seven bream the first day you fish. The next day the fish will be crammed in the swim, and you should enjoy a bonanza.

Worms are equally as good as maggots, if not better. The local lads will fetch you a tin full for two or three bob. We took ten cwt of groundbait and 40 gallons of maggots to share between ten of us. That was more than ample. My best bream weighed just under 6lb. Put that with the 2lb rudd I caught and you have two fish which would please any specimen hunter.

Tom Bedder - another angler staying at Ballinasloe - had a huge 20lb 10oz pike take a 2lb bream. And he landed that on float tackle.

Since I've come back, my phone hasn't stopped ringing. Everyone wants to know whether we were chased by masked men with machine guns.

I can only repeat that everywhere our party went we found no trouble at all. I've been going to Ireland now for the last 15 years and this latest trip equalled them all.

Ballinasloe wasn't the only spot I fished in Ireland. There were the rudd and bream of the Prosperous Canal, and the river where roach come two a minute. But I'll tell you about those places another week.

THE IRISH ROACH ARE UNBELIEVABLE!
[June 22nd,1972]

THE ENORMITY of the scale of the roach population explosion in Ulster and parts of the Irish Republic defies description. This must be the biggest single move forward in coarse fishing in the British Isles this century.

Perhaps we are lucky to be around while history is being made in this way, for the present roach population is growing steadily and spreading. The spread worries the South. There's a ban on pike livebaiting to prevent roach being carelessly released, but the main river systems are bound to become heavily stocked.

Only British anglers who have been to Lough Erne can imagine how big that is. You could tuck Rutland Water into one of the small corners...yet, so far as I had time to discover, there are roach everywhere.

In between the days spent fishing the recent Benson and Hedges Open at Enniskillen, there was ample time to sample the local pleasure fishing. Everyone who roved around looking for out of the way places reported the same sequence of events – a few minutes to get the swim primed properly and then it filled with roach.

The locals have netted their home waters for many years to obtain bream for pig food. Goodness only knows how many fish have been taken away, but one thing's for certain – there's no way anyone can tell the difference, simply because there isn't any. This is a fertile area so vast and unexploited that even man, ingenious though he is, will find difficulty messing it up. Some of the recent visitors to the Erne for the Benson and Hedges match were so impressed they said they would leave their tackle behind and return as frequently as possible - English fishing getting the equivalent of a thumbs down.

Virtually every factor taken into account is favourable. The lough and river system is so big that flooding is no problem. The fishing is predictable, accessible, and everyone can catch.

The Erne system, unlike the Shannon, has permanent water colour. It has that peaty-brown stain that comes from flowing in and out of bogland. Whether this is good or bad is, at least so far as casual visitors are concerned, impossible to tell.

The colour must help us keep the roach fishing, since peaty water is better than clear stuff, but there may be questions about the effect of peat on the long term stock. Could be there are so many roach that few of any of them will grow extra large, but the stock is bound to settle down to what is sustainable in time.

One oddity of the situation is that the roach don't prime on the surface as they could be expected to do in such situations. "There's an easy explanation for that," said our Irishman I discussed it with. "They daren't come to the top for if they do they lose their space down below!"

One fear is that the roach will mess up the bream stock. Certainly the bream can never again have it all to themselves, but considering how few people ever bothered with the bream that isn't really a problem. There should be plenty of fish of both species for everyone.

The perch are already bigger than in most Irish rivers. There were quite a few of 1lb caught and the run of the mill fish were perch of 6oz to 12oz – much better than was found some years back.

The facilities for anglers are superb. We could have fished out of the bedroom windows of some hotels – three were actually on the water's edge.

There are, in fact, plenty of hotels for holidaymakers. So

far as the fisheries are concerned, there's space for 2,000 anglers at a time.

I've been told that it's 99 per cent certain the Benson and Hedges match will be repeated next year, and there's no need for anyone to attach the slightest significance to the fact that part of D and E Sections fished relatively badly.

Any other time they could both have been exceptional hotspots. All depends, it seems, on the time of year and the temperature. That helps resolve the whereabouts of the fish in the river.

Although this was late May, the roach still hadn't spawned. A couple of fish were opened up to reveal that it would have been another three weeks before the fish actually spawned. The locals make the point that most of the fish come out of the lough into the river to spawn. Which is good theory. But how then does one explain the fact that wherever we fished in the bigger waters we caught roach?

Maybe there are localised concentrations, but one thing's for sure: if all the roach in Lough Erne moved into the Enniskillen town water the river would become solid with fish. There'd be no room for any water!

I can thoroughly recommend the Benson and Hedges to everyone. It really is a wide open contest, and if you look at the results, the thing that sticks in the mind is that although Kevin Ashurst won it overall, lots of what might be considered lesser-lights got into the money placings.

You need simply the ability to catch fish, to keep on catching fish and to keep your cool while others all around are knocking out enormous weights.

Whether or not this is good or bad practice for the English match circuit is arguable. Maybe the gruelling run of winter pegs, for instance, will be less bearable after comparison with the River Erne....but at least you'll know how good I was once!

200LB OF BREAM IS NOT A DREAM

[May 17th, 1973]

A 200LB NET of bream in five hours...it sounds impossible, doesn't it? But that's the sort of result I'm hoping to see at next week's angling gala at Ballinasloe on Eire's River Suck. And if anyone does hit the 200lb jackpot, it'll be a Leicester angler!

You may think that I'm sticking my neck out, but I'll bet that the majority of the big names travelling to Ireland won't have the right tackle to take one of those huge nets of fish. My old mate Tom Bedder is the current holder of the Irish five-hour match record with an incredible 161lb from the Plassy water on the Shannon. But I'm certain that this weight can be bettered from the Suck where there are even bigger fish. And there's the added incentive of a special prize for the first man to break 200lb.

But back to this tackle...the Leicester anglers learned last year in Ireland that to put up any sort of real performance you need heavy gear. And by heavy I don't mean a nine-foot swingtip rod and a 3lb line. You'll probably laugh when I tell you what tackle we're going to use for these bream. But I think Dick Walker would approve. I'm talking about a Mk IV Avon rod coupled with a line from 5lb to 7lb!

These Irish bream just can't be put off once they've got food in their heads I'm sure they follow your line down to the bottom so they can chew that worm to pieces. So the thicker the line, the easier they find it! Of course I'm exaggerating, but you could almost believe it were true.

Irish bream are big animals, completely different from English bream. The more stuff you chuck at them, the more they seem to like it. We'll be bringing them in from anything up to 25 feet of water. And when you remember that they grow to well beyond 7lb, you can soon see the need for the heavy line.

I'll probably start off by using a size 10 hook, but I'll be prepared to go bigger. If you're aiming for the double ton, you've got to average 40lb an hour. Say each fish averages 4lb and you're talking about one fish every six minutes. This is where you need a rod that punishes the fish, so you can reel it straight to the net. You can't waste time playing the fish.

A golfer doesn't use an iron if he's trying to drive 300 yards. Likewise, an angler shouldn't use a normal match rod to try for 200lb.

The swingtip rods on the market - like our Persuader - are designed to take a light line and handle fish from 8oz to 4lb. These are the general run of English bream. In a five-hour match in the Fens, the usual ceiling is around 50lb. And using one of these rods I could manage 80lb comfortably. But if you put a 7lb line on a Persuader, it just wouldn't be working properly. The line would take all the strain and the rod would have nothing to give. That's why we have opted for the big fish rods.

And believe me, the Irish bream are big. A three-pounder is a rarity, while the largest fish I saw caught last spring weighed 7lb 14oz. In fact one angler at Ballinasloe weighed in four bream for 28lb. Now if you start catching bream at 7lb a time, that 200lb total seems even more of a possibility. You would want only 16 fish for a hundredweight. And these shoals are around. Last year every fish weighed in by one section of anglers was 7lb plus.

You'll soon know if you sit on one of these bumper shoals. There will be 20lb in your net after a quarter of an hour. Then it's just a case of hustling each fish out as quickly as possible, and putting a couple of balls of groundbait in as soon as your bomb hits the bottom.

In my original example, when I said that you must average a fish every six minutes, this would give you three minutes to bait-up and get out again. You might get a bite within a few seconds of going in, so you could build up some extra minutes when you could have a groundbaiting session.

Another way of improving your catching rate would be to have a second rod behind you already baited. This would be cast out as soon as the bream was in the landing net, gaining you vital seconds as you unhooked your fish.

These giant bream shoals are not in every swim. The recent Birmingham versus London match proved that. Both Kenny Giles and Clive Smith would have caught if the bream had been all the way along. In fact, it would be easy for a pleasure fisherman to have a blank day if he sat in the wrong area. But in a match, it's odds-on that someone will sit on the shoal.

To give you some idea how large these shoals can be, five of us took 165 fish for 500lb from just one 30-yard swim. One of us fed the swim while the rest of us fished almost on top of each other in the rush bed. But in a match, that swim would be fished by just one angler. The fish were still feeding when we packed up to go to the prize presentation in Ballinasloe. Yet come the match days and I drew in pegs 1-10 twice. And on both days this section was won with 6lb.

Irish bream need to get used to groundbait before they will really feed. The results of last year's Ballinasloe contest went 17lb on the first day, 41lb on the second and 111lb on the third. By the final day the bream had really got their heads down. I shall probably take a minimum of 20lb dry for the first day and see how it goes. But I shall be prepared to use a lot more.

STORM RUINS THE GRAND FINALE
[May 31st, 1973]

A GIANT thunderstorm frightened the River Suck's bream into hiding on the last day of the Ballinasloe Angling Gala. It was a great shame as the stage was set for a grand finale with a two hundred pound performance.

The locals said that as the river runs between beds of peat, the vibration from the heavy rain upset the fish.

The first match was won with just 29lb, but when the second yielded a fantastic 116lb we all expected mass slaughter on the final day. Yet it was won with just 15lb 8oz! But that's fishing...

It was the pleasure anglers who really caned those bream. One man had a catch estimated at more than 300lb. Can you imagine that? At the end of the day he was running out of keepnets, never mind bait.

Another six anglers from Sheffield took around 800lb of those black beauties, while Leicester's Gobio Gather's went beserk and took an unbelievable 1,000lb. Gerry Colver's worm mine kept that shoal busy but still they ran out.

These bream were really big, some of them running to well over six pounds. Swinton angler Bob Goodwin took 21 fish for 100lb so you can get an idea of their size.

Next year, the organisers are moving the match four miles to the stretch that produced these mammoth hauls. So we should really see some action. At the moment it's a race between the Plassey water on the Shannon and the Suck at Ballinasloe to see which can produce this 200lb winning bag.

Now you're probably wondering what I caught. Well, I don't mind admitting that I blew-out because I just couldn't beat the luck of the draw. The first day I was drawn in an almost fishless area and took a meagre 2lb 11oz. And on the second day I drew a peg on the edge of a vast shoal of bream, and took 31lb. To my left the angler caught 7lb, while the weights to my right went 22lb, 30lb, 116lb, 86lb and 26lb.

I started off with a size 10 hook and worked down, but I did not have an opportunity to get to the size 6 and seven pound line. The fish just moved away. I took all my fish in 35 minutes and if I had taken my hand off the rod, the fish would have pulled it in. I only had a chance to use two pints of worms and six pounds of groundbait.

None of our crowd did any good, taking only ounces on some days. It was a big disappointment, but we all enjoyed ourselves.

I drew a bad peg in the final match and didn't bother to fish. I expected a huge weight to win so I was shattered when it was won with 15lb 8oz. If I had known that was the target, I would most certainly have fished. But so many good men drew favoured pegs I didn't bother. Instead I went rudd fishing and took about 12lb in an hour. Rudd made up most of the weights on the final day with the bream scared off. A Leicester angler took one of 2lb 2oz during the match so you can imagine the scope there for a big-fish hunter. And even a pike of 16lb-plus was landed.

My own bream were quite small by Suck standards - nine fish for just 31lb! I had my doubts about the pre-match groundbaiting carried out by the organisers. Asking three men to throw in hundredweights of groundbait is no easy task. Which swims got groundbait, and which didn't, is anybody's guess. Better, in future, to let the anglers do their own pre-groundbaiting.

My advice to any angler visiting this fantastic water this summer is give the swims time to work. It's no good sitting down the first day and crying that you haven't caught a hundred weight. Keep feeding and eventually those bream will arrive, even if it's three days later.

I should think that at least 20 anglers caught a hundredweight of bream during last week. Remember you only need between 20 and 30 fish. But all the catches came after the swim had been groundbaited solidly for three or four days.

You can try your chosen swim for a couple of hours each day to see if the bream have arrived. If they haven't then you can while away the time catching rudd.

And when those bream do move in, you can expect sport that is quite unknown in England.

ARE THOSE BIG IRISH BREAM BAGS ARE A THING OF THE PAST?
[March 12th, 1975]

ANGLERS who doubt that fishing itself imposes changes on the behaviour pattern of fish stocks should consider some of the trends now becoming apparent in the more heavily fished Irish rivers.

Until angling tourism reached its peak four years ago, the

Irish fish had never been subjected to pressures of any sort. Which explains why worm, the most natural of all natural baits, was the only bait to do a good job on the bream.

There are many Irish waters where this situation will continue, simply because they are either never or very rarely fished. But waters that have taken the brunt of the pressure have shown, and will continue to show, that this pressure induces a reaction from the bream Of all the bream rivers the River Suck has taken the heaviest load, primarily because it is one of few in Ireland with banks good enough over any length to provide a match fishing venue.

In the early days Irish bream fishing was muck or nettles. You either whacked out a mammoth bag of big bream, or you failed, perhaps being spared a water-licking by the friendliness of the perch population.

The first signs of change have shown as the result of worm anglers feeding with maggots. That is simply because maggots are so necessary at home that British visitors to Ireland couldn't feel happy about prospects over there unless they were armed to the teeth with gallons of the traditional bait and feed.

The big bream were conditioned to take maggots over a period of several years, but the biggest change has come with small bream at last showing up in strength. Because of this heavy maggot feeding, the little bream are now 'educated' to the point where they will prevent many of those so common water-lickings of past years.

That much was evident in last year's Ballinasloe Gala, a series of three contests held in a single week during our English close season. The first day followed form well enough last year. Ben Goffin, from Sheffield, yanked out over 100lb of the bigger 'slabs'. Significantly, half of Ben's catch was made on maggot. But instead of the heavyweight bream maintaining their appetites, they very largely called it a day.

I won the second contest in the series with 60lb - and that catch was unusual. True it included a dozen bream weighing a little more than 40lb, but my bag was completed by 16lb to 18lb of rudd - taken close in under the rod end on the float.

The third and final contest was the-eye-opener. I drew well, close to an area where big bream had been hammered during the free days in the week. But the expected worm and swingtip tactics wouldn't work. At last Irish bream were reacting against sheer fishing pressure.

It was the change to small hooks and maggot that brought my swim alive. I began to catch little bream, fish weighing between 8oz and 14oz. I had wasted the first half-hour of the contest on worm but maggot brought an immediate response.

The small bream kept coming - but here's the proof of the change. I twice caught 3lb bream on maggot. Each time I immediately changed back to a bigger hook and worm, hopeful that the bigger fish had moved into the swim. But each time I sat for 15 minutes without a bite. Reverting back to small hook and maggot I was quickly back into the skimmers again.

At the end of the day I had topped 50lb with just 6lb of biggish bream and 44lb of skimmers. And that was enough to make me the series winner on aggregate weight.

I scraped home narrowly in front of Ben Goffin, whose 100lb first-day total had set what at one time seemed an unbeatable obstacle.

The lesson for all the anglers who will be fishing Ballinasloe again this year is that at least some of last year's competitors would have done very much better with impressive backing weights had they scaled down their tackle and gone for the fish that were feeding.

It's all very well to go over there with the notion that you want the grand slam - a 200lb match weight of the big fellows. But once a swim fails to respond, it is time to try something else. I'm sure a 200lb matchweight will come. That's inevitable. But it will only be possible in the right swim on the right day. Match fishing remains a dedication to getting the best possible weight of fish out of every swim on the day.

My method of catching those small Irish bream is worth

explanation. I use my swingtip and a size 18 hook, but I don't watch the swingtip for bites...I watch the line. This is without doubt the deadliest method for small bream fishing over there. I have my misgivings about this slack line fishing when there is wind on the water, but if the near bank surface is unruffled then it's a killing method.

I let the line from the swingtip to the surface take enough slack so that there are two to three inches of line left floating on the surface. The line is held on the top by the surface tension of the water. As soon as that slack floating section tightens, it has to be a bite. The fish have little or no resistance to their pull, whereas they would quickly eject a bait if they feel the resistance of a swingtip. I'm not saying you can't catch small bream on a swingtip. But I do believe that you get the maximum return from a small bream swim, hitting a bigger proportion of your bites, if you use this slack-line method.

I haven't yet decided whether or not I shall be at Ballinasloe this year. I rather fancy the Winfield contest on the canal at Prosperous and I cannot make them both. But if I get to Ballinasloe I am confident I can get many more of those small bream.

It is always possible, too, that the grand slam catch, that 200lb in one day, will be made this year. The weather has been mild, the fish must spawn a little earlier than usual. So the big fellows could be in top order in early May.

IT'S COMING...A 200LB BAG OF ROACH
[April 28th, 1976]

THE FANTASTIC roach weights taken from the Irish River Bann near Portadown are interesting from many points of view, not least because the Irish themselves are beginning to show improved match form.

There was a time when English anglers first began to holiday across the Irish Sea when the local concept of rod and line fishing was primitive, to put it mildly. Nowadays the Irish anglers are no pushovers in contest fishing and they get better every year. In previous years on the Plassy water, near Limerick, and now on the Bann, the Irish anglers are showing themselves as an emerging force. This was always inevitable. They were able to adapt English methods to their own situations and they were bound to make a showing.

As time passes it is even likely that the Irish will show the same mass interest in coarse fishing as a nation that we do. They have so very much going for them. Untapped stocks of fish, existing in river systems virtually free from abstraction and with minimal pollution. The mere fact that they were able to crush a strong English contingent by 1,060lb to 684lb on the first day on the Bann proves that no-one should take them lightly any more.

With the benefit of local knowledge to help them, the Irish got it right first time. And even with the benefits from that first day's lesson absorbed, the English took another beating next day...although the margin was down from a devastating 376lb to a much more respectable 5lb.

The English anglers had won this same contest the previous year in an encounter in which the top individual garnered a mere 50lb. Perhaps it was the prospect of another 'low' weight that made the visitors go for loosefeeding again, rather than use groundbait. The Irish soon proved how wrong that was!

The advantage of groundbaiting with cereal and maggots combined was that it brought in consistently bigger fish. In rivers packed with feeding fish, anglers can produce their maximum speed but never come out on top. If the other team are getting fish averaging 12oz to your 6oz fish, it just can't be done in situations where the fish are feeding freely.

The Irish lads had their own winter league contests in Ulster to point the way. They have become accustomed to looking for top weights in the order of 90lb. We're not that lucky. We tend to think that if anyone is to reach such a weight he needs to have the help of a bream shoal.

When it is known that roach are the target species and prior form suggests (if wrongly) that the top weight will be close to 50lb, you don't see many English anglers tackling up with a 3lb breaking strain reel line and a size 14 hook.

As it turned out, George Proctor won the first day with a mammoth 134lb - that's the same George Proctor who won his section in a World Championship for Ireland at the tender age of 17.

His two-day aggregate of 212lb 10oz suggests he continues to improve and his and John Mills' 215lb 15oz aggregate suggest something much more startling...that the Bann is an even better prospect that Denmark's Ansager or Guden.

It wasn't as though those leading weights were a flash in the pan. On the second day Ray Elkington, from Leicester, turned in 90lb...and he finished seventh that day. Even the Guden can't match that. Not with roach, it can't.

Ireland can in fact now claim the credit for providing the fish for the two best match weights ever made with roach and bream. The roach record is George Proctor's with his 134lb 6oz, while Tom Bedder so far tops the all-bream weights with 161lb 14oz in the Shannon Gala in 1972.

Which provides us with another interesting piece of speculation. Are we moving into the stage where the record five-hour catch of roach will be higher than the five-hour match weight record for bream? The gap at the moment is a mere 27lb...and that isn't very much when the fish are coming fast.

None of the Bann roach were specimens. There were fish of 1lb but a lot more weighed 8oz to 12oz. Average them out at 10oz and George Proctor landed around 200 roach. That may seem an enormous number until it is examined a little more closely. In five hours fishing - 300 minutes - that amounts to a fish every 1.5 minutes.

It is when the catch is reduced to that basic one every 1.5 minutes ratio that it can most easily be seen that the figure can be improved upon. It is reasonable to believe that we shall one day see a 200lb catch of roach made in just five hours of match fishing. All of which is a far cry from roach fishing as we know it in matches in Britain.

Match weights of a stone or more of roach are rather more uncommon than people seem inclined to admit.

I'll tell you this. We may look for a 200lb single match catch from Ireland or perhaps from Denmark but I would very cheerfully accept a TOTAL catch of 200lb of roach for all the major contests I fish in England next season.

Allowing for the fact that at least on occasions I would expect chub, bream and dace as well from our mixed fisheries, I could look for a match average of around 14lb for my 30 contests...and what a season that would be!

THE IRISH ROACH TAKEOVER IS NEAR
[May 25th, 1977]

THE PATTERN of Irish fishing is changing under the fast-spreading influence of the roach. Let's face it, the Irish may have introduced all sorts of bans to stop roach being introduced to their other waters but they are already too late.

I suspect coarse anglers won't be too worried about that. The real concern is much more likely to stem from the salmon fishing faction, but I am sure there are already roach in the Shannon. It may take five years before those roach show but show they will...and I reckon we're in for some exceptional fishing in the Shannon when that happens.

Mind you, it can't happen overnight. It will probably take ten years for the roach to show in strength and longer than that before the fish grow to any real size. But, given time, the roach are destined to become real heavyweights; as good as any in the Blackwater.

I am not hinting at any illegal stocking - or any particular stocking of the Shannon with roach. To the best of my knowledge it hasn't happened that way. But pike anglers have taken roach to the Shannon and cast some off alive and returned others to the river rather than have them die.

The Erne System is, of course, already stuffed out with roach and the number and size of the fish continues to advance every year. They are already having an effect on Erne fishing in a number of ways.

I have no doubt that 100lb daily catches are now possible… and maybe match weights just as high, but the arrival of the roach has affected the other species. Not necessarily adversely though. I'm not complaining about the roach. The main thing is for anglers to understand that the fishing circumstances have now changed. In fact the well established and successful technique of preparing an Erne swim for a bream bashing session is no longer valid.

Before the roach arrived, anglers simply fed heavily day after day in the same place and waited for the bream to show up. It was almost inevitable that they would. Put enough feed into a bream swim and they'll come. But the equation is now very different. Put 28lb of bream stodge into a swim and it no longer lays there on the bottom ready waiting for bream to gobble it. The roach get it first. So with the roach immediately attracted, this means there's really no way you can build up a bream swim in the traditional manner. You can feed a swim steadily for a fortnight and the roach will eat the lot!

As the result the bream find nothing for them when they move through, probably in the night or at first light, and they just keep going. This will impose changed tactics on the anglers and the bream are also likely to change their way of life.

I think it will lead to smaller bream shoals - not fewer bream, more shoals but smaller ones and they are more likely to feed through the day.

British visitors to Irish waters holding mixed stocks are now advised to think how they can catch one species to the exclusion of the other…,if that's what they want. It figures that there's a much better chance of catching bream if roach aren't forever messing the bait about. So use a lobworm.

And anglers after bream must also adopt another change.

They are advised to sit closer together rather than space themselves out. Instead of spreading six men through 100 yards of bank space it is now better to get the six in 40 yards. The concentrated groundbait will then be much more effective from the bream's point of view. There's a better chance that some will be left on the bottom for the bream to find as they move through. In fact I see no reason why three men should not fish what amounts a single swim...if they're after bream.

The policy of feeding heavily remains as necessary as ever. In fact I continue to be surprised that so many anglers will spend £100 on the necessities of an Irish holiday and then knock their own chances by saving on groundbait. If you really want to get the best out of it you should be prepared to spend £10 on swim feed for a week's fishing. It will be money well spent for it will ensure that you get value for money from the £100 you will already have spent!

You can never take too many worms to Ireland. The more you take and use the more fish you will catch. I was over in Ireland three weeks ago. Emerald Isle Holidays organised my trip and I went to Cavan, fishing at Carrafin Bridge and on the Woodford River near Ballinamore.

I had one 60lb catch of roach in four hours plus a couple of 2lb 8oz bream without pushing myself at Ballinamore and 40lb in five hours at Carrafin. In each case the roach were 2oz to 10oz fish.

I can't really commit myself to catching massive quantities without an incentive of some sort. Had both these sessions been in matches I'm sure I would have done very much better. I might even have touched 100lb. I had one spell of 25 roach in 15 minutes but I can never be bothered to keep up that scoring rate when I'm fishing on my own. In fact on one occasion I packed the roach in and tried to sit it out for the bream. I got five...all of them foul-hooked no matter how I tried I couldn't hook a bream in the mouth. That will soon change once the water warms up.

[Chapter Seven]

Ivan Marks on...
EVERYTHING ELSE

> *Black cats, spilt salt, broken mirrors....these are omens I never ignore. Like most gamblers I'm as superstitious as a medieval monk. I'll do anything to keep Lady Luck on my side, even if it means crossing the road to avoid walking under a ladder.*

CLOSED SEASON NONSENSE
[April 20th, 1972]

MY FLOAT is gliding down the Severn. I tense as it reaches the 'hot spot' and seconds later I am playing my umpteenth chub of the match.

Already there is 30lb in my net. But as the scalesman helps me lift out the fish, I wake up with a jolt! I often get this dream in the close season. It's my favourite fantasy trip when I can't fish. Have you noticed how nice waters look the week after the season ends? The weather warms up and the rivers run into form.

The Severn is usually in marvelous condition by the middle of April. Yet much of this river is unfishable in winter due to flooding. I believe that river authorities and angling associations should get together and stagger the dates of the close season for different rivers. This way anglers could have fishing for 12 months of the year. The Trent, Severn, Broads, Ouse and Nene could still have a two to three month rest - but at varying times. The Severn, for example, could be closed for February and March when the river's at its worst, and reopened to angling in April.

Fish spawning depends on the weather. If it's warm they'll spawn early, but if the water temperature remains cold they'll spawn late. Last winter was very mild and I believe that many fish spawned before the season ended. Roy Marlow and I have already seen shoals of tiny fry swimming around in several lakes.

I've caught roach and perch from the Nene near Wansford that have been in spawn before the season ended. And dace in back-end Severn matches often show signs of spawning by being rough to the touch. So the close season as it stands at present is no guide to when fish spawn. It just means that we are prevented from fishing many rivers when they are at their best. A lot of nonsense is spoken about spawning fish refusing to feed - my wife Linda hasn't given up eating now she is expecting our child!

Before the East Suffolk and Norfolk River Authority stopped the Whitsun break in their area, I used to spend the Bank Holiday on the Broads. Fleet Dyke, near South Walsham Broad, is stuffed with bream at the end of May. Yet if you fished there during the season you caught only the odd fish. Sport in the dyke was unbelievable. It was easy to take 80lb or 90lb of bream in a sitting. The fish were cleaning themselves after spawning and were ready to feed.

This kind of opportunity would give a novice angler the chance of a big weight, something he would be unlikely to repeat during the season.

At Easter seven of us motored down to Essex to fish a size-limit roving match on a gravel pit. I've won this event before with bream, so I was fairly confident...provided I could get the right peg. But by the time we got to the draw everyone had picked their swims!

I walked around for two hours without my tackle. The swims were crowded out and when a 6lb bream was hauled in I realized there was only one peg would give me a winning chance. But there was a snag. Two anglers were already fishing there.

I asked if they minded me sharing their swim. One chap objected so I went back to munching sandwiches. When I finally found a vacant swim I was ten yards away from my rod when the float vanished. I missed that bite, so I held my rod. Down went the float again, but this time I was talking to my mate.

I reeled-in and to my surprise the rod went double. I had contacted a big bream, but only fleetingly. I had several other bites afterwards, but missed them all. I suppose it wasn't my day. None of the Leicester anglers caught a fish, but we had a laugh and a joke. And that's what counts.

I spent most of the match walking about, yet I was weighing up swims for the future. Next time I shan't miss that draw!

The Likely Lads will soon be heading south again in the close season. Our sights will be on Marcos Lake, near

Staines. It's a strange water divided in two by an island. If you draw the wrong side of the island, your chances of catching are very poor. But big weights can come from the other side. When we match fish the London waters local anglers will help us with information. In turn we swap our match knowledge.

OPENING DAY IS STILL A THRILL
[June 15th, 1972]

CATCHING fish for 12 months of the year makes me take angling for granted. I don't get excited any more about big nets of fish. It's something I've grown to expect. But I'm still like a small boy when it comes to Opening Day. After three months of filling in time at trout reservoirs and London gravel pits, the thrill of competing on the big match circuit is always fresh.

The river championships are the grand prix of the angling world. And this season they are going to be a lot, lot harder to win. Competition is really hotting up in the match world as many younger anglers are learning the skills which win.

And don't be surprised this season to see roach turning up in winning catches on the big match waters. The Nene, Welland, Witham and Relief Channel will all provide nets of these fish on the right day.

Roach still won't beat the bream, but the angler who is able to include a few in his bream bag could be the winner by a few pounds. Anglers fishing the Severn at Stourport report a roach revival and I believe the Cam also now holds plenty of these fish.

Do you remember the TV film made on the Likely Lads two seasons ago? The cameras filmed me catching roach to more than 1lb from the Dimmock's Cote match stretch. Many anglers watching the programme thought it must be a different river. A weight of roach in a match there was unknown. But after a low start that day I caught 11lb to finish second. If a boat had not ploughed up my swim, I would have won the match. Perhaps today that weight could be doubled.

Despite the usual predictions of pollution and disease from the gloomy Joes, I believe that this will be a bumper season with plenty of big weights. The mild winter means that weed growth should flourish. I'm always happy if I draw near a weed bed in a match. This means there are fish about, because weed provides both shelter and food.

River authorities tend to start weed-cutting soon after the start of the season. This disturbs the feeding habits of the fish although it may please some anglers. I would prefer to put up with the chance of snagging in the weed and getting bites rather than fish a swim which the fish have deserted.

Lots of waters could produce fish on bread at the start of the season. Howard Humphrey used flake to take 28lb of bream in last week's Linesman summer league match at St Ives, Hunts. But the main bait for the serious competitor after bream will still be the gozzer maggot.

The new NFA match rules come into force tomorrow, allowing catapults, throwing sticks and swimfeeders. This means that a lot of good anglers whose throwing ability handicapped them in the past will come into the reckoning. But the Leicester anglers don't mind more opposition. We're all confident we're going to do well. If we weren't, we wouldn't go fishing!

But match fishing isn't all pools and prizes. At the start of a new competition season, there's the chance to renew acquaintance with anglers you probably haven't seen for six months or more.

Now I'm running a tackle shop, I won't have as much opportunity to practice on Saturdays. So I shall have to make the most if the mid-week sessions, including finding time to practice on the Bristol Avon.

One match I must make certain of qualifying for is the Woodbine Final in Denmark. The money and the fishing make that match too good to miss.

Most pegs on the Guden will give between 30lb and 60lb of fish, and there are some outstanding pegs where the sky's the limit - Johnny Parsons proved that with his latest two 90lb hauls. If this particular stretch is continually fished by visiting matchmen, the roach will probably become harder to catch. But continual groundbaiting might persuade more bream to move in.

I've no doubt there are a lot of other rivers waiting to be discovered in Denmark which are as good - if not better - than the Guden. I've always said that an enterprising travel agent who ran weekend package holidays in the close season to Denmark or Ireland would be on a winner. The anglers could fish a match on a really good water for worthwhile prize money.

Last season I went to Eniskillen on the River Erne along with nearly 200 other anglers just for the weekend. We fished a competition where the top weight was a staggering 66lb of roach. I caught 26lb and finished nowhere! What a match that was. So just imagine what the weights would have been if the bream had fed.

THE DAGGERS IN MY BACK
[September 14th, 1972]

THE BIGGER the name, the bigger the cheat. That's the cry of hundreds of disgruntled matchmen who fail to do well week after week. They relieve their frustrations by accusing the top anglers of fiddling. There are that many daggers in my back that I shouldn't be able to walk!

This is one of many reasons why I hope that the proposed Matchmen's Union gets off the ground properly. I shall know more about its aims after I've attended a meeting in Leicester next Wednesday.

Accusations of double drawing are always flying around at the end of big opens. So I would expect the Union to press for a uniform procedure of a sealed draw to be adopted by all match organisers. This would help kill these cheating rumours once and for all - and make the draw watertight. Match organisers should write an angler's peg number next to his name on his match ticket, and keep it for checking. Then if, say, he was found fishing peg one when he had drawn 20 he could be disqualified.

Double drawing was more prevalent five or six years ago when there was less money at stake. Now the game is too big for minor cheating. Any angler caught would be banned indefinitely.

I'm willing to let anyone draw my peg for me and I'll fish there. Last season I drew three pegs for Roy Marlow, and they were all winners!

Roy asked me to draw for him in the Nene Championship, and again on the Severn. In the Clubs' National on the Welland the team captain is allowed six pegs. Everyone drew except Roy and myself. I picked mine out, asked Roy if he wanted to win and gave him the card. He won!

Drawing a good peg is only half the battle. It's the weight written on the card which decides whether or not you are in the money. And that in turn depends on the accuracy of the scales.

I've been weighed-in on some scales that weren't fit to weigh potatoes! Yet as long as it's the same for everyone, I wouldn't care if they were spring balances.

But, of course, scales used in competitions are all different. This is why they should be checked and rechecked before the weigh-in. I trust the scale stewards to do their job accurately and efficiently. And it was fortunate for me that I had two good men weighing my fish in the Great Ouse Championship.

An angler wanted to fish my swim directly after the contest. So he asked that my fish be kept in a keepnet rather than returned immediately. I'd weighed in exactly 35lb, when I slipped on two good bream. The fish scaled 6lb odd. Then they started to jump about and the next time I looked at the scales they were registering 5lb!

Every time those fish bounced the scales showed a different reading. The stewards weren't satisfied with the scales and fetched another set.

Luckily the fish already weighed were still in the net, and this time they scaled 35lb 10oz. Now I won that match by just 2oz. What would have happened if those fish had been returned after the first weighing? The scales would have robbed me of victory. So this is another field where I expect the Matchmen's Union to investigate.

I've little complaint about the pegging on rivers where I fish, except the Witham where the 14-yard spacing is barely sufficient. But I realise that on some waters especially in the South, it could be improved. The same applies to the pools payout. I've no grumbles here, but in other areas it could be different.

I know that some anglers wonder about what happens to the ticket money. What they don't realise is that day tickets can cost up to 25p a head. Then there's the pegging fee to be taken into account, plus all the costs of organisation.

I don't worry about the money prizes available. I'm there for the pools. If it cost me 50p just to fish a match with good pools and no other prizes, I'd still take part.

One improvement I'd like to see is better control of spectators on the bank. I'm a kind character at heart and can't tell people standing behind me to buzz off. To get rid of them I usually go for a walk along the bank.

And this is where I run foul of the rules as they stand. If someone complained I could be disqualified for leaving my peg. Yet surely it is the organisers' job to see that contestants' prospects are not interfered with by spectators.

Last season I was fishing on the Trent when a small gallery gathered just downstream of me - right where I was catching my fish. I asked politely if they would mind moving upstream of me. And they did...right into Johnny Rolfe's swim! After the match Johnny came up and said he never wanted to draw next to me again. Good organisation can stop this sort of situation developing.

So I'm looking to the Union to achieve great things. There is certainly room for improvement in some open match administration, and I hope the Leicester anglers will be able to co-operate with the Londoners to get things moving.

TAKE A KID OUT FISHING
[September 28th, 1972]

MOST towns have a sign welcoming motorists. Leicester's no exception, but if I had my way it would read: "Welcome to Leicester, matchangling capital of Britain."

The consistent success of its anglers has surely earned the city this title. Yet I would say that we have no more than 30 anglers competing each week on the open-match circuit.

The reason why so few can do so well is because we are constantly swopping information and ideas. No serious rivalry exists between the different groups. Everyone is happy as long as Leicester anglers are winning.

This system started with the Black Horse Angling Club, where young anglers were encouraged and taught the basic skills by more experienced anglers. The club would fish matches where novice anglers were paired off with the top men. For two hours the older angler sat patiently with his pupil explaining the correct tactics to use. He was allowed to fish for only the last three hours, and if he found anything new he would break off fishing to tell his partner. At the finish both anglers' catches were weighed together.

This concept helped both anglers – the newcomer would benefit from the older angler's experience, while the teacher could often learn from his pupil. Remember that to remaina top match angler, you have got to retain an open mind. I'm always willing to learn, even from a schoolboy.

There are days when fish will take a bait that is scurrying about with the wind, rather than accept one carefully controlled!

I'm always on the lookout for future 'star' material, young anglers who can be coached and tutored along the right path to success. I've got my eye on three youngsters at the moment who have all the makings of top class men.

No angler can go on for ever, and it is only right that what he has learned over the years should be passed on. I've no worries that giving this information will work against me. I'd always back a crafty old 'un against a young angler.

My greatest success to date must be with Phil Coles, a National Champion at 18. And when he gets a car, he will be taking young anglers fishing. But I've got a great deal of pleasure from watching other anglers shape up.

Look at Robin Grouse. Five years ago his angling rating was zero. This season he can count his winnings in the hundreds.

Robin offered me a couple of quid to teach him how to fish! I refused the money but offered to take the boy along. First we went to the Welland, then the North Bank. I caught while Robin watched. I taught him how to cast accurately with the big peacock floats and put a ball of groundbait round his tackle. He was impressed and eager to learn. And as soon as he got home he was on to his dad to buy him a complete new set of gear.

Since then, Robin has put in a lot of hard work which has paid off with wins such as the Nene Championship. He has risen from the back-runners to the Likely Lads second team.

Johnny Essex started as a very successful club angler. He asked us for information, and we helped him achieve open match fame. Now he, too, is a firmly-established Likely Lad.

Leicester and District, which spawned the Gobio Gatherers, has some very good anglers among its ranks. I regard this association as a 'nursery' for the Leicester AS National team and future Likely Lads. Already I've creamed off Phil Coles, Peter Jeyes and Robin Grouse.

Although we are all good mates, it is an angler's ability that confirms his place in the team. If we think he is going to let us down, then he is out.

The Leicester system of talent spotting should be adopted all over the country. Good young anglers would be put on the right tracks from the start without wasting many years in the wilderness.

But in the meantime it is up to the young anglers themselves to ask the stars to help them fish. They'll find that most of the big names are quite approachable and willing to help.

Everyone in Leicester knows me as Ivan, and they know that I don't mind people watching me fish. But I can't just go up to a lad, take his rod and say fish like this...he might get the wrong idea.

If I don't know someone, I still have to wait until he asks me to help him. And of course many youngsters are just too scared. So my advice to them is summon up your courage and have a word with the stars. But don't bother them in a match. Just sit quietly behind to watch and learn. You'll pick up far more in five minutes from watching anglers like Clive Smith or Kevin Ashurst in action than from whole day on your own.

Too many young anglers are handicapped from the start by poor tackle, and by reading books and articles where they talk of heavy lines and big hooks. A 12-year-old doesn't appreciate that he's expected to wait a week to hook one of those monster carp he's read about. Yet light line and small hook would see him catching fish straight away. Young anglers should be taught to play a fish on light tackle rather than heave it in on heavy gear.

If a young lad is really keen, he should be bought a good rod and reel which he can handle in keeping with his size. You don't expect a young golfer to bash away with a stick! Then he should start off in club matches, asking the senior men to help him. The younger the angler, the quicker they pick up new tactics.

When he's proved himself at this level, it's time to move on to the bigger matches on a water that suits his style and experience. It would be little point sending a lad used to running water up to the Witham. If he can find someone to pay his pools, all well and good. But at first he would be well to stick to the smaller sweeps until he gains in confidence.

Young anglers often have a lot more spare time which they can use practising to find out the effectiveness or otherwise of different methods.

Helping a youngster with his first faltering steps in matchfishing can pay dividends for the tutor. The exchange of information is two-way. Remember that the lad might always stumble on something which in turn could help you win a slice of the action.

I'M MR SUPERSTITIOUS
[November 2nd,1972]

BLACK CATS, spilt salt, broken mirrors....these are omens I never ignore. Like most gamblers, I'm as superstitious as a medieval monk. I'll do anything to keep Lady Luck on my side, even if it means crossing the road to avoid walking under a ladder.

I was born on the 13th and that fateful figure has been my lucky number ever since. It started when I drew a peg where the number added up to 13 and then won the match. Since then, that number has given me great confidence and helped me to win whenever I've drawn it. I always prefer to draw late at a match, putting my hand in the bag only at the last moment.

I always believe the last pegs to be as good as the first. It was the same when I played soccer...I always made sure I was the last player on the field. Silly perhaps, but luck and superstition are part of my life.

You'll never find me fishing a match without a scarf tied round my neck. My original "lucky" scarf is so tattered and torn that I've acquired two or three more. And if I can't find one before the whistle I tear the car apart in the search!

I took my original scarf with me to Ireland this year as a good luck charm. One of our party, Ray Elkington, didn't catch a fish during the first few days so I lent him the scarf …you've guessed, he came back with 50lb odd. Coincidence or fate – we can only guess. But I'd have a heart attack if I lost that scarf.

I've also got a lucky float that has won me more matches than I can to remember. It's a green and black antenna which I've used to win both the Nene and the Welland Championships. There's that many coats of paint on it, that I'm sure there's no balsa underneath. If I break my line above that float, everything stops until I get it back. It was the same with the groundbait bowl which Kevin Ashurst lent me before a big match. I won the event so I asked Kevin if I could keep it. I used that bowl for the next three years and enjoyed a fantastic run of success. Then I lost it and my luck disappeared as well.

My mother-in-law has a huge snail's shell standing on her window sill. Yet if that ornament is moved from its place – even for a spot of dusting – I am unhappy. I first saw the shell at a fancy restaurant – the sort of place where you can't read the menu – during the Likely Lades "do" one evening. I was strangely attracted to it so I shoved it in my pocket. And later gave it to my mother-in-law. Now the first thing I do when I walk in her house is to look for the shell. I've adopted it as my lucky mascot.

Lots of anglers ask me what's happened to Tiger, the little Jack Russell terrier I used to take to all the matches. Well, he's still as frisky as ever but rather than leave him in the car all day I keep him at home. If he got out of control on the riverbank he could get me banned from a competition, and tickets are hard enough to get hold of anyway.

When my luck is running I play it all the way. A couple of years ago I finished second in the big Wraysbury three-day open. To celebrate the following day I went horse racing with Robin Grouse and his fiancé. Two races had already been run and I saw that the horses I fancied had both finished well. So I splashed out my match winnings on the next four races and, incredible though it may seem, picked four winners on the trot!

Sometimes I get strange premonitions that I'm going to do well in a big-money contest. Three years ago I was travelling back from Torquay when I turned to Linda – now my wife – and predicted that I was going to win the following day's Welland Championship. I never normally make predictions but this time I felt so confident that I did. And sure enough I won the match.

It's rare that I dream about fishing. I just take each match as it comes, but there was one dream which I shall never forget. I saw my mate Brian Dexter drawing a sweep ticket out of a hat. Then some horses flashed by and he shouted that he'd won. The following day at work there was a sweep for the Lincoln. And as soon as Brian picked his horse I rushed round to the books and put on £5 each way. Even I was shattered when it came home at fourteen to one!

At the moment my luck is definitely out. I'm having a bad run in matches and who knows, it could last as long as two years. To do well, you've got to draw a good peg. And this is something I can't do at present.

Roy Marlow suffered a similar run of bad draws last year until he asked me to draw his peg for him – with the permission of the organisers I hasten to add. I picked some good pegs for Roy, including first and second on the Severn. My luck was in and I could do no wrong. But when it's out I can do no right. I shall never forget an unlucky trip to Ireland when a few of us paid a visit to a greyhound breeder. This chap bred all the best dogs so when he showed us a young animal which he thought was unbeatable we couldn't wait to get our money on. The gate went up, the dog shot out and stopped dead after 100 yards. We couldn't believe our eyes, especially when it repeated its go-stop performance in another race and we lost our money a second time. The owner was so disheartened that he gave the animal away. It was only later that he learnt it was colourblind and couldn't see the hare under artificial light. In daylight over the hurdles it broke all track records! Luckily we were able to recoup some of our losses.

THE TRENT IS THE BEST WINTER MATCH WATER IN THE COUNTRY

[January 18th, 1973]

THE TRENT is now the best winter match water in the country. Every week contests on the river are won with double-figure catches, sometimes topping 20lb. You'll find the Likely Lads there most weekends, even though the money isn't as good as on the Witham. And I'm betting it won't be long before we see some 30lb or even 40lb matchweights recorded.

Big weights of roach were commonplace before disease and pollution struck the river five years ago. Then catches slumped to an all-time low. But now, I'm glad to say, they're picking up magnificently.

I'm hoping for a repeat of the day in September '65 when I weighed in 39lb 14oz 8drm from the Shelford shallows. Then I still only finished second behind Kevin Ashurst who set a new six-hour match record with 41lb 11oz.

The match was a Nottingham AA charity open where the organisers allowed competitors to make as many draws as they wanted. I walked across the fields to the river with Kevin who firmly predicted he would win the match at the peg he chose. I replied that if he won the match, I would finish second. And so events proved.

I was just a few pegs away from Kevin and the match turned into a race. We could both see each other hammering roach 'on the drop'. Casters were still the killing bait in those days and we both had to wait some time for the roach to show.

Our swims were only two feet deep which meant that we were getting in twice as many casts as the anglers downstream in the deeper water. We got a bite as soon as our floats hit the water.

At the weigh-in Jobnny Moult was in front with 33lb until the scales arrived in our section. I briefly held the river's match record until they weighed in Kevin. Third with exactly

39lb was Harold Booth, brother of tackle dealer Ken. And the 20th man had 23lb. What a sensational match!

Nowadays Salford is bugged by boat traffic at the weekends, but the shallows are still unbeatable on the right day. The last Worksop open match on the Trent at Winthorpe was won with chub as you probably read. My pal Dave Downes had 16lb 10oz while Sheffield's Ken Littlewood took 15lb 7oz – both weights of chub.

Now anglers are asking whether the Trent rates an all-out chub assault with wasp grub, cheese and luncheon meat. I believe anglers could burn their fingers if they tried this in matches. The Trent is first and foremost a roach river and it would be too chancy to try for chub from the start.

It's worth recalling that in 1963 a Derbyshire angler hit the headlines by taking 170lb of chub from the river near Newark on legered wasp grub. And I've no doubt this would be the bait for an adventurous matchman to use.

Chub are not caught only in the lower river. I've seen odd ones landed at Hazelford, Hoveringham and Shelford. But the tidal river below Winthorpe Weir seems to hold the most.

It's the same with bream. A few are always caught at Winthorpe and ten years ago pleasure anglers used to take 20lb bags at Crankley Point, Newark. But who would dare to go all out for bream in a match? Perhaps an angler quivertipping with a shedload of groundbait could surprise us all.

The point about the Trent is that it holds such a varied head of fish. Anglers have caught trout, barbel and even carp. Who knows, perhaps barbel will eventually dominate the river as they do the Severn?

Remember that in the days of the writer "Trent Otter" - no, I'm not quite that old! - huge barbel hauls were taken below Nottingham. Nowadays odd barbel are being caught at Shardlow above Nottingham and at Newark. And as the river gets progressively cleaner, I expect them to turn up even more.

The Trent River Authority can certainly take a bow for

helping to restore the river. They've done a fantastic job in restocking and improving the quality of sewage effluent.

It wasn't so long ago that you couldn't fish on the bottom without picking up muck. Now you can cheerfully put a shot down and reel in a clean hook.

The roach are getting bigger as well. There are plenty over a pound being caught now that so many good anglers are fishing the river. This is why it is so difficult to win a big Trent open. Fifteen years ago a top angler could win from an average peg. Now there are so many big names about that one of the cracks must draw a winning swim.

Pete Warren is the hot property on the Trent this winter. Pete's a marvellous angler and he's been having the luck of the draw. I drew near him two weekends ago and we both finished with similar weights. Pete tackled the river with extremely light float tackle while I fished quite a bit heavier. They were two different styles yet they both paid off.

That's the beauty of the Trent. There are so many roach in the river that if you present your bait correctly you will catch fish.

SCIENTIFIC INVESTIGATION IS NEEDED ON OUR RIVERS
[April 4th, 1973]

THE CLOSE season is a farce, especially now the recent change in law has further confused the situation. No one seems to know if they can still fish some enclosed waters without running the risk of prosecution.

But don't get me wrong - I still think that there should be a close season to protect fish when they are at their most vulnerable. But who said fish spawn between March 14 and June 16? There seems to be no scientific evidence to fix the present close season between these dates. It's a relic from the days when anglers used to take home their catches for the stewpot. Then, it was probably thought necessary to protect fish stocks for three months from overculling by hungry anglers. But this reasoning has no relevance today.

The close season applies from the high moorland country in the North right down to the Southern lowlands. Yet you can't tell me that a roach living in a cold Cumberland lake, fed by mountain streams, spawns at a similar time to a roach living in a warm, shallow Sussex pool. The fish in the south would surely spawn earlier.

What is needed is a complete scientific investigation on all our major rivers to see just when and where the fish spawn. David Moore of Liverpool University, is conducting this type of experiment on the River Nene, and I see no reason why it shouldn't be extended to other rivers. Many waters such as the lower Nene, Trent and parts of the River Ouse are kept at an artificially high temperature by the presence of power stations returning warm water. So when do the fish in these rivers spawn?

You could see carp fry in our local canal at Leicester twice a year which suggests that the continual presence of warm water encouraged the fish to spawn twice. The Trent is perpetually warm so it could be that the roach here spawn more than once a year. Again only expert investigation will tell us more.

If the close season was staggered to give full protection to breeding fish in different areas then anglers would benefit. In the North, the close season might run from May to July, while in the warmer South just March and April might suffice to protect the fish. Anglers would always have somewhere to fish while the stocks would not be harmed.

Fish are at their most vulnerable when cleaning themselves after spawning. They lose their slime and could pick up disease from too much handling. On top of that, they become stupidly easy to catch.

I can remember taking Gerry Colver to the River Wensum during one of those close-season breaks the Norfolk River Authority used to allow. The dace were stacked tight on a gravel run and Gerry must have taken 90lb. They were crawling up the rod in their eagerness to feed. At this time of year they are so rough to the touch they almost take the skin off your hand.

I'm glad those Norfolk Bank Holiday breaks have been stopped. They made the close-season even more of a farce. The river authority allowed them just to attract holidaymakers to the Norfolk Broads. But now the Broads are no more than a glorified boating lake, anglers interests have been completely discarded.

During this close season I'll be doing some trout fishing - I'm not very good - and perhaps visit a few pits in the London area where coarse fishing is allowed. In May I shall be busy at the National Tackle Show in London for a week, as well as visiting Ireland, and then France to look at the World Championship venue.

I've also got to find time for a couple of team meetings to decide on our plans for the next match season. The weeks soon pass and before you know it, the season is on us again. I find trout fishing rather boring as the competitive angle is missing. Yet it's somewhere to take the wife on a Sunday when most spots in the country are crowded with cars.

I can't see why trout anglers are so against the use of spinners. Their lures and stickle flies represent tiny fish and look just like a little spinner in the water. I use a bigger hook to catch a pound trout than I do for a three-pound bream. But of course trout don't get the same chance to become hook shy. Once they are caught, mine get a swift bang on the head!

BOATERS AND ANGLERS DON'T MIX
[June 7th, 1973]

I HOPE the sun doesn't shine too much this summer. Then perhaps we won't have so many boats cruising through our swims like the Seventh Fleet.

I'm sure that the new season will produce better results

than the last, which was one of the worst I can remember. But the threat of increased boating traffic is now a greater danger to our sport than ever before. You can virtually write-off the Norfolk Broads now that they are no more than glorified boating lakes. But the writing could really be on the wall for rivers like the Nene and the Witham, as there seems to be more boats on these waters each summer than ever before.

The matchman pursues his sport for no more than five hours while the boatman has all day. Yet boats still persist in charging past lines of anglers, spoiling their sport. Small wonder we get angry when a churning propeller scares our shoal of bream into another angler's swim. I think it's true to say that selfish boat traffic in the past has cost hundreds of matchmen a lot of money.

The boating set is entitled to its enjoyment, just as we anglers expect ours. But let there be more give than take. For a start boats could slow down when they see a match being fished, or, even better, wait until the anglers have gone home before churning up the water.

On parts of the Trent, the water skiers keep off the river until the angling competition has finished. They have their fun from half past three to the early evening. And on the Great Ouse at Huntingdon, I've noticed that the local yacht races don't start until the anglers have weighed in. So I take my hat off to them. Let's just hope that some sort of compromise can be reached to avoid that obscene abuse which greets every passing craft.

The recent rain should do a lot to help the rivers and get the fish feeding. On the Welland, the bream should be moving downstream from their spawning grounds earlier than usual. This means that we can expect the low numbers on the permanent pegs to produce some good weights, which they didn't do last summer. The guide will be the Welland Championship which takes place in the middle of July. For the last two years it's been won from the 600s to 800s, but now I think that the bottom end will fish.

I can remember it being won from the 20s years ago when hand-sized bream played an important role in Welland matches. For my money I rate the 250s. This area always holds fish and produced some weights in last year's Second Division National.

The Nene fished below itself last year. Those 'funny' bream - I daren't call them hybrids or fishery biologist David Moore will be after me - vanished, and this badly affected summer weights. I hope they will be back this season and we will soon know after the first few weeks.

I rate pegs 60 to 170 as the area most likely to give you a few fish early on. But don't expect to win here with just one species. A typical catch would be mainly hybrids, or silver bream, a few roach and one or two pound-plus bream. And it is these last fish which could win you the match.

Whether casters would be any better than maggots at the start of the season, it is difficult to say. It's a matter of trial and error. You can't make your mind up until you've had a few fishing sessions. If it were possible to predict the right bait before a match, it would make winning a lot easier. When the top boys hit the right method from the start, they make a 'mess' of it - that's a Leicester expression for slaughtering the opposition, would you believe?

The river I expect to show the greatest improvement is the Trent, which fished exceptionally well last winter. But now the water is so much cleaner, it should fish just as well in the summer. Remember Jim Todd won a match there with 20lb right at the start of the season.

The summer bait on the Trent is definitely tares, judging by the reports of catches I hear. But I still haven't got the confidence to use them in a match. Perhaps someone will sit down next to me and show me how to use them, while I stick to casters. And at the finish we'll see which bait has worked the best.

My first two matches are on the Relief Channel, and don't think that I'm joking when I say that I might not even get a bite. One year I fished five matches on the Channel on the trot without even a flicker of the swingtip. And I was using the same methods which won me last year's Great Ouse Championship.

When the water is clear, the fish sit tight and you have to draw right on top of them or wait for another angler to make a mistake. If it's coloured, then the bream start to move and get their heads down on the feed.

MATCHMEN AND THE SPECIMEN HUNTERS CAN LEARN FROM EACH OTHER
[June 14th, 1973]

SPECIMEN hunters are often critical of match fishermen, and vice-versa. Yet what a lot could be learned if only the two factions would get together.

At times you'd think they practised different sports judging by some of the letters you read in Angling Times. The main difference in attitudes between them is that whereas the matchman has only five hours to catch his fish, the specimen hunter can wait five weeks. Time is on his side. This is why the specimen man is content to leave a big bait where a big fish can find it.

The matchman, on the other hand, must work hard to draw the fish into his swim by ground baiting, and then try to catch them.

Who is the most skilful? I'd welcome the opportunity to fish a contest against someone like Dick Walker, or Fred Taylor - just for a laugh and a joke - to see how I would fare. Mind you, for me to stand a chance it would have to be a water where there were some medium-sized fish – stuff from a pound to three or four pounds.

If it were a water holding only big fish, then I would have to choose a water holding stacks of small stuff for my round. And of course, this would prove nothing.

The specimen hunter and the matchman view a swim from different outlooks. Say, for example, a shoal of chub were sporting under a far-bank willow tree. The specimen hunter would devise some rig to take his bait across to the fish, where the match angler would try to draw the fish across to him by feeding.

Matchmen often read the water differently from the specimen hunter. At the end of last season, Fred J Taylor took Roy Marlow and I to the River Test. We both spotted a swim we fancied but Fred told us we would be wasting our time there. Well, after a couple of blank hours, Roy moved into this swim and promptly caught a 4lb 8oz chub plus some grayling. Now they call this swim the 'chub peg'.

The swim was a quickish run opening out into a bend. And both Roy and I saw something in it which Fred hadn't appreciated. No doubt a specimen hunter would appreciate a swim boiling with swirls and eddies where the matchman would take one look and give up in disgust. The difference is that the big-fish man's methods would be right for this sort of swim, and the matchman's wrong.

And this is why each faction could learn so much if they dropped their prejudices and got together.

In many ways, specimen hunters are more progressive at legering techniques. Fred Taylor showed me a little dodge to cope with the problem of mussel beds that I'd never thought of before. Fred uses plasticine or putty to make his bomb which he moulds round three-quarters of an inch of matchstick tied to his paternoster link. Then, when he snags his bomb, the matchstick breaks on the strike leaving the mussel with a mouthful of putty. It's a simple trick, but typical of the many experiments that the big fish men regularly try out.

Certainly too many match anglers approach their fishing in stereotyped fashion, and in this respect they could learn from the specimen hunters. Remember that no angler has ever finished learning.

Certainly, on the other hand, the matchmen could teach the big-fish boys a thing or two, especially about feeding and bait presentation. For example, why do they ignore casters - a bait on which I have caught every fish that swims. Casters have proved themselves on every water in this country, as well as on the Continent and in Ireland. So what would they do on a private lake?

I believe that casters represent some sort of natural food, and encourage the fish to start feeding in a swim. An angler after big fish could fill his swim with them the night before he starts fishing. Unlike maggots, which would just crawl and bury themselves in the mud, the casters will stay there until the fish find them.

The Leicester anglers recently fished a private lake at Stow-on-the-Wold, Gloucestershire, where angling is allowed during the close season. And we found that the carp were queuing up to take our floatfished casters.

I can't see any reason why some specimen hunters should automatically choose a big hook for a big fish. Provided there are no snags in the pond or lake, surely a size 12 hook to say a five pound line would be strong enough to play most carp. Every year twenty-pounders or thereabouts are taken from the North Bank on tackle much lighter than this.

Of course it might take an hour to get a big carp out on this tackle. But to me this is the skilful part of catching a specimen fish.

THE BIG CARP ARE COMING...
[November 21st, 1973]

DON'T LAUGH, but in five years time you may see me chucking out a King Edward or half a loaf in matches on Peterborough's North Bank.

This season has proved beyond any doubt that there are big carp on the Bank, and lots of 'em. Let's face it, carp have won and made up the places in recent matches. And many anglers have got themselves attached to these 'animals' only to come unstuck after playing them after hours and hours.

Lots of matcrmen won't think much of this idea. But to

catch them in any number, we have got to ask specimen hunters like Dick Walker just how he would tackle them. It's not a question of swallowing pride, it's either ask the right man, or don't catch.

No matchman, no matter how good he thinks he is, can put a man like Dick Walker down. He's caught far too many big fish for that.

These big carp have probably swum downstream in the hot water from the Electricity Cut and are obviously breeding like hell, or someone is putting in some clouters without us knowing. They will be a threat to match tactics in a few years but perhaps in a different way to what may seem obvious at first sight.

Specimen hunters could easily go and walk away with the money by sitting it out with one bait for five hours. But on the other hand they would be giving us all their little fish, which they consider are a waste of time!

Being pegged next to a carp angler in a match would be like having an empty peg next door. Of course, they could just as easily get stuck into a 20lb carp and wipe the smile off our faces.

It's going to take a lot to get me chucking a big carp bait on heavy gear. I just haven't got the right temperament. Matchmen have got to be working with their rods all the time and fiddling about. These carp boys can sling out their spuds, lumps of bread or worms, and that's it for five hours. They're a different breed altogether.

But who knows, they may have the right answer and bang out 60lb of carp while we are going all out for the bream and roach.

I take my hat off to anyone who can get a carp out on normal match gear. I hooked one at Farnborough lake and never saw my float for 20 minutes. It ran all of 70 yards, and the nearest I got it to the net was when I hooked it. Minutes later, I hooked a 6lb 14oz bream and just wound it in. That's the difference between carp and bream.

The time it takes to get these carp out, presents another

problem. How long do you give anyone to beat a hooked carp? A 15-minute time limit or something like that will have to be strictly imposed if these matches are not going to become a joke. Without any limit, an angler could easily hook one on the last throw and be playing it four hours later with everyone else packed up and ready for the pay-out!

But if we do start using heavier gear, carp could easily win this way. Say 20lb is the probable winning weight and you have only caught a couple of pounds of roach on normal light tackle with half an hour to go, it might then pay you to put that big bait out in the hope of catching a double-figure carp. It will be like doing the pools. People moan about how lucky someone is to win £ 500,000. But if you don't fill in the coupon, you can't win anyway!

The North Bank carp could, to a smaller degree, become like the Severn barbel and be the only match-winning fish.

If we do get a carp explosion on the Nene, it will please the average angler no end by giving them more than a good chance of beating the big boys. The North Bank is a top man's water, the payout proves that. But if these carp do take over, and I think there's a good chance they might, even they will go for them and forget the roach and bream.

Anyone who doubts reports of Nene carp should take a look over Peterborough road bridge at spawning time. I once saw a massive black shoal which must have contained many hundreds of big carp. And those were only the ones I could see. How many actually were there must be staggering.

One angler this summer floatfishing the middle at the Dog-in-a-Doublet sluice, 700 pegs away from the Town Bridge, hooked and lost several carp in an afternoon. That's how many carp there are in the Nene! And has anybody thought about those carp that have been caught in the Welland this summer? Who knows, a similar thing just could happen there too.

THE OLD DODGES TAKE SOME BEATING IN WINTER

[December 12th, 1973]

WINTER team fishing is for hard men only. There's no room for softies in this game. Over 4,000 anglers fish in Angling Times League fixtures and many, many, more battle for places in other winter events up and down the country.

Choosing a strong team appears to be an easy matter to the average angler. But ask any hard-pressed team captain who is faced with making decisions that can make him the most unpopular man for miles around. Every man he picks must be dedicated, and most important of all, he must be a real sticker, who is content to sit glued to his basket for the whole match - even if he knows in his mind that there's not a single fish in front of him.

Anyone who knows me will laugh their heads off when they read that. I admit that I like a wander about in the summer. But I only do it when I know I'm not in with a dog's chance.

I'm a different bloke altogether in winter when I fish in a team. If a team captain hears that one of his lads has gone for a walk when things get hard, he must drop him. There's no other choice. It's not fair that the other team men, who have fished their hearts out, should carry men less dedicated.

A good summer angler is usually a good winter man, but no matter how brilliant his summer record, he should not be included if he can't stay on his basket for five hours.

Past records, no matter how outstanding, don't weigh in. All the big teams know this and it is usually quite easy to pick a 12 man squad. But when it comes to picking 35 anglers, the team captain has really got his work cut out.

Then there's the angler who arrives without enough bait. It usually happens that this type of bloke always drops lucky and draws the plum peg, only to run out of bait well before the end, automatically wrecking a real chance of his team winning with a big weight. Things like this should be sorted out at regular team meetings before each match.

How do you keep concentration for five freezing hours? Every winter man knows that 5lb in the hard months is worth a good 20lb in summer. Bites can come in the last half hour, or perhaps only once or twice during the whole time. Miss them, and you don't really deserve your winter league place.

This is why a lot of really brilliant summer anglers who expect action all the way don't collect in the winter. Remember that most league matches are won with very small weights. Even the Trent, a really good winter river, where our lads are fishing in the Angling Times League, only produced a 3lb average last year. Most waters are much harder, and a bite missed through lack of concentration can make the difference between a second and first team place.

To keep alert for those precious bites, you must be warm. If you are cold, you shiver and lose concentration for those vital moments. Roy Marlow is a perfect model of the ideal winter angler. He can sit it out all day for two or three bites which he rarely misses. He will find a method and stick to it for five hours if he knows it's right for the day, and keep alert the whole time. That's the sort of winter league man you want.

Take plenty of flasks and food to the bank and wrap up as warmly as you can. Some of the really old dodges take some beating. I don't think that there's anything to beat the wind or keep in the body warmth like brown paper.

The old timers, who had to find ways of keeping warm without the benefit of modern all-weather clothing, always used it. A good idea is to get a really big brown paper sack like those you get in supermarkets. Cut out holes for your arms at the corners and one for your head, and slip it on next to your skin, covering your shoulders and body right down to your behind!

It may sound daft and a bit old fashioned, but try it. You will be pleasantly surprised at the difference. Another old wrinkle is to rub the backs of your hands with Vaseline. This keeps the circulation going through your hands into your fingers. Both are very old dodges but they work. I don't feel the cold much myself. But when I do, these are some of the tricks I turn to.

WHAT DO WATER AUTHORITIES DO FOR US?
[January 1st, 1975]

S O THE cost of fishing licences, in some areas at least, is about to rise. We don't know by how much, but increases are coming. It is very easy for the Water Authorities proposing increases to trot out the usual run of reasons why increases are necessary - inflation is an acceptable enough word these days not to raise too many eyebrows.

But I ask the question: is it enough for Water Authorities to plead inflation as their reason for asking us to pay a bit more? I will never haggle over pennies or even more than pennies if I think I am to get value for money. The question is, of course, do we get value for money from Water Authorities in fishery terms?

It's too early in the life of these new undertakings to say yes or no to that one. I would dearly like to be able to give an unqualified yes. I suspect, on the other hand, that in three years' time my answer is more likely to be no.

The main trouble with whatever fishery authority we have at the time is that it is so often a situation of 'them and us'. They don't see problems at our level. They don't answer our questions, certainly in ways we understand, about fish stocks and other problems.

Who, for instance, ever sanctioned the permanent pegging of the Coronation Channel at 12 to 13 yard intervals? No one who knew anything about match fishing could have been involved in that decision.

Why don't they find out what distances have to be in

fishing terms before they act? Same goes, of course, for the North Bank of the Nene, which is also unsatisfactorily pegged - 16 to 17 yards instead of 20 yards. That's not so bad as the Coronation Channel but, it is a limiting factor on catches.

So there we have just two examples of fishing money being badly spent and strictly in need of being spent a second time. Can we have confidence in the authority spending extra money wisely?

We would be right to suspect that a great chunk of any extra income will be used right away to pay higher salaries. That's alright so long as the people getting those salaries are doing a good job of work for us.

There are anglers who would argue that our rivers would be little the worse for it if fishery departments were disbanded altogether. I think I can speak for all anglers, certainly the ones I know, when I say we are looking for something positive from fishery authorities, some genuine forward-looking attempts to give us better quality fishing.

Take this national fish farm idea. It will cost an enormous amount of money to build, staff and run. My guess is it is one of the things we shall have to do without in the present financial climate.

Which doesn't upset me very much, because this country isn't short of fish. It is short of fish in most of the popular fisheries but that's another matter altogether.

Do we really need to breed bream in a national fish farm at colossal expense when the tidal reaches of the Nene, and Great Ouse all hold super stocks of these fish?

In the past I have taken 20lb a day bream catches from both the tidal Nene and Great Ouse…when close season fishing. The shutters have come down on that now…so no one now fishes these areas and the fish might just as well not exist for all the use we make of them. Daft isn't it? The fish are in wonderful condition. Everyone I have ever caught has been in mint condition.

So when are we going to have them moved from where

they do us no good into the over-fished and under-stocked areas where we desperately want them? I refuse to believe these tidal places can't be netted. On slack tides there could be as much as two hours during which a large netting team consisting of most, if not all, the bailiffs in the Anglian Water Authority could retrieve huge quantities of these fish – and there are some cracking roach as well as bream.

We can't get fish from Holland and Denmark now, so let's utilise what we have nearer home. Isn't it even possible that a King's Lynn-based trawler could get the fish out for us?

I don't profess to know the best way to get the fish out, but I am sure there's a way. Perhaps it's more accurate to say 'where there's a will there's a way.'

We see precious little sign of authority accepting the challenge of getting these fish but there must be several hundred thousand pounds worth there for the taking.

Fishery people will continue to insist our fisheries are as good as ever they were, but we know different. People are praising the results in the Great Ouse at Littleport and Ten Mile Bank, for instance but everyone who fishes those two sections knows they are not so good as 20 years ago.

The Anglian Water Authority should be able to supply the rest of the country with fish instead of importing from Europe...and make a profit out of it.

SPECIMEN HUNTING IS TOO EASY
[August 6th, 1975]

WHAT IS the main difference between specimen hunters and match anglers? Not the size of the fish they hope to catch, that's for sure. For match anglers are just as much big fish anglers as anyone else. No, the main difference is in the approach.

Specimen hunters fish at times when the fish are ready for one of the day's main meals. Match anglers, on the other hand, by the very essence of the organised fishing they are obliged to do, have to catch fish between fish's meal times. Realistically, it is much easier to catch fish at times when they are thinking about a meal, than it is when they've just had one.

Which helps explain why match anglers use small baits. No one has steak for afternoon tea, do they? I really think it's time someone put match angling and specimen hunting into perspective. I've waited a long time and nothing has happened so it seems I shall have to do it myself.

You see - if you didn't already know - match anglers are midday specimen hunters. None of us wants 2lb bream from the Welland when we can catch 4-pounders. And a 4lb bream is a specimen fish for the Welland. In relative terms, it's as good a fish for the water as a 7lb barbel from the Hampshire Avon or a 20lb carp from Redmire.

Specimen hunters have often taken a rise out of match anglers because they use tiny hooks. Match anglers say "They use meat hooks!" Who's right?

Both are right. Part of the art of angling is matching the hook to the bait. I wouldn't dream of fishing a lobworm on a size 20! We take much the same attitude over line breaking strains. We both use lines we think are right for our fishing.

The essential difference is that match anglers are fishing during midday, during maximum daylight, whereas specimen hunters often either fish at night, or dawn or dusk or on weeded water where line thickness isn't the disadvantage it would be in the middle of the day.

Hang a piece of rope from a beam inside a crowded room and switch off the light. What happens. People are constantly bumping into that rope because they can't see it. But if you hang a length of 3lb line from the same beam and leave the lights on no one bumps into that, simply because everyone can see it.

That really explains the difference between us. We both use lines that are right for the times we fish. Catching big fish after dark must be the easiest fishing we have. It's really like ambushing them when they are foraging for food. Fish that feed by smell - carp, tench, eels and bream, for example, the mainly bottom feeders - can always be caught easier in poor than in good light.

Surface feeders, on the other hand, fish like rudd and bleak, can best be caught at the crack of dawn when they suddenly come to peak activity. It figures that if anyone fishes at the time when fish are feeding really well they can catch those fish on almost anything edible the fish can get into their mouths.

If I ever fished Redmire I've no doubt I would tackle up in exactly the same way that the current Redmire anglers do. But if, let's imagine for a moment, Redmire became a day-only ticket water with pegs every 20 yards, it wouldn't be long before tackle was scaled down to match dimensions.

It's a well-known fact that pleasure fishing is much, much easier than match fishing. Pick your swim on the Welland in the week and you have a fair chance of a 40lb catch. I doubt if there were six 40lb match catches from the Welland all last season.

It follows therefore that if you are not only pleasure fishing but are also fishing at times when the fish are most interested in feeding, then your catches will be correspondingly higher.

I'm not interested in fishing in the dark, but I reckon it's easier to take 100lb of Welland bream in the dark than it is to get 30lb in daylight. A specimen hunter, because he fishes as an individual, can fish for the fish on his own terms. The odds are on his side. The match angler is fishing against the odds – against the other fellows, at times of maximum daylight and when the fish are still digesting their last meal.

I suppose there are degrees of skill in pike fishing. But fishing for fish like pike and zander is the classic example of the use of time rather than skill to make contact. You have only to read Angling Times each week to learn of pike hotspots which produce big fish with fair regularity. All you need do then is locate one of them, bung a bait in, leave it there long enough and eventually you'll catch yourself a pike. It may not be a big one. So you fish on and on - or even use three rods - and eventually you will catch yourself a big pike.

As I said earlier, I suppose there are degrees of skill in pike fishing. But basically, let's be honest. it's easy. Dead easy.

All of specimen hunting is easy compared to match fishing. Techniques are easier, the fish more gullible, the tackle much stronger and - I've got to say it - the anglers are therefore not so skilful. They don't have to be. No doubt most of them could be if it were necessary....but it's not.

Specimen hunters should, of course, be far more grateful to match anglers than they are. We fish the difficult waters at difficult times. Just imagine what it would be like if we were all dyed-in-the-wool specimen hunters. Ninety per cent of the swims in our rivers would never be fished at all.

In fact, if we were all forced by some strange law to be specimen hunters in quest of the biggest fish to be found anywhere in Britain, the number of anglers in this country would drop to 10 per cent of the present total in 12 months.

1975 – WHAT A YEAR!
[December 24th, 1975]

FOR MATCH angling, 1975 will be remembered as the year of the spectator. First the Gladding Masters final drew a crowd around 5,000 to Coombe Abbey; then the Lawden Masters attracted 10,000 to Evesham.

These two events proved once and for all that people will come and watch the stars in action. Now that the South are talking of scrapping size limits, it only remains for a sponsor in the London area for example to set up something similar.

I'm sure that the crowds would turn out to see the big names fish in the South. All we want is a sponsor with the money. So far, the Midlands have responded with reasonable support for this type of event. Now let's see what the South can do.

This year's Gladding will always be remembered as the

year John Wilkinson did the double. Well done John. Who knows? Perhaps you'll make it three on the trot and set an all-time record.

The Lawden Masters was a fantastic match for everyone who took part and watched. Just one fish could have turned those top three places upside down. I led for four-plus hours and then fell down during those last vital 30 minutes. But congratulations to Lloyd Davies. It was a great match...but wait until next time.

The National Championship...well that's one match I'd rather not remember. In matchfishing you've got to accept the downs with the ups. It was a great disappointment for Leicester, but one of the best teams in the country won. We won the National on the Severn - Birmingham's home water in 1971. So I suppose you could say that honours are even.

Kenny Giles pulled off a fantastic feat in Denmark putting over 100lb on the bank. But I just wasn't surprised that this man won. He's one of match fishing's true professionals. A great angler. And that's not just my opinion. Ask Kevin Ashurst as well.

The World Championship proved once again that English anglers are the best all-rounders in Europe. The first time we had a chance to use an unlimited line, we came up trumps. Ian Heaps' performance was out of this world.

I know there's little glory in finishing second, but I believe the English team will now go from strength to strength. So far we're the most consistent team in the match. And I firmly believe that the England lads will be climbing the winners' steps in the next three years.

Our biggest handicap as a team is that we are not together for long enough before the match. It's not like soccer where Don Revie can have a dozen internationals to try different players and sort out a top-class squad.

We don't even have a chance to fish a friendly against the Continental cracks. We're together for just one week. I would expect in the future for an England squad to stick together for at least two years. Team manager Stan Smith has been criticized for changing the team. But Stan has got to try out different anglers.

And there's nowhere in this country where conditions are similar to World Match day. There you're talking in crowds of thousands watching your every move. You've got to have the big-match temperament. The strongest of nerves can crack under the strain.

The French and Belgians are now showing great interest in the English style of fishing. They will always be masters of the pole, but they've got the sense to realise that styles are changing. And they are not going to be left behind. Those countries are looking for a young team that will master the English style in three or four years.

But to come back to home, I must say that the coarse fishing generally has been poor. Big weights have been caught, but there have also been a lot of dry nets. The Welland has been as patchy as I've known it, while the Nene has probably been one of the worst rivers in the country. It's now a hard job selling open match tickets for the North Bank, whereas three years ago it was a battle to get your hands on one.

One of the few rivers to show an improvement is the Warwickshire Avon. The match record has consistently been broken there, and I can only put it down to the river running a lot cleaner.

Of course the Severn has been as fantastic as ever. Ask Fred Bailey. That man's probably had more match-winning weights over 20lb this season than any other angler.

The Relief Channel is still recovering from the fish disease which hit it at the time of the 1967 National. It's still a big-fish water, but a few small fish are now showing.

The Trent is fishing its normal self. And Dave Thomas is still working his weekly miracle. Give it a couple of weeks and Pete Warren will take over. These two anglers have styles that can't be beaten.

I'm looking forward to 1976 as I always look forward to a new fishing year. My resolution? To persuade as many anglers as possible to take home their rubbish and leave their pegs cleaner than they found them. Anglers just can't afford to lose any more waters through a thoughtless minority.

Happy Christmas!

MATCHMEN DON'T HATE PIKE
[March 24th, 1976]

IN VIEW of the now long-running controversy over big pike, I think it's about time the matchman's point of view was known. I can't, of course, speak for every contest angler but as far as I am concerned pike are very welcome everywhere I fish.

I say that without any real interest in the fish from an angling point of view. I don't often catch a pike but when I do the fish is put back alive.

It's the pike's function in a fishery that is important to me. It takes out the sickly fish, the ones that might otherwise spread disease which would impose far greater losses than the pike inflict on healthy fish.

Neither would I kill a very big pike - and there's a simple reason for that. Pike eat pike. They do it more regularly than some people might suppose. Isn't it a known fact that one of the very best baits for a really big fish is another pike. Nothing fits more snugly into a pike's belly than another pike. Which means that every time a big fish is killed then numbers of smaller pike survive that would otherwise have been eaten.

Twenty pound pike will polish off five-pounders without a second thought. So if you kill a specimen pike, you are automatically ensuring that more of the smaller pike grow through to specimen weight. A big pike could eat twenty other pike in a year, maybe even more in some cases. So, you see, Nature has her own way of dealing with losses.

Pike can be a nuisance when they interfere on the days

when a match angler is building up his swim. But, by and large, they do their killing job quickly, with a minimum of fuss and disturbance.

Zander are different altogether. They hunt in packs. They herd shoals of tiny fish up to 2oz in weight, corner them and then attack indiscriminately, taking many more young healthy fish than do pike. In my book it's better to lose all the big, sickly fish, plus as many big but healthy ones, than masses of healthy mini-fish.

In most of the waters I fish where pike are present in average to large numbers the match season is concluded by late September. The pike are only then becoming active. I don't see much sign of pike activity in the summer. Which means that pike anglers and match anglers are perfectly compatible on the same fishery - simply because, among other reasons, they mainly use that fishery at different times of the year.

I don't want to hog a water for a full season and it would be selfish indeed for match anglers to dominate a mixed fishery where others can also have a good time.

As I have said, pike can at times be a nuisance, but it is always possible to get them out of the swim by using a little craft. Next time you have pike trouble, simply bring in a small fish slowly and allow the pike to take it. It then follows that if you have the time you can play the pike out and maybe net it. On the other hand, if the fish is so big you cannot beat it, at least you can force it to run out of your swim. Then pull the bait out of its mouth or lose it in another part of the river, far away from the spot where you are fishing for your roach or whatever.

Roy Marlow landed a pike weighing at least 20lb while fishing with a 1lb breaking strain hooklength at Four Mile Bar on the Welland two years ago. Which proves that, if only occasionally, big fish can be beaten on very light gear. So long as the hooklength nylon doesn't foul the pike's teeth, you must have a chance - if you can spare the time!

The good pike fishermen are much the same as competent

match anglers. They know how to locate fish via experience - which explains why the top pike anglers get more than might be considered their share of the specimens.

It's a question of reading the water and of being able to work out why pike should be in one place rather than another. I think the average pike angler would do very well to take a leaf out of our book when he is searching for fish. He should feed an area with cloud bait and maggots to get the food-fish active. Then, with their attention diverted from survival to feeding, they are more vulnerable to pike attack.

Pike know that they have a better chance at such times and they are much more likely to become active feeders.

Another point here: assume there are, say, 500 food fish in the area you intend to fish for pike. Isn't it far better to concentrate them into a small area via swim feeding?

That way the pike have to move to an area you have determined if they are to fill their bellies. And once that happens they are much easier to catch. You waste less time. I hope these comments of mine put the record straight. I wouldn't like any pike anglers to think that their fish are in any peril because of match anglers. That just isn't so.

Pike, to me, are as important as any other species, even though I don't fish for them myself. I last tried it 15 years back, but then there isn't time to do all types of fishing well. So I choose match fishing...

ANGLERS ARE THE NATION'S WHIPPING BOYS
[April 17th, 1976]

WE REALLY are the nation's whipping boys, aren't we? Despite all the fanfares of trumpets that hailed the setting up of water authorities and the fishery sections that went with them, coarse fishermen are worse off than ever they were.

Quietly and without too much fuss and bother the Middle Level Commissioners are digging out sections of the Fen boat link in preparation for the huge boat rally to be held on the Nene in August.

The traditional spawning beds of Twenty Foot bream in Whittlesey Dyke have been ruined. Some of the drains have been getting a water-level binding treatment calculated to minimise the effect of boat wash and no one says boo to that particular goose.

Empingham is already getting past a joke. We've seen what has happened to the Welland. It has had its worst winter in living memory. Might just as well have been frozen over for all the good it's done us. The river has been stagnant all the year and the super stock of roach and bream have shut up shop on us. Through most of the autumn and winter it has been a struggle to get a bite and even now, in the concluding days of the season, sport is below its best.

The writing is on the wall for the Nene. That's bound to go the same way as the Welland once the river is considered clean enough to be pumped into Empingham. The Nene will then become another no-flow fishery at a time when everyone should know that it is flow more than anything else that keeps the fish feeding.

Unfortunately that isn't the end of the Nene's problems. If the flow through Peterborough becomes non-existent then the town's effluents, previously carried downstream into the tidal and out to sea, will simply accumulate in the North Bank stretch.

Coarse fishing hasn't, it must be admitted, been aided by the prolonged dry weather spell that's been with us for months. But once we catch up on the rain now overdue it's a certainty it will be shot straight up the pipes bound for Empingham.

So the Nene and the Welland below the extraction points are destined to become miniature Relief Channels. That means gin-clear water and no fish activity.

We already know what can happen to fish in deep still waters like the Relief Channel when nothing is done to stir up the water. The Nene and Welland could finish up in a much worse plight than the Channel simply because they lack the depth and width. This is a situation which can please no one but the pike fishermen.

Welland pike are numerous along the full length of the popular match length. Two Leicester anglers bagged 23 - best of 15lb - in one day in the Four Mile Bar area. And they've had double figure catches from the same section on many other days.

The pike are well and truly on the increase and there's a debit side to that. On those rare occasions when it may be possible to get the roach and small bream going it's a near certainty that the pike will intervene. They will be swim-raiding all day and it is likely to become virtually impossible to keep the roach and bream feeding.

All of this was so predictable but the plain truth has to be that no one really gives a damn about the quality of coarse fishing. It is time every coarse fisherman stopped believing the propaganda spilled out from those mammoth headquarters' buildings we are helping to pay for.

In terms of actual achievement there's nothing at all. We must be as green as grass to put up with it. And I suppose because we always have, authority thinks we always will. As I said recently, it's time we held our fishery managers to account for the state of our coarse fishing. If they can't do a better job than they are doing now it's time that many of them moved on to something else.

It would be interesting to know just how many thousands of working hours and pounds of our money are wasted at the Institute of Fishery Management's annual playtime - when they all gather to talk themselves dizzy with theory, and, hopefully, to impress us with their word power. There's a better word for that but we are not allowed to use it here!

ZANDER SPELL BIG TROUBLE

[December 6th, 1978]

DICK Walker was way off the mark when he suggested in his column two weeks ago that there is furious argument about the merits of zander in our rivers. There is next to no argument at all.

I reckon 98 per cent of anglers either reject or actually hate the species and only two per cent have a good word to say for it. I am convinced that a vote by all anglers in the Great Ouse area would show that sort of majority.

I go further. The real danger is that zander will be transplanted about the country by the more zealous of that two per cent. If they do and some are caught in the act then they should go to jail for the offence.

It is blatantly criminal that anyone should introduce zander to such a wonderful water as Coombe Abbey Lake...but I know one angler who caught two little zander there last winter. Don't tell me they swam all the way!

Now it's inevitable that some of us should prefer some sorts of fishing to other sorts. There aren't many keen club anglers who have much interest in pike fishing but pike are an accepted part of the scenery. Zander will never be so accepted simply because they are foreign and damaging to the British scene.

All sorts of rubbish has been foisted on us by the zander-lovers and their sympathisers, such as 'the fish are good to eat'. Is that, I ask you, why we go fishing, to catch fish to eat? Of course it's not. And it beggars the argument to suggest that to have any validity. Advance it a stage furtherand assume crocodiles are good to eat - and their skins are useful - and we might just as well say let's have some of those in at Grafham and Redmire...and the Cumberland game rivers.

Make no mistake about it. All hell would have broken loose if someone had introduced zander or any other predatory species into a game river. The man who performed the deed would have been instantly retired...without pension.

No-one can refute the argument that the zander are steadily eating their way outward from their first home, the Great Ouse Relief Channel, and that every water they move into is eventually the worse for their presence.

No-one can lay all the blame for the decline of the Great Ouse on to the zander. But if a river suffers a decline, for whatever reason, that decline is inevitably accentuated by the arrival in strength of yet another predatory species.

It is already becoming apparent that the pike in the great Ouse area occupied by zander are less healthy than they used to be. They are thinner, leaner fish...which suggests they're either not getting enough to eat or that they have to work harder for what they swallow.

Fortunately the signs are that the Anglian Water Authority's scientists are looking at the species objectively and not through rose coloured glasses. There's no doubt at all that the present staff at all levels would have nothing to do with a zander stocking...and neither would any other water authority anywhere in the country.

What, Dick Walker asks, are zander living on? Why are they fat and well, rather than skinny? I don't pretend to know all the answers to that but I do suggest that if zander eat the little fish and pike eat the bigger ones then the fact that the pike are leaner than they used to be implies they're having difficulty getting food of the right size.

No doubt pike are scoffing a lot of zander. No doubt zander are also scoffing a lot of zander. Could in fact be that small zander form a major part of the bigger zander's daily diet. Zander are reputed to breed at a furious rate so it has to be a fact they eat their own young. Pike do too, of course.

Given time, a lot of time, and a river free from all other problems, and the zander problem would at least to some extent solve itself. There would be fewer pike, of course but who gave the then Great Ouse River Board the right to reduce the calibre of the pike fishing in the Great Ouse? It doesn't concern me too much - my main interest is elsewhere, but pike are good sport to other people.

If Dick Walker knew the rivers of this country as well as his writing sometimes suggest he does he would know that zander-free rivers - let's take the Nene and Witham as examples - have at least quantities of smaller fish showing up in catches. Those fish may be gudgeon and bleak and tiddlers of other species but they show up.

When did anyone last catch even 2lb of fish weighing an ounce or less each from the zander-affected Great Ouse or the Relief Channel?

We need large quantities of small fish in all our rivers and I happen to believe that if some of those fall into the category Dick Walker describes as 'stunted' that doesn't matter a jot. All anglers want first to catch something. Beginners of all ages are delighted with small fish. Only later, with experience and by taking the branch road into specimen hunting, does one need to catch big fish for maximum pleasure.

Even 30 years ago many of our rivers - or many sections of them - were incapable of producing outstandingly big fish. That was never a crisis. People enjoyed themselves because they caught plenty of little ones instead.

Why then, asks Dick, if there are so many zander in the rivers, don't match anglers fish for them? Why are fish baits banned by the NFA? It is an inescapable fact that competition anglers give gudgeon a much higher rating.

I suspect that zander fishing, if it became a widespread matter, would prove to be pretty flat for most of the time and unproductive. Zander are pack fish. They hunt in packs and most zander anglers would agree that they get their 'runs' in quick succession after a pack has moved in.

Then the fish tail off somewhere else for a while. Pike don't hunt like that. They lay up once they've had their fill but zander are fish-frighteners as well as killers. They've even been spotted harassing and killing big bream. They are a species we could do without, but we appear stuck with them.

For goodness sake let's not have them spread around any further and faster than is otherwise inevitable.

POWER STATION CARP
[January 2nd, 1980]

THERE'S no doubt that many more anglers are able to catch carp these days – simply because carp are one of few species that are around in greater numbers than 20 years ago.

There are many more carp lakes these days holding fish of various ceiling weights from only a few pounds probably up to 50lb and maybe even beyond, but the biggest increase I see is in river carp. Perhaps that's understandable – because I fish more rivers than lakes – and the Trent on current form is perhaps the biggest piece of carp fishing that's available to all and sundry in this country.

Mind you, the situation is not of complete progress everywhere. In some instances the quality of the carp fishing has deteriorated. The Nene and the Leicester Canal are both examples of what can happen to a river carp fishery when local power stations cease to function. The loss of the warm water outfalls seems to do a number of things but the carp suddenly become hard if not impossible to catch. Their season is immediately shortened as they react to natural temperature fluctuations - perhaps for the first time in their lives. Small carp almost immediately seem to vanish and only the bigger ones are conspicuous by their presence!

Whereas it used to be possible to take 20lb of small Leicester Canal carp at a single sitting (plus another 20lb of other species), catches these days are limited to the occasional single fish. They're bigger, 10lb and more sometimes, but overall it is no substitute for what's been lost.

The Nene in and below Peterborough is exactly the same. Five years ago the match length of the Nene was suddenly chockfull of little carp. Everything was set for a carp explosion on the scale that it happened on the Trent. But, alas, those carp just disappeared. There were, it seemed, thousands of little common and mirror carp. They vanished overnight when the power station stopped working and haven't been seen since.

No doubt some of the fish survive and there's still the chance of tussling with a really big one, but carp will not now figure in Nene contest weights with quite as much emphasis as they might have done.

The Severn Trent fisheries people have looked at the Leicester Canal in some detail and have reported that the carp are no longer there in strength so the fish aren't playing hide and seek. They've gone. But gone where? Maybe some went out of the length, moving downstream, but odds are, unfortunately, that most of them must have died, unable to cope with the loss of warmth perhaps.

Mind you, carp have the ability to play hard to get. I fish a private lake which was stocked with 400 – and 400 into three acres is a fair stock of carp. In the early years the carp fed well enough but they are a much more difficult proposition these days. No doubt they could be caught if I was prepared to lay siege to them and leave two or three baits in the water, night and day through full weekends, but I don't fish that way.

Some of the Lancashire canals and lakes used to hold quantities of carp but again the same favourable factor applied – the water had an artificially high temperature thanks to nearby power stations.

Now I like fishing for carp. They are good sporting fish and they can be stocked into rivers instead of roach and bream...but only, I think, where the power station influence exists. In all other circumstances they are probably a better stillwater species.

There must already be 30-pounders in the Trent. Match anglers have landed carp over 20lb and all the signs are that the fish are continuing to grow both in size and in numbers. It could very well be that the Trent may one day hold 40 and even 50-pounders...so long as the power stations stay in business.

There must be big fish in the entire length from Shardlow right downstream to Collingham – which is a lot of carp fishing in one stretch!

The remarkable increase of the carp stock is down to the fact that Trent carp spawn very regularly and successfully, probably every year, whereas carp in unheated waters are much less productive. This in itself, as much as anything else, confirms that if carp are asked to perform the same role as roach and bream in a river fishery this can only be a complete success in Trent-like situations.

There are, of course, carp in a number of heavily-fished match water, in the Welland, in the Great Ouse and many others no doubt, but the fact that these fish figure very little in angling events is a confirmation of their limited value in river fisheries.

But where there are power station outfalls in business it seems that carp stockings are well worthwhile and should be carried out. Match anglers have, of course, landed large numbers of big carp...and lost many others. Only on the Trent perhaps it is really worthwhile fishing exclusively for carp. Elsewhere tackle and tactics must reflect the fact that carp are relative strangers to keepnets.

But, just to prove that sizeable carp can be landed on frail tackle, Roy Marlow landed one of 12lb while fishing a size 22 hook and a 1lb breaking strain reel line. It took him 45 minutes and he had to walk the fish up and down the bank a bit but Roy won in the end.

I CHALLENGE DICK WALKER TO A MATCH
[January 9th, 1980]

I T GETS a little wearing for people to continually counter advice I, and others, give on tactics to catch fish when writers who ought to know better make a habit of countering what we say.

The business of big hooks and big shot being the right approach to fishing is so grossly misleading that, if taken literally, it can mean advising people to fish for fish that aren't there!

Big hooks and big shot, even lots of bit shot, may have been used in huge catches made years ago but times have changed...fish stocks have changed, pressure on the remaining fish has intensified. It is altogether much harder to catch fish now than 20 years ago.

People who advise big hooks in all circumstances really are leading most of the country's anglers astray and they also do nobody any favours at all with some of their odd shotting theories.

Now I'll put my words to the test. I here and now challenge Dick Walker and any five specimen hunters he cares to name to fish a six-hour contest against Marks and five others on Coombe Abbey Lake or on the Trent, fishing 10am to 4pm.

My side will use hooks ranging from size 24 to size 14 with the opposition to use hook sizes 14 up to size 2. So far as Coombe is concerned, just to make it more interesting, only fish weighing 1lb or more to count at the weigh-in!

If the challenge is fished on the Trent then only fish of 8oz each or more will be eligible to weigh. All styles allowed. Let spectators be the judge of the team using the right tactics both during the contest and at the weigh-in.

If people who fish the Trent and Coombe Abbey Lake aren't doing it right then let those people who say we're not doing it right prove it...so that everyone gets the message.

I'm not saying that the specimen hunter's logic is wrong - I'm sure we can learn from them - as they can learn from us – but let them prove that big hooks are better than small ones, that big baits are best, that we don't shot properly.

Come on Dick Walker, how about it? It would make an opportunity for hundreds of Angling Times readers to actually see you fishing for coarse fish.

It's all very well to say that shotting patterns drawn to illustrate words on shotting techniques don't look like that in the water. A shotting rig doesn't necessarily assume the required presentation unless the angler helps it to happen – by the use of tension and/or the lack of it with the rod top.

The slower moving water may be nearer the bottom in a flowing river and big shot sink faster than small shot. No-one is arguing about that. But I know what my shotting patterns do for my bait presentations...they catch me fish I wouldn't otherwise get anywhere near.

Presentation is very much more important these days – as all keen coarse anglers know full well. The only reason our catches ever rival those of 20 years ago is because of the improvement in fishing tackle and fishing techniques.

Collectively we owe a very great deal to casting reels, fine nylon line and improved float and legering techniques. Dick Walker has said that we often put the big shot in the wrong places. It should be closest to the hook.

I can't think of any situation where I would ever put a big shot closest to the hook. One of the prime reasons – to beat the bleak – no longer applies, because the bleak have become as thin on the ground as most other species.

And, if a big shot falls fastest, there's no disputing that a small one RISES fastest. So, in my view, that means that when running a float through a flowing river you put a small shot nearest to the hook to make the bait behave in a manner the fish find attractive.

That way you can make the hookbait rise and fall in the water by holding back and then letting the float run a foot or two. You can't do that so well with a swan shot nearest to the hook!

Part of any success formula is finding out where the fish are. And that means the level they are swimming in as well as the actual area they occupy.

The Trent for instance, is false in many ways. It isn't a natural river since it is fed with warm water...and you catch your fish most often in the warmer layers, not in the colder ones. It isn't enough to fish the bait on the bottom all the time...when the fish aren't there!

Leicester anglers may not be quite as prominent these days as they were when the fishing was easier, but Nottingham and Barnsley anglers – the two best teams in the country in my book – are winning wherever they go. And they're catching fish to do it...of course. Doesn't matter much to them whether they fish the Welland, Witham, Trent, Nene, Thames or any others you care to name...they are catching more than their share. They fish 'on the drop' style with their shot spread through the distance between the float and the hook.

Imagine for a moment that you are trotting a river with a float taking the equivalent of one swan shot. Anglers from both those teams would do as I do and split that shot up in such a way that the bait could be fished effectively in the lower half of the depth.

But put all that swan shot on close to the hook and you will only get your bites in the bottom two inches of the river. That won't do on most rivers I know.

Dick Walker and people like him who offer advice to the whole of the angling fraternity must particularise their advice and clearly define its limitations, or they lead anglers astray.

There is, of course, one great difference between match anglers and people who fish as they do and specimen hunters and anglers who share their logic, that's timing.

Specimen hunters fish at times of the day or night when fish show the greatest interest in food. Match anglers fish are more convenient times – bearing in mind that more often than not they collectively have to travel greater distances and then fish for shorter periods.

Match anglers fish at times when the fish are hardest to catch. That's a necessary fact of life; no complaints about it. But if we adopted the specimen hunter's approach and used big hooks (assumedly that also means big baits) we would be in danger of a water-licking eight times out of ten.